Meditations
and Devotions
on the Millennium
Development Goals

A Prayerful Guide

Sales of this not-for-profit book will benefit the following:

Imagine No Malaria (www.imaginenomalaria.org)
United Methodist Global AIDS Fund (www.2020aidsfreeworld.org)

to all children

that their future may be
more just,
more peaceable,
more sustainable.

and yes, in a world
more friendly and loving,
more humble and forgiving,
more kind and caring.

Meditations and Devotions on the Millennium Development Goals

A PRAYERFUL GUIDE

By Liberato C. Bautista

with

Deva-Marie Beck
Ann Marie Braudis
Nguepi Ndongo Donald
David Hallman
Manoj Kurian
John L. McCullough
Jo Anne Murphy
Jacqueline Sylvie Ndongmo
Athena Peralta
Mira Shiva

Forewords by

Caryl M. Stern
James Winkler
Salil Shetty

Contributors: Shalom R. Agtarap • Susan Aguilar • Patria Agustin-Smith • Maria Teresa Alvarez • Patricia Archer • Rebecca C. Asedillo • Alexander D. Baumgarten • Marta Benavides • Margie Briggs • Marc Brown • Natalie Brown • Ellen A. Brubaker • Alexandra Buck • Donna Burkhart • Rebecca Burkhart • Joel A. Capulong • Ronald Paz Caraig • We Hyung Chang • Neal Christie • Janice Clark • Joe Connelly • Jose Pepito Manansala Cunanan • Alvaina Daniels • Christopher de Pano • Christine Dial • Demi Diaz • Norma Dollaga • Meredith Duarte • Ashita Eleanko • Billie Fidlin • Pihaatae Francois • Haniel R. Garibay • Mário Gerson Monteiro da Costa • Linda Gertenbach • Gary Girao • Betty Gittens • Thorsten Göbel • Jay Godfrey • Maike Gorsboth • Boe Harris • KeTia Harris • Jessica Hawkinson • Richard K. Heacock, Jr. • Cindy R. Heilman • Betty Henderson • John S. Hill • Mote Houma • Judy Huff • Aquilino Javier, Jr. • Anne Johnson • Jonathan Jonas • Rodolfo A. Juan • Joseph Kim • Mark Kim • Eunchun Timothy Kim • Rebekah Cypert Krevens • Casey R. Laggan • Sophony Lamour • MyungRae Kim Lee • Sung-ok Lee • Dahlia Leigh • Rubylin G. Litao • Joan Lucarelli • Gladys P. Mangiduyos • Jane D. McCarthy • Robert McClean • Jonathan Melegrito • Connie Semy P. Mella • Donald E. Messer • Kimberly Miller • Etta Mae Mutti • Fritz Mutti • Jörg Niederer • Lloyd Nyarota • Harriett Jane Olson • Wilson Paine • Kathleen Pearson • Chita Rebollido-Millan • Joanne M. Reich • Johnny Riingen • Necta Montes Rocas • Martin Roth • Ann Brookshire Sherer-Simpson • Richard A.D. Siwu • Ryan D. Smith • Gheeta S. Smith • Harold S. Stanton • Deanna Stickley-Miner • Kathleen Stone • James E. Swanson, Sr. • Jeremiah Swen • Sinnathamby Thevanesan • Cherian Thomas • Linda Bales Todd • Molly Vetter • Vivencio L. Vinluan • Linda Warren Seely • Rosemary Wass • Kayon Watson • Jill Wiley • Carol Windrum • Akuila Yabaki • Andrew Yamamoto • Katey Zeh • and NPAC/ Northern Philippines Annual Conference/Board of Church and Society /Social Principles Workshop (Delmar Abella • Romulo Agpaoa • Max Aguinaldo • Delilah C. Bacud • David Balboa • Norina Balunsat • Bonifer Baquiran • Excelsis Biteng • Domingo Calayan • Jovita Conciso • Lolita Diaros • Honey Estraza • Oscar Ferrer • Janet Florentino • William Florentino • Lourdes Garcia • Thelma Gonzaga • Atanacio Ilac • Abraham Javier • Emerson Javier • Samuel Martinez • Modesta Miguel • Florentino Mina • Marilyn Pascual • Chita Pico • Rodel Pico • Alexander Pre • Benjamina Quilang • Lorelyn Racho • Roy Rumias • Amador Sabado, Jr. • Rebecca Santiago • Ezrael Santiago • Eric Tapulao • Crisostomo Torida • Macario Torida • Ruby Anne Torida • Dionisia de los Trinos)

General Board of Church & Society
The United Methodist Church
Washington, D.C. • New York

Editorial and Production
Liberato C. Bautista
Joseph D. Kim
Wayne Rhodes
Michelle Whittaker

Concept and Design
Liberato C. Bautista

Graphics, Layout and Design Execution
Lolourien Siwu

Interns
Rebecca Burkhart
Christian Ciobanu
Maria Jansson
Nicole Kuruszko
Casey Laggan
Joann Lee
Wilson Paine
Plamena Zamova

The **General Board of Church and Society** is the international public policy and social action agency of The United Methodist Church. It challenges United Methodists to work in areas of social concern and develops resources to inform, motivate, and train United Methodists on issues of social justice in the society. It is headquartered in Washington, D.C. and in New York where it maintains its United Nations Office.

MEDITATIONS AND DEVOTIONS ON THE MILLENNIUM DEVELOPMENT GOALS: A PRAYERFUL GUIDE

Copyright © November 2011
General Board of Church and Society of The United Methodist Church

Information about this publication may be obtained from the United Nations Office of the General Board of Church and Society of The United Methodist Church, 777 United Nations Plaza, Suite 8G, New York, New York, USA 10017.

ISBN 978-1-4507-9931-7

Millennium Development Goals logos courtesy of the United Nations Development Program. All scripture quotations in this book are the copyright of their respective publishers.

Back cover artwork by Jet Pascua

Printed by The Kutztown Publishing Co., Inc.
Manufactured in the United States of America

This book is printed on paper that contains 50% of recycled fiber.

Typeset in Athelas, Cochin, Futura, Tarzana, and Century Gothic.

 A publication of the General Board of Church and Society of The United Methodist Church

Washington, D.C. • New York

Contents

My prayer has been answered. That this book be finished and get printed. You now have it in your hands. And what a relief! Even better, the feeling is exhilarating, having 150 people co-write it.

The devotional writers in this collection come from many places around the world: Asia, Africa, Caribbean, Europe, Latin America, North America and Oceania. Many are people that I or colleagues know, have met and worked with. They wrote in response to a request to contribute to this project. I could not be happier or more thrilled for the expanse of both location and expertise that these devotionals represent.

Assembling 107 devotionals into one collection was not easy. Collecting enough devotionals for each of the eight MDG goals was even more difficult. While it was important that each writer chose the goal he or she wanted to address, it also proved to be a challenge. It took some time to have enough for each of the goals to have balanced representation.

Still, some goals have more devotionals than others. Interestingly enough, and sadly too, the goals with the least writers are the ones that are in most danger of showing real progress. These are the goals dealing with the reduction of child mortality and the improvement of maternal health. In fact, this publication took longer to print partly because I had to seek writers for these important goals.

But here it is. After a little over two long years of preparation and anxious anticipation, this prayerful guide to the United Nations Millennium Development Goals is available.

I am extremely pleased that three important and wonderful people have agreed to each write a foreword to the book.

Preface

Ms. Caryl M. Stern is President and Chief Executive Officer of the United States Fund for UNICEF. The United Methodist Church's collaboration with the U.S. Fund for UNICEF spans half a century, especially with the Trick-or-Treat for UNICEF campaign. This book is dedicated to children partly in honor of this collaboration and for the inspiring work and dedication of the U.S. Fund for UNICEF for the well-being and human rights of children.

This book would not have gone to print without the foreword of the General Secretary of the United Methodist General Board of Church and Society, James Winkler. Jim's witness in the global public square, advocating for gospel imperatives of justice and peace, models a deep spirituality that the devotions in this book equally exuberantly exhibit.

Mr. Salil Shetty wrote his foreword in February of 2010 while he was the Director of the UN Millennium Campaign. Staffs from the UN Millennium Campaign office have been invaluable in resourcing GBCS about the MDGs. More information about the campaign is available at www.endpoverty2015.org.

 Events sponsored by the General Board of Church and Society (GBCS) proved to be the best and largest sources of devotional writers. Most events were held in Washington, D.C., and New York, but many were in other places around the world as well. Many were organized by GBCS's offices of Education and Leadership Formation, Peace with Justice and United Nations/International Affairs.

I am indebted to colleagues at GBCS who have promoted this project to their own networks to solicit writers. These included events like Social Principles training, gatherings of young clergy, young seminarians, ethnic young adult interns, Peace with Justice gathering, and the seminars on national and international affairs. Other writers came from our network of UN advocates, the Isaiah Circle.

One particularly unique source was the Social Principles Training that I and a colleague,

Joseph Kim, conducted for the Board of Church and Society of the Northern Philippines Annual Conference. Four devotionals in this collection came from workshop groups in this training event.

I am greatly indebted to the commentary writers. They have been gracious to work with my timeline and instructions. They are colleagues whose commentaries on the goals are filled with knowledge, expertise, and experience. This collection is made richer by their contributions.

Before this book, there was the newsletter called **pers.pec.tives**. It was jointly published by the United Nations offices of GBCS and the Women's Division of the General Board of Global Ministries (GBGM). The fall 2005 issue of **pers.pec.tives** focused on the MDGs, with a meditation and eight devotionals. It was published as a resource for the UN Sunday commemoration that year. The meditation I wrote for this book borrows from and expands on that newsletter version. Its eight devotionals are also included here. Encouraging comments about the newsletter became the seeds that grew into this book. Colleagues at GBGM have contributed devotionals and also helped to bring in others to write.

Like any book project of this magnitude, a number of people were involved in its production. I give them my profuse thanks for bearing with me and my schedule. Joseph Kim who worked with me in our United Nations New York office until the first quarter of 2011 helped me the most. He was the custodian of devotionals that came in many different forms, from many different peoples, and in many different delivery modes. Joe and I worked with wonderful volunteers and interns like Rebecca Burkhart, Christian Ciobanu, Maria Jansson, Nicole Kuruszko, Casey Laggan, Joann Lee, Wilson Paine, and Plamena Zamova to put the devotionals in a format that made my work easier.

Editing the substance was not all there was to finishing this book. Copy editing is what makes the final product presentable and more readable. My biggest thanks go to Wayne Rhodes and

Michelle Whittaker of our GBCS Communications office. Wayne knows best my style of writing and therefore he usually makes me look better in print. I can't wait to see the Web version of the devotionals that Michelle is preparing.

The beautiful layout and graphics of this book are the handiwork of Lolourien Siwu. Lourien is trained in computer science, animation, visual effects, and graphics arts. It is a wonder that she survived all my pretensions to art and my impositions on how art is to be represented even on a book about appalling subjects such as poverty, hunger, even disease. While I conceived the design and layout of this book, including the cover and title, I had no talent like Lourien's to put them in a manner and form that made this book handy and appealing.

In the end, though, whatever shortcomings this book may present, the responsibility is mine. It is already my pleasure that you are reading a copy, hopefully your own.

Liberato C. Bautista
New York City
16 August 2011

Caryl M. Stern
President and CEO
U.S. Fund for UNICEF

September 2000 marked a pivotal month in the history of the world and for children – it's when the leaders of the world gathered at the United Nations for the Millennium Summit. That year, representatives from 189 member states of the U.N. convened to discuss poverty reduction strategies and ways to increase global security and create higher standards of living for all. The leaders agreed upon the Millennium Development Goals (MDGs), where by 2015, the world would achieve measurable improvements in the most crucial sectors of human development.

For children, meeting the MDGs is critical. They are the first to die when basic needs such as food, water, sanitation, and health care are un-met. Moreover, helping children reach their full potential is a way to also invest in the overall progress of humanity. Investing in children means ac-celerating the achievement of development goals, since children constitute most of the world's poor.

This is where UNICEF comes into the picture. UNICEF is the only inter-governmental agency dedicated exclusively to children. It is mandated to promote and protect children's rights, health, and well-being. From work-ing with local policymakers to affect health-care and education reform, to providing access to clean water and adequate sanitation, every UNICEF action is a movement toward the MDGs.

For half a century, The United Methodist Church has partnered with the U.S. Fund for UNICEF as part of their traditional, annual U.N. Sunday celebration. Through its General Board of Church and Society, the United

Foreword

[H]elping children reach their full potential is a way to also invest in the overall progress of humanity. Investing in children means accelerating the achievement of development goals, since children constitute most of the world's poor.

Methodists continue to support the Trick-or-Treat for UNICEF campaign. This long-standing collaboration has been integral to UNICEF's mission to save and protect the lives of children and realize the MDGs.

In the year 2000, during the Millennium Summit, almost 11 million children – more than 29,000 a day – died before the age of five, mostly from preventable causes. Today, the number of children under the age of five dying each day has significantly dropped to 21,000. That is dramatic progress. The most exciting element of this reduction is that we can see that the drop in child mortality is actually accelerating, in spite of the fact that the overall birthrate has risen. In other words, we are truly on our way to the day when zero children will die from preventable causes. And with partners like you by our side, we are certain to get there.

Many people have contributed to this book – representing a full spectrum of religious, political, and social views. I may not agree with every one of them, but what I do know is that we are all united by our deep belief that every child deserves the opportunities for health and a hope-filled future. On behalf of the children we serve, our many thanks for your passion and dedication to saving and improving the lives of the world's children.

James Winkler

General Secretary, General Board of Church and Society of The United Methodist Church

I have been in countless settings in which a meeting or event or day has begun with devotions. The best of those devotions uplift us, connect us with the Divine, focus and prepare us for the day and the tasks at hand. Inspirational words, relevant scripture passages, and personal experiences combine to shed new light on a problem or stir us to action. May this devotional guide related to the Millennium Development Goals be helpful to your prayer life and instructive to your ministry.

I have spoken many times in local churches and other venues about the Millennium Development Goals adopted by the nations of the world. They are a "Jesus Agenda!" In a world plagued by pandemic poverty and environmental degradation, the Millennium Development Goals reflect the mind of Christ. Each and every one of the Goals can coincide with his teachings.

In a world plagued by warfare and a growing gap between the rich and poor, positive change can sometimes seem impossible. However, great strides have been made in the fight against numerous diseases. Hundreds of millions of people have been lifted out of poverty in recent decades.

Still, the struggle for human empowerment and ecological healing continues. Only sustained effort, hard work, and the insistence of people around the world will reorient policies and priorities toward the accomplishment of the eight goals.

We must find a tipping point for the continued improvement of the global situation. Achievement of the Millennium Development Goals

Foreword

In a world plagued by pandemic poverty and environmental degradation, the Millennium Development Goals reflect the mind of Christ. Each and every one of the Goals can coincide with his teachings.

is relatively inexpensive when weighed against wasteful spending on weapons, alcohol, gambling, pornography, tobacco, plastic packaging and a host of other useless items.

The accomplishment of the MDGs, one building on another, can create momentum and stability that can move the entire world into an era of peace and prosperity. This is not a pipedream. These goals have been established with great care and expertise. They are serious and practical goals.

They are goals we have all been working toward for many years, but a better and more coordinated global focus can make them a reality.

My own church, The United Methodist Church, has long been devoted to education, health care, and economic empowerment. We are committed to the fight against malaria and AIDS. We do none of this in isolation. Only in concert with governments and other NGOs can our ministry have the impact we desire.

I pray this devotional guide will prove to be a valuable spiritual resource for you.

Salil Shetty

Director, United Nations Millennium Campaign *

"We will spare no effort to free our fellow men, women and children from the abject and dehumanizing conditions of extreme poverty, to which more than a billion of them are currently subjected. We are committed to making the right to development a reality for everyone and to freeing the entire human race from want."

This was the promise that 189 heads of state made to their people ten years ago. Since then, progress has been made in the fight against extreme poverty but not nearly enough. Today, 50,000 people continue to die every day as a result of poverty. A woman dies every minute in pregnancy and childbirth. Around the globe, 72 million children still do not go to school. There are just five years left until the 2015 deadline by which time world leaders have pledged to achieve the Millennium Development Goals (MDGs) in order to eradicate extreme poverty and its root causes. Time is running out. But it's not too late. In September 2010, the United Nations will host the largest gathering of heads of state since the Millennium Summit in the year 2000, to review progress on the MDGs.

This is not a time for idle talk or more empty promises. We as citizens must use the time from now until September to tell our leaders in no uncertain terms that we expect them to deliver concrete, breakthrough plans at the summit, outlining exactly what they will do in order to deliver on their promises by the 2015 deadline. We expect them to implement policies and plans that serve the needs of their people, particularly the poorest and most vulnerable. Their plans must include clear mechanisms for accountability to their citizens.

We cannot deny that today, the world has the financial resources needed to end extreme poverty once and for all, but also the technological knowledge and know-how to realize the MDGs. What is lacking is the

Foreword

Eliminating extreme poverty is therefore no longer a matter of "can we?" but a matter of "will we?"

politicial willingness to take the actions necessary as well as the mechanisms to hold governments to account. Eliminating extreme poverty is therefore no longer a matter of "can we?" but a matter of "will we?"

The global economic crisis has given governments an additional excuse to set us back on accomplishments already made and has the potential to jeopardize future progress. However, a project like the one that you hold in your hands can refocus and redirect our efforts to honor the true call of the MDGs, which is for every citizen to expect the basic necessities of life: the right to food, education, health care, dignity and human rights. Simple entitlements, which if guaranteed, will ensure a healthy population and a peaceful planet.

The United Nations Millennium Campaign greatly values its continued collaboration and partnership with The United Methodist Church, specifically through the United Nations Office of the General Board of Church and Society. Collaborating on "Meditations and Devotions on the Millennium Development Goals: A Prayerful Guide" is another chapter in this productive partnership.

We look forward to continuing our partnership over the next five years to scale up and deepen our work to support and inspire people from around the world to take action to ensure that the Millennium Development Goals are realized. My hope is that you will join us in the fight to end poverty.

There is a lot we can do collectively and individually. Resources such as this one provide the inspiration and guidance to get involved in the global movement to end poverty. We can be the generation that ends poverty. We should refuse to miss this opportunity.

Let us continue to send a clear message to our leaders: We will no longer stay seated or silent in the face of poverty and broken promises to end it.

At the time he wrote this foreword, Mr. Salil Shetty was the Director of the United Nations Millennium Campaign.

When Poverty is No More

Liberato C. Bautista
Assistant General Secretary for United Nations and International Affairs, General Board of Church and Society of The United Methodist Church

The poor may indeed be with us always. But poverty need not be.

As a young boy I grew up knowing what poverty meant. I was born to poor farmers. My father finished seventh grade and my mother third grade. But they were hardworking and persevering. Both my parents worked extra hard to provide for necessities such as food, shelter, clothing, health care and education.

Produce from our small rice farm and small orchard gave us food and cash, but not enough to provide for all our basic needs. Each member of our family helped provide for these needs.

Education was a priority. Our parents imbued us with its importance and necessity. We had to be serious in our studies. Graduating from elementary, then high school, then college was every parent's wish for their children. From our parents' perspective, education was the most tangible legacy they can leave behind – not land which they did not have enough; not cash savings for there was none.

We all went to college as self-supporting students. Some of us finished our degrees, others didn't. Skills and knowledge acquired from high school and college augured well for our adult lives. But primary education already provided us with the knowledge and skills to move on to adolescent and adult life.

Fundamental to our understanding of the lofty aims of the United Nations Millennium Development Goals (MDGs) is a decent, dignified daily existence where necessities of food, shelter, clothing, education, decent job, and health care are available and within reach.

Suppose a brother or a sister is without clothes and daily food. If one of you says to them, "Go in peace; keep warm and well fed," but does nothing about their physical needs, what good is it? In the same way, faith by itself, if it is not accompanied by action, is dead.
(James 2:15-17 NIV)

Therefore I tell you, whatever you ask in prayer, believe that you have received it, and it will be yours.
(Mark 11:24 ESV)

Introduction and Meditations

I

The provision of basic needs is important to understand poverty. Personal circumstances, for sure, play a role in one's economic standing from the start. I believe that every human being desires to have the wherewithal for a decent, dignified life.

But how one's circumstance interfaces with prevailing public policies and social forces greatly affects how basic needs are either met and provided for or denied or become inaccessible and unaffordable. Government plays a big role in determining such policies.

The infrastructures necessary for sustainable development in the town where I was born and grew up in the Philippines could only have been put up with government support. Our town is rural and agrarian in economy much like most of the Philippines. There was no electricity in our town until after I finished high school.

Early in life I learned the dignity of labor. I also learned that progress beyond poverty needed more than what we had to scrape by. Social progress and sustainable development requires the intentional collaboration of everyone in the community: of the poor and needy, of decision and policymakers, and of civic groups, in fact, of the entire citizenry.

Central to the MDGs is partnership. Goal 8 speaks of the creation of global partnerships for development. That cannot happen unless we take seriously the participation of all stakeholders in defining and pursuing what that progress and development is.

Human endeavor to better the human condition is one thing. It is another to have economic and political structures democratically governed so that people can participate in bettering their condition. Development, if it is to be beneficial should be people-centered. That, too, must be a key understanding for the MDGs to succeed.

Poverty and wealth will always be relative under any economic and political system. The political infrastructure and the economic architecture of a country, including how it relates to the ever-globalizing economic situation, affects making public policy in such areas as trade, finance and commerce. Public policy certainly reflects how the poor and the vulnerable are treated in society.

How compassionate is society towards the poor and vulnerable? Does the national budget bend toward their needs? Are the so-called safety nets funded so that aside from eking out a living, the poor and vulnerable may also get much needed assistance through public coffers?

[D]evelopment cannot happen unless we take seriously the participation of all stakeholders in defining and pursuing what that progress and development is.

These questions are very germane to the MDGs. The goals and targets are for society's extreme poor and vulnerable. It is for those who will never be able to fight for their rights in the halls of power. Their poverty multiplies over their vulnerability.

Let us be clear: The poor are among us, and among them are the extreme poor. Extreme poverty is the MDGs' target. Anyone who makes just a dollar a day is poor. But the MDGs, say Goal 1, aim at those who do not make close to that amount. The very first target of the MDGs is therefore halving the proportion of people whose income is less than one dollar a day.

Meeting the 21 targets of the eight MDGs is crucial. They will show that the goals made a difference in the lives of the poor and vulnerable by the time the calendar flips to 2015. Fewer than 5 years to go, and the record is both encouraging and discouraging: The multiplicity of crises of food, fuel and finance continue to dwindle public resources, and are affecting the determination of peoples and governments to meet the goals.

The resources coming from civil society included here remind us that our enthusiastic support for the MDGs is nevertheless happening at the same time as the "worldwide food, energy and environmental crises were reinforced by the devastating effects of the financial and economic crises. The combination of these crises is threatening the socio-economic roots and stability of the Global North, and inflicts even greater burdens, with debilitating effects, on the Global South, cancelling monetary socio-economic gains achieved over the last three to five years."

The Civil Society Development Forum of July 2009 declared:

"Now, more than ever, UN Member States must reaffirm their commitment to fulfill the promises they made with regard to Official Development Assistance, and for member states and the international financial institutions to take into account the conclusions and recommendations of the UN Conference on the World Financial and Economic Crisis and Its Impact on Development held in June 2009 in New York. These recommendations reminded all States and international financial institutions to ensure adherence to the social and economic rights of the most vulnerable, especially their right to health."[1]

---

[1]Outcome Document, Threats to the Health and Sustainable Development of Nations, Civil Society Development Forum, 6-9 July 2009, Geneva, Switzerland, sponsored by CoNGO (Conference of Non-Governmental Organizations in Consultative Relationship with the United Nations).

How compassionate is society toward the poor and vulnerable? Does the national budget bend toward their needs?

3

The crises, indeed challenges, behoove us to gather political will from the people, muster political courage from their leaders in government and at UN and international institutions, and exhibit political wisdom at every negotiating and decision-making table.

A promise that as yet is to show real improvement in poor people's lives may yet be frustrated by 2015. Even then, ministry with the poor is a core Christian mission that owes its mandates from the Christian gospel and therefore goes beyond any deadline, official or otherwise.

How indeed can we fill a bowl of food closer to hungry mouths, or put pencils closer to fingers itching to write, or make water available to bedsides of birthing mothers hoping for safe child deliveries? How indeed can a mosquito net get to those who need it the most, especially in the continent of Africa, so that people, especially children, need not die from this needless killer called malaria?

To get serious means that all stakeholders – governments, international institutions including the UN, and civil society – collaborate under rules of transparency and accountability in monitoring the progress of the implementation of the targets through indicators available to all to see and examine.

But indicators mean nothing unless actual programs are monitored as to whether they are making a difference in the lives of poor people.

The *Imagine No Malaria* campaign is one such project, focused on Africa. It has gone from simply a campaign into a movement of people, grassroots and experts alike, working to prevent the disease. Empowerment of people goes hand in hand with strengthening the capacity of United Methodist infrastructures on the ground, such as churches, clinics, hospitals, and schools, to do diagnostic tests and distribute anti-malarial medicines.

Education has gone beyond awareness-raising about the disease to reaching out to as many people as possible to train them to extend the same knowledge and skills they have so that malaria can be avoided. Communications networks are being upgraded so that knowledge sharing is faster and more efficient, something needed about a disease-bearer that flies and knows no sovereign boundaries.

Imagine No Malaria is a program that ties all the MDG goals together. This program shows the virtue of cooperation among governmental, intergovernmental, non-governmental, and

4

philanthropic groups. It shows how much more can be accomplished when working together, and when the people most affected are valued as stakeholders in addressing their health and community needs. Good stewardship of the campaign resources entails transparent accountability mechanisms that include health boards in Africa.

Governments remain crucial in the success of the MDGs. The extraordinary display of international cooperation among Heads of State and Governments was hailed in 2000 as something new and exciting, albeit expressed as promise and pledge, to mobilize global financial resources to address extreme poverty and other intersecting obstacles that are fundamental to achievement of sustainable development, peace and security.

Governments declare poverty thresholds and poverty lines. They aggregate data that the World Bank calls a "poverty profile."[2] Such profile includes "distinguishing characteristics of the poor, such as access to markets, assets, disability, education, employment, ethnicity, family size, gender, marital status, occupation, race, and urban and rural location." Information from such profiles is usually the basis for poverty alleviation programs. The MDGs fit in such a program.

Cost of living is a predictor of poverty. But indicators do not sum up our understanding of poverty or the difficulty of defining it. The fact remains that those in the lower rung of the economic ladder are impoverished. Their impoverization is primarily the result of the inequitable distribution of resources. The rich and wealthy nations of the world – the developed countries – bear great responsibility in the mobilization and equitable distribution of such resources.

The Social Principles of The United Methodist Church declare:

"In spite of general affluence in the industrialized nations, the majority of persons in the world live in poverty. In order to provide basic needs, such as food, clothing, shelter, education, health care, and other necessities, ways must be found to share more equitably the resources of the world. Increasing technology, when accompanied by exploitative economic practices, impoverishes many persons and makes poverty self-perpetuating. Poverty due to natural catastrophes and environmental changes is growing and needs attention … Conflicts and wars impoverish the population on all sides, and an important way to support the poor will

[2]World Bank 1993 Poverty Reduction Handbook.

[T]he fact remains that those in the lower rung of the economic ladder are impoverished. Their impoverization is primarily the result of the inequitable distribution of resources.

be to work for peaceful solutions."[3]

The poor may indeed be with us always. But poverty need not be. The poor themselves are key to strategically altering this condition. Their participation in crafting the direction of their lives and their communities is the necessary antidote to their vulnerability, indeed, of their impoverization.

In 1982, at the Second Fosdick Convocation on Preaching at the Riverside Church in New York, I heard a powerful lecture by Peruvian priest and theologian Father Gustavo Gutierrez. Under the theme "Speaking Truth to Power," I recall him saying: "The news is not that the poor will always be among us. The news is that they are organizing."

The 1980s was, of course, a time when major agendas for cultural, social, economic and political transformation were taken on by a variety of social movements. It was a time of community organizing to fight for social, economic, civil and political rights. The poor not only asserted the dignity inherent in themselves, they also fought for their protection through human rights mechanisms.

The sustainability of communities was not only an economic concern, but a political one. Poverty eradication was understood, for example, in church and ecumenical circles, as a concern of justice as much as of peace and the integrity of creation.

I still remember the call to fast for one day at the Sixth Assembly of the World Council of Churches in Vancouver in 1983. The fast was called in solidarity with the poor and hungry of the world.

I was a United Methodist delegate coming in as a young person from the Philippines. I came from a poor country, and I myself from poor origins. I sensed that was the case for many of the other young people at the assembly.

In response to the call, a good number of us decided not to fast. Youth delegates and stewards alike declared that we came to Vancouver to eat. Not only to eat, but to eat three times a day, with plenty of fruit snacks in between. We made the point that where we came from, many of us did not have the luxury of more than one meal a day, if at all. In a country and at meeting with plenty of food and plenty wasted each meal time, we were going to eat three times and nourish

The poor may indeed be with us always. But poverty need not be. The poor themselves are key and strategic in altering this human condition.

[3] E) Poverty. ¶ 163. IV. The Economic Community, Social Principles of The United Methodist Church, 2008.

ourselves while food was available.

The action was not to disrespect and devalue the spiritual and covenantal power one derives from fasting. On the contrary, it was to force upon our consciousness the effect of unequal sharing of available, even abundant, resources. In that consciousness is the power of acknowledging our dependence equally on prayer and action. We realized that unless joined, faith and action, prayer and deed are not efficacious.

The MDGs, if they are to succeed, must be implemented with the intent that charity cannot be the framework under which they are pursued. Rather, that justice becomes the ultimate aim of any poverty alleviation program.

The fundamental critique against the MDGs arises from the notion that poverty eradication cannot be addressed by the benevolence and philanthropy of the rich. The building blocks on which the eight goals are founded must be human rights. That is, the inherent dignity of each person bestows on them fundamental human rights to life and the securing of rights to food, shelter, clothing, health, education, decent job, etc.

To whomever greater wealth is endowed and achieved lies the greater responsibility to care for and share with those having less. Eradicating poverty will have to mean altering the relations of production so that every human being involved in it partakes equitably of the produce. Also, every resource used in the production, both that of human labor and of natural resources, is treated with care for the sustainability of humanity and the entirety of God's creation.

The spirituality I derived from the conversation with fellow assembly participants about the act of fasting, and our decision to eat instead, was so powerful. The notion of solidarity among poor and non-poor alike was so compelling as to have subverted notions of charity in favor of justice.

Spirituality is abundant and robust when we can pray as well as mobilize resources to empower and provision the poor. The devotionals in this guide, and the prayers said and deeds called for, exhibit this spirituality so abundant of grace and so robust of hope.

The poor may indeed be with us always. But when the poor have God on their side, that is a transformative and liberating moment. The poor may not always side with God, but God siding with them is incarnation at its most subversive. We have Jesus in us because he has

The building blocks on which the eight goals are founded must be human rights.

chosen to in-dwell with us no matter how we reject him.

Philippine witticism includes a wisecrack about drivers of the jeepney, a popular mass transport vehicle among Filipinos. The jeepney brings more souls to heaven than a Sunday preacher. Knowing how drivers navigate traffic-ridden metropolises like Manila, you can perhaps imagine how much passengers pray just to survive the ride. These passengers and the poor alike realize that they have nothing to lose when they pray. In case the compassionate and merciful God to whom they pray is listening, they might just get their prayers answered.

When the poor participate in altering their condition from being destitute to empowerment – as subjects rather than objects – they join God who loved them first, the God who took their side.

And so the poor pray. They cry out loud to the Lord for help. There is a saying in the Philippines that the poor pray unceasingly more than the rich. Former Philippine President Ramon Magsaysay said it another way but compellingly: Those who have less in life should have more in law.

The warning, Jesus' admonition actually, in John 12:8 (NIV), that "You will always have the poor among you" is crucial to our understanding of Jesus' commitment to the poor and their cries.

But wait. Don't stop there as is usually the case. The entire verse says, "You will always have the poor among you, but you will not always have me."

How indeed are we to have Jesus? It seems to me that to have Jesus is to follow his footsteps. We follow Jesus' footsteps by following what he has commanded us to be and to do. We are to be his disciples, inviting and making disciples of him who are ready to transform the world in the ways that reverence God and God's love, justice, and peace.

Deuteronomy 15:4-11 expresses best what it means to obey God. Jesus surely had these verses in mind as he was contemplating the demands of the Sabbatical year whose concern is for the poor.

4However, there need be no poor people among you, for in the land the LORD your God is giving you to possess as your inheritance, he will richly bless you,5 if only you fully obey the LORD your God and are careful to follow all these commands I am giving you today.6 For the LORD your God will bless you as he has promised, and you will lend to many nations but will borrow from none. You will rule over many nations but none will rule over you.

[7]If anyone is poor among your fellow Israelites in any of the towns of the land the LORD your God is giving you, do not be hardhearted or tightfisted toward them.[8] Rather, be openhanded and freely lend them whatever they need.[9] Be careful not to harbor this wicked thought: "The seventh year, the year for canceling debts, is near," so that you do not show ill will toward the needy among your fellow Israelites and give them nothing. They may then appeal to the LORD against you, and you will be found guilty of sin.[10] Give generously to them and do so without a grudging heart; then because of this the LORD your God will bless you in all your work and in everything you put your hand to.[11] There will always be poor people in the land. Therefore I command you to be openhanded toward your fellow Israelites who are poor and needy in your land.

Solidarity with and preferential option for the poor entail giving of ourselves and of our resources openly, generously and abundantly. Those who have been provisioned abundantly are to abundantly provision those who are of greater need. That is justice and equity; it is having Jesus live in us. It is following after our Lord who has blessed the poor.

When we give openly and generously we participate in the dynamic of abundance and empowerment that continually cancels out human deprivations and vulnerabilities. Concern for the poor points to a moral compass whose moorings are justice and compassion.

Jesus lives in us when we follow his genuine commitment to the poor and challenge greed in the manner he rebuked Judas, who would rather that the perfume which Mary anointed on Jesus was sold. Alas, Judas' protestations were not like the solidarity we knew Jesus had with the poor. Judas was after the possibility of dipping his hands into the cash proceeds from the sale of the perfume. Where greed abounds, justice suffers. But where justice prevails, abundant life prospers.

Prayer and deed, worship and work, faith and action – they are intrinsic to each other. The devotionals and resources in this book are exactly about these: prayer followed by a call to perform a deed for the day and resources that describe global challenges we face and that suggest actions we may take to address them. This prayerful guide to the MDGs is a collection of devotionals, resources, forewords, and this meditation. Altogether they inform and educate our prayers so that our deeds may lead to action that sanctifies and glorifies our God.

The Council of Bishops of The United Methodist Church, in the foundational document of its Pastoral Letter called "Hope and Action for God's Good Creation,"[4] speaks of God blessing human beings "with the capacity to read the signs of the times and to respond with intelligence and faith."

The bishops say: "God has inspired human beings to envision new futures and to invent the tools necessary to make them a reality … God is bringing people together to plan and to act upon emerging realities."

The bishops say public leaders "are working at a feverish pace to reshape the rules of engagement between humans and the earth," and "Christian and interreligious communities are speaking out boldly on the interrelated nature of the present crisis."

In this forthright witness to God "doing a new thing," the Bishops highlight the interconnected nature of poverty and disease, environmental degradation, and weapons and violence.

This prayerful guide on the MDGs is a contribution very much in line with the bishops' invitation to "turn from fear and concern to hope and action." The bishops urge us to do so with a combination of prayer, study and action that calls "for transformation of lifestyles, systems, and structures" that speaks well of our biblically and theologically grounded "Wesleyan passion for social holiness."

The guide was meant to show that the eight MDGs coincide with many programs the church has engaged even before the MDGs' enactment.

This guide comes as an expansion of the fall 2005 issue of **pers.pec.tives**, a newsletter my office, the United Nations Office in New York of the General Board of Church and Society, and the Women's Division of the General Board of Global Ministries, jointly published that included a shorter version of this meditation plus eight devotionals.

The guide, from the start, was decidedly Christian in orientation. It was meant to show that the eight MDGs coincide with many programs that the church has engaged before the MDGs' enactment.

While most of the devotional writers are United Methodists from many parts of the world, the

---

[4] A Call of the Council of Bishops of The United Methodist Church to Hope and Action for God's Good Creation. Nashville, TN: Cokesbury, 2010. pp. 17-18.

project has taken on an ecumenical and interreligious character. Others beyond the denomination who are equally concerned with the MDGs have contributed either a devotional or a commentary. And then there are the resources that come from secular groups: the UN and the Conference of Non-governmental Organizations in Consultative Relationship with the United Nations (CoNGO). These resources are not footnotes to the devotionals. The devotionals and resources meet at the nexus where prayer and action cross each other.

It has been my privilege to work with these devotionals as I assembled them into this book. I have been blessed many times over as I read and reread each devotional. My spirituality has been challenged and deepened by the stories of people whose lives are lived according to God's will and Jesus' examples.

As a young United Methodist in the late 1960s, I grew up reading "Siled ti Kararag," the Ilocano version of "The Upper Room." My faith as a Christian was developed in The United Methodist Church. Here I learned how faith and action are entwined; how prayer and advocacy are linked; and how our personal faith can turn into public witness for God's justice and peace.

As a regular member, and eventually the National President of the United Methodist Youth Fellowship in the Philippines, I realized how spirituality and discipleship are deeply meshed with social witness and advocacy. I went to high school at the United Methodist-related Thoburn Memorial Academy on the first year of martial law under then President Ferdinand Marcos. I went to college at the time of the most brutal suppression of human rights in the Philippines. The profligacy of the Marcoses contrasted with the economic deprivation and exploitation that was the daily fare of the majority of Filipinos.

As a youth leader, I taught Sunday School and led studies of the United Methodist Social Principles. These principles and their rootedness in the Gospel of Jesus Christ and the best of our understanding of our Wesleyan heritage have sailed us through the political storm that has seen many, including church members and religious leaders of my own peers, killed and imprisoned in the Philippines. These people dared to struggle for freedom, justice and democracy in a land bereft of them. The United Methodists among them point to the Social Principles as a primary source of their inspiration to pray and act. That was certainly the case for me, then and now.

Prayer and action for the eradication of poverty and the elimination of hunger must be high

Prayer and action for the eradication of poverty and the elimination of hunger must be high both as devotion and agenda for any Christian.

both as devotion and agenda for any Christian. Achieving the MDGs can be vehicles to express our faithfulness to our God whose will is to live life abundantly. Meeting the MDG targets must make us fully aware of the justness of siding with the poor, who are indeed blessed.

A nd what exactly are the MDGs? And why should Christians be concerned about their fulfillment?

At the United Nations 2000 Millennium Summit, 189 Heads of State and Governments firmly committed to work together to build a safer, more prosperous, and equitable world for all. These world leaders committed to eight Millennium Development Goals (MDGs), which originally had 18 quantifiable targets that have expanded to 21.

The Summit's Millennium Declaration reaffirmed commitment to the purposes and principles of the Charter of the United Nations, calling such principles timeless and universal in an increasingly interconnected and interdependent world. The Summit recognized the need to build a world "through broad and sustained efforts to create a shared future, based upon common humanity in all its diversity."

Six fundamental values essential to international relations in the 21st century were lifted up at the Summit: freedom, equality, solidarity, tolerance, respect for nature, and shared responsibility. These values inform key objectives that the Summit identified: peace, security and disarmament; development and poverty eradication; environment; human rights, democracy and good governance; protecting the vulnerable; meeting the special needs of Africa; and strengthening the UN.

I have been fortunate to serve as the main representative at the UN for the General Board of Church and Society of The United Methodist Church for the past 14 years. I have seen how crucial the mandates of the UN are, and how equally crucial the work of non-governmental organizations is in fulfilling those mandates.

Even more, I have seen how crucial the role of faith-based bodies like our denomination and an agency like GBCS is in raising the ethical and moral dimensions of public policy in all arenas: local, national, regional and global.

The UN is an institution designed to address the human condition. That's a big task for an organization with little resources at its disposal. Sometimes, even bigger obstacles to overcome

Meeting the MDG targets must make us fully aware of the justness of siding with the poor, who are indeed blessed.

are the criticisms leveled against it. The strongest defense of this institution comes from Dag Hammarskjöld, one of the UN's beloved Secretaries-General. He said the UN is "not created in order to bring us to heaven, but in order to save us from hell."

The MDGs are a set of targets aimed at alleviating the poorest of the poor from endemic, lingering poverty. To renege on this task that the MDGs address will be a failure of political imagination. Not achieving the goals will mean consigning the extreme poor into further vulnerability, marginalization, and exploitation.

The MDGs committed the UN to sustainable development and to the elimination of poverty. With the MDGs forming part of other internationally agreed development goals, the UN has put in place people-centered development at the heart of global, national and local agendas.

The MDGs come to us by way of decisions and actions of previous world conferences that defined and crafted wide-ranging agreements on human rights, women, sustainable development, migration, climate change, population, social development, financing for development, etc. Like the MDGs, these internationally agreed development goals are themselves waiting to be fulfilled.

At its 2004 General Conference, The United Methodist Church expressed strong support for the MDGs. It resolved to call on governments worldwide to implement the Millennium Declaration and the MDGs that emanated from it.[5]

The United Methodist Social Principles remind us that all economic systems are under the judgment of God. The MDGs, too, fall short of the gospel measure of life in its fullness. The fullness of the MDGs comes from the larger array of internationally agreed development goals.

At the center of United Methodist mission are two focus areas directly related to the MDGs: combating the diseases of poverty by improving health globally and engaging in ministry with the poor.

As a denomination our work with and among the poor predates the MDGs. Ministry with the poor and ministries of healing are central to the work of the Christian faith. But at no time as a denomination have we been more intentional than now in linking with other institutions in achieving a greater synergy to address poverty and global health.[6]

Ministry with the poor and ministries of healing are central to the work of the Christian faith.

[5] See Resolution # 6025. Globalization and its Impact on Human Dignity and Human Rights. The Book of Resolutions of The United Methodist Church, 2008).

[6] See www.ministrywith.org for more information.

The poor may indeed be with us always. But poverty need not be. Even more so, our commitment to justice must then become a commitment to eradicate poverty and eliminate hunger. It is a commitment that might just indeed "make poverty history."

The MDGs are a step in the right direction. Surely not enough but their targets are urgent. Their achievement will contribute to obliterating the blight of poverty and hunger. And yes, perhaps even the scourge of conflicts and wars will be slowed down. To be freed from want is to be freed from fear. Freed from want and fear, people live in dignity and in peace and security.

In this century we now have the knowledge and technology to address hunger, poverty, and diseases that afflict the human race. It is time to mobilize the necessary wisdom, will, and commitment, to put them to work to do so.

Excuses will be frowned upon. It won't be acceptable if the presidents, prime ministers and royalties renege and backslide on their promise in 2000 that they "will spare no effort to free our fellow men, women and children from the abject and dehumanizing conditions of extreme poverty, to which more than a billion of them are currently subjected."

Social Watch, an NGO dedicated to poverty eradication and gender justice, in its statement to the 2010 UN Summit on the MDGs, said that "to invest in the poor, through social services or even direct cash transfers makes for a better stimulus package for the economies as a whole than subsidizing the already rich."

Social Watch contends that this "match of the ethical imperative with economic good sense is simple: In times of crisis affluent people save when they can and risk-aversion demoralizes investors, whereas those living in poverty can only spend any support they get."[7]

The lackluster commitment to financing for development, including the anemic flow of official development aid, including commitments already made by governments and international financial institutions to the MDGs, unless scaled up, are going to imperil achievement of the goals.

There is no illusion that the MDGs are enough to eradicate hunger, eliminate poverty, or even to educate every boy or girl. Still, there is normative power in the slogans "Make Poverty History" and "Stand Up. Take Action. End Poverty Now."

There is no illusion that the MDGs are enough to eradicate hunger, eliminate poverty, or even to educate every boy or girl.

[7] Statement on the 2010 Un Summit. We need Justice, Not Business as Usual", Dar-es-Salaam, April 2010.

My prayer is that we seize on the moment to act upon the MDGs. While they are not enough, they are nevertheless pointed in a direction where resources that are otherwise budgeted for wars and other unsustainable activities should rather go to reducing the blight of poverty and the pangs of hunger.

Empty coffers and grumbling stomachs make for chaos and conflict. Achieving the MDGs may help avert this.

Achieving the MDGs, according to the campaign Stand Up Against Poverty, entails addressing a host of other issues: public accountability, just governance and the fulfillment of human rights; trade justice; debt cancellation; gender equality; climate justice; increased quantity and quality of aid and financing for development; as well as peace and security.

The prophet Micah is instructive in what is required of us at such a time as this:
"He has told you O mortal, what is good; and what does the Lord require of you but to do justice, and to love kindness, and to walk humbly with your God? (Micah 6:8 NRSV).

The MDGs show possibilities for justice, kindness, and humility to be experienced in our lives. They can become common global goods that animate the way we transact our social, economic, political and cultural relations.

It's amazing how something clearer and compelling happens when one reads and re-reads a biblical text. Reading Micah 6:8, the beauty and the force of a biblical and prophetic injunction comes to the fore. The sequential enumeration of the eight MDGs finds resonance in this Micah text. The first three goals correspond well to the justice call; the second three to kindness; and the last two to humility.

To do justice. Isn't this what the first three goals are about: addressing extreme poverty and hunger; ensuring that boys and girls complete primary education; and promoting gender equality and empowerment of women?

The MDGs help address injustices that consign people to poverty and powerlessness. The MDGs point to the empowerment and strengthening of people's capacities so that they can be freed from want and enabled to build sustainable communities. Justice as a criterion of sustainable development points to the provision of choices that are varied and plural, and the capacity to make choices in structures that are democratic and participatory.

Empty coffers and grumbling stomachs make for chaos and conflict. Achieving the MDGs may help avert this.

Food sustainability and food sovereignty must be pillars of poverty eradication. We must protect and insulate the rights to food and to work, from both political indecision and economic exigencies, as these rights are tangible measures in eradicating poverty and eliminating hunger. In short, they are crucial to achieving the MDGs.

To love kindness. Isn't this what the second three goals are about: reducing by two thirds the mortality rate among children under five; reducing by three quarters the ratio of women dying from childbirth; and halting by 2015 and reversing the spread of HIV/AIDS?

The MDGs point to our common vulnerabilities, as peoples and communities, and in so doing, help engender a kind, compassionate society where the vulnerable and marginalized are freed to live with their dignity intact and their human rights enhanced. Kindness in society entails the securing of safety nets for the vulnerable and the marginalized.

Health is central to the MDGs because it is at the core of poverty eradication and sustainable development agenda. Good health is not just the outcome of poverty reduction and development; health is a way of achieving them.

GBCS, supported by the UN Foundation, has sponsored two programs that address maternal and child health. These are "Operation Healing Hope" and "Healthy Families, Healthy Planet." These programs assert that "political stability, economic security and human survival on a vulnerable planet all depend on healthy populations born of healthy mothers."

To walk humbly. Isn't this what the last two goals are about: ensuring environmental sustainability and developing a global partnership for development? The MDGs enhance our common humanity. The call to humility is itself the call to revere our God and Creator who reminds us of life's finitude, the cosmos, our human communities and relations.

The last two sets of MDGs are a reminder that not only is the planet our common habitat, but that assaults on it redound commonly to our peril. Humility reminds us of the finitude of the physical environment as well as the human capacity to tinker with it. Humility enables us to acknowledge that the earth is the Lord's and the fullness thereof (Psalm 24:1) and that the resources in it, finite they may be, are a common inheritance to be enjoyed by all.

Care for the earth and care for humanity must be the highest agenda for global cooperation and partnerships. Even as the UN is being reformed to be better and more efficient, it must not

Kindness in society entails the securing of safety nets for the vulnerable and the marginalized.

give up and slacken on its mandate to secure, enhance and protect the global commons that are our natural patrimony.

The MDGs challenge our capacities to address the goals that are at once global in dimension yet aching to be localized. They matter to impoverished, marginalized and vulnerable peoples and communities. They challenge our willingness to muster courage and mobilize for action on matters that strike deeply into the core of our Christian calling to be a just, loving people. Like John Wesley, may we then "watch over one another in love."

"Development emergency" is the term used by UN Secretary-General Ban Ki-moon to describe the dire situation poor countries are in five years from the MDG deadline. The moral challenge that the MDGs pose before us emanates not from their urgency, as they surely are urgent, but that they are doable if only there was enough political will to redirect already available resources for their achievement.

The ethical compass must surely point to the achievement of the MDGs. The MDGs should be baselines to start from and not ceilings to reach. As baselines, it would be downright immoral if we fail to act upon them knowing that we have the resources to address diseases of poverty, to address gender equality, to provide basic and primary education, and to make childbirth and maternal health safe.

The MDGs are of monumental proportions. When ethical demands arising from the goals stare us in the face, I pray that we welcome divine mediation. Even principalities and powers compete to define what love requires and ethics demands. It is moments like these when the faithful must pray and act together and preach the full gospel of love and compassion, of justice and peace, and of mercy and grace.

To participate in the implementation of the MDGs requires from people of faith the inner strength to love so that we can move on to care justly, kindly, and humbly. The MDGs compel us to address the vulnerabilities of "the least of these" (Matthew 25:40), for to them the urgency is real.

The devotionals that follow are a rendering of the MDGs in ways that I hope will summon divine illumination, biblical inspiration, and personal witness. The writers have shared their

The ethical compass must surely point to the achievement of the MDGs. The MDGs should be baselines to start from and not ceilings to reach.

17

stories of faith and witness whose junction is action on behalf of God's blessed: the poor. Their devotionals come with biblical verses in which God's words and the witness of God's disciples speak to the human condition and the state of our planet today.

Each writer ended his or her devotional with a prayer that lifts up every human endeavor to God's throne of grace. In so doing, we hope that such efforts may be found pleasing and sanctified, and meet the gospel demands of love and grace, of justice and peace, and of compassion and forgiveness.

Each devotional includes a deed for the day that calls the reader to do something doable and tangible. Small acts and little steps perhaps, but nonetheless such deeds can become strong and effective if done by many, and if done collaboratively.

The quote for each day comes from many sources. They are intended to supplement our understanding of each goal and inform the course of action we may take to address it.

In all, my hope is that our individual and collective actions will help achieve the MDGs in ways that satisfy the gospel demands of justice and peace.

An investment in the achievement of the MDGs is an investment for today and the future.

We will have consigned our children and our youths to a bleak future so hard for them to undo and unmake if we renege on our responsibility to mitigate the spread of ever-more virulent diseases such as HIV/AIDS, malaria and tuberculosis, but also non-infectious diseases including mental health; or if we renege on fighting hunger and malnutrition that are primary causes of death among the world's peoples; or if we renege on helping the UN to end the scourge of and penchant for war.

The scars of wars and the painful grind of an empty stomach on our young are not what make for a just, peaceable and sustainable future.

And so this meditation. And so this prayer. That in God's own good time, even as we may always have the poor with us, poverty need not be because we have resolved to collectively bless the poor by the equitable and just sharing of our resources.

The scars of wars and the painful grind of an empty stomach on our young are not what make for a just, peaceable and sustainable future.

ERADICATE EXTREME POVERTY AND HUNGER

Commentary by Athena Peralta

Poverty is quite simply the biggest threat to life; and the critical work to eradicate this scourge is at the very core of our faith and witness in Christ. Above all, Jesus taught us: "Love your neighbor as you love yourself."

The scandal is that we have more than enough resources in the world to guarantee that the "least of our brothers and sisters" lives in fullness and dignity, that none is forced to sleep in the street on empty stomachs.

Growing up in the Philippines, where politics often colludes with multinational businesses, where landless farmers are among the hungriest, where indigenous peoples – dispossessed of their mineral-rich ancestral territories by "development projects" – are forced to take on dirty, demeaning and dangerous jobs in the cities, I quickly learned that poverty is manufactured: There is nothing natural or preordained about it.

Tackling the roots of impoverishment entails transforming structures of trade and finance that concentrate political power and economic resources in the hands of a few. It means carving and enlarging spaces for people and communities to participate fully in making economic decisions that affect

MDG 1 – Eradicate Extreme Hunger and Poverty

Target 1.A: *Halve, between 1990 and 2015, the proportion of people whose income is less than $1 a day*

Target 1.B: *Achieve full and productive employment and decent work for all, including women and young people*

Target 1.C: *Halve, between 1990 and 2015, the proportion of people who suffer from hunger*

their lives. It is about ensuring people's equitable access to land, technology, health care, education and training. It has to do with investing in the really important things: basic needs such as food and water, social reproduction and ecological protection.

We won't be able to take on any of these challenges with any success, if we don't see women as equal partners in fighting poverty. In my family and community, women have always been in the frontline of struggles to put food on the table and safeguard other basic needs.

(Athena Peralta is an economist based in Manila, Philippines, and currently serves as a consultant for the Poverty, Wealth and Ecology Project of the World Council of Churches. The WCC promotes Christian unity in faith, witness and service for a just and peaceful world. An ecumenical fellowship of churches founded in 1948, today the WCC brings together 349 Protestant, Orthodox, Anglican and other churches representing more than 560 million Christians in over 110 countries, and works cooperatively with the Roman Catholic Church. WCC's project on poverty, wealth and ecology "encourages churches to explore and advocate for alternatives to economic globalization. It is an attempt to bring churches and ecumenical partners from North, South, East and West together to reflect and act together on finding new and creative ways to use global wealth to eradicate poverty. It encourages them to create new synergies between different standpoints on poverty, wealth, and ecology." WCC is headquartered in Geneva, Switzerland.)

For such a time as this. In the 1990s, I attended my first National Gathering of Bread for the World in Washington, DC. The attendees were to lobby senators and representatives on behalf of legislation to alleviate hunger in Africa. Since I had never visited a congressional office or called my senator or representative, I was apprehensive about what I would say. I didn't want to hinder the proposed legislation. I reviewed the information many times to be well prepared, but I had to ask God to prepare me for the visits. After praying and asking God to be with me and to put the right words in my mouth, I felt at ease.

I thought of Queen Esther who spoke to the king to save her people. Esther's uncle Mordecai, urged her to speak to King Xerxes after he had ordered that all of the Hebrews should be killed. No one but Mordecai knew that Esther was a Hebrew. By law, no one could approach the king without being invited. If Esther approached the king, she risked danger or even death. She told Mordecai to have all the Hebrews fast and pray for three days.

God provided Esther the wisdom to approach the king and the courage to speak for her people. God gave me the courage and words to speak when I visited the congressional offices. **(Donna Burkhart, Erie, Pennsylvania, USA)**

Admitting that business-as-usual hasn't worked, and agreeing to change mindsets, and really change the way that everyone works. That's a big call for the agencies, for donor governments, for governments in the big countries where there are hungry people.... (Vanessa Rubin, Care International)

1

ERADICATE EXTREME POVERTY AND HUNGER

Bible Reading

Speak out for those who cannot speak, for the rights of all the destitute. Speak out...defend the rights of the poor and needy.
(Proverbs 31:8-9 NIV)

Prayer

Lord, please give us the courage of Queen Esther to speak up on behalf of the world's hungry and starving people. Grant us wisdom to speak the words to legislators so that they pass laws eradicating global hunger. Amen.

Deed for the Day

Call, e-mail or write your representative or senator to pass legislation, like reforming foreign aid, to alleviate worldwide hunger.

1

ERADICATE EXTREME POVERTY AND HUNGER

Bible Reading

And the king will answer them, "Truly I tell you, just as you did it to one of the least of these who are members of my family, you did it to me." (Matthew 25:40 NRSV)

Prayer

Dear Lord, help us to recognize your abundant grace through the people who acknowledge you as their God and share their abundance to those in need. Amen.

Deed for the Day

Help facilitate access to abundant resources and answer the needs of poor people.

God's abundant grace. My first church assignment as a United Methodist pastor was Kalayaan, in the province of Laguna in the Philippines. Livelihood in this rural area centers on fishing and farming. Many families are poor, like Elaine's. Elaine, a daughter of church members, is a very thin, frail and underweight young girl. One time she insisted on joining us on our way to a fiesta in nearby Lumban town. The car being already full, she sat on somebody's lap. She was so underweight and possibly undernourished that having her on someone's lap was not burdensome. Most families who are members of Kalayaan church, like Elaine's, are poor. When Elaine's father got sick with asthma, there was not enough cash to buy medicine and to visit a doctor. Her mother earned very little money working as "katulong," or household help, and as laundry woman.

To support church members like Elaine's family, I asked for help from the Methodist Committee on Resource Development, a Philippine group providing loans and loan management training. With loaned capital, Elaine's family put up a small business in the neighborhood selling banana cue and other snack items. With the small profit they earned, they were able to meet some of the family's immediate needs.

Other livelihood projects were introduced to church members and the community, including making rug and "taka," or paper maché, along with other livelihood activities. The small profit made from sales of their products augmented the meager incomes of families and sustained their basic needs for a healthier life. Elaine completed high school and is now working in a nearby shop, enabling her to support her siblings. God's grace is abundant indeed!
(Joel A. Capulong, Antipolo City, Philippines)

We at UNICEF are convinced that working together with committed partners, and with an appropriate plan of action and a commitment to resources, we can make that dream a reality for each and every child on earth.
(Carol Bellamy, former Executive Director, UNICEF)

Seeing the poor as our neighbors. A bridge in Massachusetts connects South Hadley, a small white upper middle class town to Holyoke, one of the poorest urban cities with a Hispanic and Puerto Rican population. The bridge is less than 400-feet long, but is called the "5,000 Mile Bridge" representing the distance from Puerto Rico to South Hadley where many live as if they are 5,000 miles from the poor in Holyoke.

In the Gospel story, we find the distance between the rich man's table and the gate where Lazarus was living. The rich man lived as if a chasm was fixed between him and Lazarus, as if Lazarus was 5,000 miles away. Poverty, at its heart, is the issue of distance. Global poverty exists in the distance between the rich and poor, exacerbated as the developed nations live and make decisions as if there is a chasm between them and the rest.

Jesus lived and died to bridge the chasm that his society and religion created. This is why he crossed many boundaries and traveled to the other side, and loved others as our neighbors. Ending poverty begins only when we see the poor in our community and the world as our neighbors. A young father on a Haiti mission once told me, "Haiti is far away. But if you look from Heaven, it is just next door to us!" **(We Hyung Chang, Massachusetts, USA)**

Achieving the MDGs will also require targeting areas and population groups that have clearly been left behind – rural communities, the poorest households and ethnic minorities, all of whom will have a hand in shaping our common future. (Sha Zukang, UN Under-Secretary-General for Economic and Social Affairs)

ERADICATE EXTREME POVERTY AND HUNGER

Bible Reading

Son, thou art ever with me, and all that I have is thine.
(Luke 15:31 KJB)

Prayer

Through the love and life of Jesus you have bridged the chasm between you and us, O God. Help us to have the same love of Jesus to bridge the chasm that keeps the poor apart from your blessing on all your children. Amen.

Deed for the Day

Find the poor at the gate of your house, your church, your city, and the world. And get to know them.

ERADICATE EXTREME POVERTY AND HUNGER

Bible Reading

"Who are you Lord?" Saul asked. "I am Jesus, whom you are persecuting."
(Acts 9:5 NIV)

Prayer

Creator God, we have much work to do. Give us the courage to take responsibility for our actions both past and present, and to implement change, and be Your voice among all peoples. Amen.

Deed for the Day

Seek out your state's or community's historical relationships with indigenous peoples. Learn how to help correct the wrongs committed on them.

Poverty among Native Americans: As a United Methodist woman, it was our church's School of Christian Mission that awakened me to traumatic injustices that were inflicted upon the indigenous American Indian populations. These injustices remain a silent and mostly hidden part of US history. America was not "discovered." Before Europeans invaded America, its native peoples were a vibrant people who sought no land ownership, knew no source of greed, and wanted no other life than to commune with their Creator. When Europeans claimed their land, raped its landscape for resources, inflicted their values upon this land's rightful constituents, and herded them into reservations, the onslaught of persecution and racism started. It has not stopped to this day.

Poverty among tribal nations in the United States is alarming but widely ignored. The Pine Ridge Reservation, with a casino whose financial gains only benefit a few, continues to experience poverty at all levels. Care for the most vulnerable remains elusive among American Indians.

Poverty and persecution, especially by travesties in religious boarding schools, are the suffocating sources of many problems in Native communities. The wounds are generational and very deep. We need to take responsibility in our share of making these happen. The Apostle Paul journeyed forward to make amends for his wrongdoings, to do all he could to right the wrongs, and provide pathways to new life and redemption. We also must. **(Billie Fidlin, Glendale, Arizona, USA)**

Let us show solidarity with people living in poverty everywhere. Let us all stand up together to end poverty once and for all. (Asha Rose Migiro, UN Deputy Secretary-General)

There is enough. The Sermon on the Mount brings together food security and human rights as two aspects already inextricably linked in Jesus' time as it is today. These aspects underline the important finding that hunger is not so much a problem of production, but of distribution – of lack of realizing the right to food and of justice to the poor.

Being in Southeast Asia at the end of 2007, I witnessed how the onset of the Global Food Crisis and the dramatic price hikes hit the poor particularly hard. Never in history have we been further removed from Millennium Development Goal One, despite record harvests and the availability of unprecedented amounts of food. There is enough for everybody – if we share it adequately.

We know what explains food insecurity, hunger, and malnutrition: highly unequal income distributions; inadequate social protection schemes; weak protection of agricultural workers; gender, ethnic and other types of discrimination; poor connection to markets; high input prices; insecure land tenure systems; inequitable international trade systems, and many more.

Poverty and hunger are rooted in deprivation of power, security and influence. Poor people are disempowered agents, deprived of the benefit of rights, possessions, land tenure and political influence. Reducing poverty and hunger calls for more rights and self-determination – for greater scope for constructive participation that shifts the balance of power in the poor's favor. Poverty cannot be fought in the long term by outside experts, donors or companies. Only the poor themselves can do it. Jesus already knew. **(Thorsten Göbel, Stuttgart, Germany)**

Mere economic growth has already been shown to be an unsustainable, inefficient – and in some cases, ineffective – way of addressing the global poverty crisis. (World Council of Churches, UN General Assembly Hearing with Civil Society on the MDGs, June 2010)

1

ERADICATE EXTREME POVERTY AND HUNGER

Bible Reading

Blessed are they who hunger and thirst after righteousness, for they will be filled. (Matthew 5:6 TNIV)

Prayer

God of love and mercy, we grieve about the more than one billion poor and hungry people on this earth. Give us hunger and thirst for righteousness against our lethargy and indifference. And provide us with the power to engage for the realization of all human rights, universally. Amen.

Deed for the Day

Ask your political representatives what they are doing for the effective realization of the universal right to food (Not food aid!).

ERADICATE
EXTREME POVERTY
AND HUNGER

Bible Reading

For I was hungry and you gave me something to eat, I was thirsty and you gave me something to drink, I was a stranger and you invited me in. (Matthew 25:35 NIV)

Prayer

Creator God, giver of life, help us open our hearts, minds and spirits that we may know better our mission in this time and place that you have called us to walk. Help us embrace our journey with wisdom and courage. Amen.

Deed for the Day

Teach and feed a child and help prepare the path for healthy future generations.

Little learning with empty tummies. Born into the Ojibwe and Dakota indigenous tribes, many traditional values were passed on to me. My early journey found me teaching in the late 1970s in a small town in Northern California. Children of migrant workers from Mexico, families who arrived from Vietnam and indigenous Native Americans filled the combined first grade classroom. These children spoke many languages, had many traditions, and held great pride, something I deeply understood. Poverty and hunger were things we shared in common, for I was barely making ends meet.

There were no school meal programs; snacks and lunches were brought from home if we had food to bring. Only a little learning and teaching can take place with empty tummies. I made many trips to ask the school nurse's office for instant breakfast mix to help ease the hunger of these little ones. To provide good education, the school and community committed to good nutrition. With breakfast and snack programs, learning became easier.

Preparing the path for future generations had begun. My heart and spirit hold much respect for those that prepared my path and I thank God, our Creator, each day for the sacrifices of those early generations. Now it is our turn. **(Boe Harris, Seaford, Delaware, USA)**

Individuals...are...volunteering to make a difference. They remain the true champions of our work towards the Millennium Development Goals.
(Kofi Annan, Former UN Secretary-General)

Poverty thresholds differ. In the process of adopting our son Brett, my wife Suzanne and I were brought to tears as we read that our son's birth mother Maria was at peace with the decision to make Brett available for adoption. She knew that the poorest family in the United States would be able to provide for her son better than she could because her income in Guatemala was "a few cents a day" from making tamales.

I thought I had seen poverty in my native Appalachian hills, but I've been insulated from real poverty. Around adoption time, our adoption agency invited us to participate in its mission project to provide school supplies and uniforms for children who live in a dump in Guatemala City.

The US Department of Health and Human Services established US $10,830 as the 2009 poverty threshold for a single person. Well over one billion citizens of the earth live on one dollar per day, which is an annual income of US $365. It could be less. It takes just over twenty-nine of these people to meet the US "poverty" threshold; twenty-nine people trying to survive on what our nation identifies as not enough for one person.

Millions of Marias live on "a few cents a day," and every four seconds, one of them dies of starvation. Jesus says it best: "You give them something to eat."

(Jonathan Jonas, Marion, Virginia, USA)

If we fail to meet our aid commitments, we miss a chance to speed our own economic recovery. Fiscal stimulus has the biggest impact when it is directed to poor people.
(Asha-Rose Migiro, UN Deputy Secretary-General)

1

ERADICATE
EXTREME POVERTY
AND HUNGER

Bible Reading
Late in the afternoon the Twelve came to him and said, "Send the crowd away so they can go to the surrounding villages and countryside and find food and lodging, because we are in a remote place here."
(Luke 9:12-13 NIV)

Prayer
Gracious God, help us love our neighbors enough to share from the abundance you have entrusted to our care. Amen.

Deed for the Day
Set aside a weekly day of fasting and contribute the money you would have spent on food to feed the world's most impoverished peoples.

ERADICATE EXTREME POVERTY AND HUNGER

1

Bible Reading

But now I will come, says the Lord, because the needy are oppressed and the persecuted groan in pain. I will give them the security they long for.
(Psalms 12:5 GNT)

Prayer

Forgive us if we keep praying but do nothing to help alleviate the plight of our brothers and sisters in dire need of material and moral support. Give us the courage to denounce the evils in our society that do not serve the interests of the poor. Amen.

Deed for the Day

In times of disasters, join a relief and rehabilitation operation. At all times, advocate for economic policies that support sustainable development and for political policies that include the poor in decision making.

Typhoons that crush hope and snuff out life. Typhoon Ondoy struck my country, the Philippines, on September 26-27 of 2009. In its wake were 400 people dead, with many injured and missing. There were massive destruction and loss of properties. In the aftermath of this disaster, I saw thousands of people crowding in different evacuation centers. It was horrible to see both the living and the dead gathered in one of the evacuation centers.

I volunteered for one of the church groups doing relief distribution. I realized after going to the communities affected by Typhoon Ondoy that hunger and poverty will take a long time to eradicate. My worry is that it would last forever. The majority of those who were severely hit by Typhoon Ondoy were the poorest of the poor. The urban poor dwellers that had nothing even before the typhoon struck were devastated even more by the typhoon. Those hit were people who live on less than a dollar a day. A bag of rice, dried fish, sugar, salt, mongo beans, pack of oil, stuff that makes a bag of relief goods, would, in fact, look like luxury even for just two to three days of relief operation.

Sadly, the Philippine government was caught unprepared for this disaster. It took almost two days for the government to respond. By then many had lost their lives, limbs and properties. The government's response included blaming the victims. Government agencies continue to be criticized for mismanaging relief operations. Our people suffer from hunger and poverty, with or without natural disasters. But a typhoon not only breaks the backs of urban poor dwellers. It also crushes their hopes, if not snuffs out their lives. We must pray and act to reverse such situation. **(Rubylin G. Litao, Quezon City, Philippines)**

Poverty alleviation is not an easy task since it is a major driver for other devastating elements such as wars, epidemics & diseases, eradicating poverty means create the atmosphere for peace and stability.
(Fatima Ahmed, President of Zenab for Women in Development, Sudan, at the UN MDG Summit, 2010)

Without a trace, and no help. Families send their strongest young sons, including minors, from places like Ghana, Togo, Benin, Nigeria, and Cameroon to European countries hoping for a better condition in life. They try to cross the Straits of Gibraltar, aboard miserable boats, from take-off points in Libya, Algeria and Morocco. Some others travel in unseaworthy vessels via Mauritania and Western Sahara to the Atlantic coast and on to the Canary Islands.

Every year, 2,000 African emigrants drown on their dangerous journey in the Straits of Gibraltar. Also, more than 2,000 Africans disappear without a trace before reaching the Canary Islands. Spanish coastguards observe the movement of boat refugees with night-vision equipments. There is information that they are able to see everything, including the multiple rapes that occur aboard the ships.

Poverty and hunger in many African countries have forced families to gamble the lives of their children in these dangerous journeys. When survivors from the sea voyage arrive on the European continent, very few people would have the slightest idea what these people have gone through, including barely escaping death.

Most of the boat people are rejected by the rich European nations and sent back to their countries of origin, into poverty and violence. Sometimes, they will be abandoned in the Algerian deserts. Only mothers with their little babies may stay in Europe, presumably on humanitarian grounds. Maybe God will ask us, when we, the rich, account our lives: In their time of need, what have you done to help my people? **(Jörg Niederer, Frauenfeld, Switzerland)**

Let us commit, each one of us, to building the political will to make poverty history. To ensuring that in 2010, we can look forward to achieving the Millennium Development Goals five years later. (Asha-Rose Migiro, UN Deputy Secretary-General)

1

ERADICATE EXTREME POVERTY AND HUNGER

Bible Reading

When the child grew older, she took him to Pharaoh's daughter and he became her son. She named him Moses, saying, "I drew him out of the water." (Exodus 2:10 NIV)

Prayer

Help us to help each other, Lord, each other's load to bear; that all may live in true accord, our joys and pains to share. (Charles Wesley)

Deed for the Day

Meet a refugee and let him or her tell you about his or her hometown! Pray for open hearts, open minds and open doors!

1

ERADICATE
EXTREME POVERTY
AND HUNGER

Bible Reading

Here is a boy with five small barley loaves and two small fish, but how far will they go among so many?
(John 6:9 NIV)

Prayer

Lord, help me to step up as I hear the stories of my hungry brothers and sisters throughout the world. The little I have that is enough for me in my eyes let me share it to feed the hungry around me.

Deed for the Day

Look in your wardrobe, pantry, pocket, and drawers and see what you can share to alleviate hunger and poverty.

Sharing food with the hungry. When looking at the story of the feeding of the 5,000, focus is mostly about the five loaves of bread, the two fish, and yes, the 5,000 who were fed. The boy who gave up his lunch is mostly forgotten in many accounts. The little boy realized that though he had enough for his own lunch, many others were hungry right there with him. So he shared his lunch with prayer and honesty, indeed transparency of what he had. Jesus used the boy's honesty and willingness to feed the people.

We have so many people who are hungry in the world even as there are those who have more than enough but do not share their wealth and resources. There are many nations in the world with no money to feed their own people even as there are a few nations who would fund the production and stockpiling of weapons but withhold funds for food and other basic human necessities. They build defenses from imagined and created enemies despite the real presence of poor people in their midst.

Sometimes we are not willing to save the needy because we underestimate our capacity to help. This boy stepped up and could have said: "I can help feed all these friends who have spent their day with me in faith." Many times we hear words that put the blame on the poor for their poverty, scolding them for allowing hunger and homelessness, and the like, to happen to them. This boy did not ask these same questions; he stepped up to the plate, shared what he had, and dealt with hunger where it was needed most urgently. **(Lloyd Nyarota, Mutare, Zimbabwe)**

Poverty is a threat to security. (Sering Falu Njie, UN Millennium Campaign)

The good of all. For over 30 years I worked with people whose circumstances precluded them from fully participating in employment: people living on daily basis unable to see beyond poverty that entrapped them; people who felt that they no longer had choices. Poverty erodes choice. Lack of choice erodes dignity. Loss of dignity saps energy. And the circle closes, leaving many unable to contribute to the economy and the development of their communities.

Men and women trapped by poverty found that when they did manage to find work, it was often low paid and insufficient to meet their family's need. In recent years the British government passed a law which ensures that everyone is paid a national minimum wage even if work is unskilled. This demands a great deal of cooperation from employers to pay the right wage for a day's work. Everyone deserves to be paid fairly for the work they do.

Sadly this is not the case in other parts of the world. Often people who work in the clothing industry and in food production are not paid a fair wage for their work. Ethical shopping helps combat exploitation in the clothing industry. Buying fairly traded produce ensures that food growers and pickers receive a fair price for their goods. Considering the source of these commodities and buying ethically is one way of working together for the good of all. **(Kathleen Pearson, Great Britain)**

The growth of ethical consumerism in developed countries has led to increased imports of environmentally and socially certified products produced by the poor in developing countries, which could potentially contribute towards the achievement of the MDGs. (Asian Development Bank Institute)

1

ERADICATE EXTREME POVERTY AND HUNGER

Bible Reading

And do not forget to do good and to share with others, for with such sacrifices God is pleased. (Hebrews 13:16 NIV)

Prayer

Gracious God, may we be mindful of how food comes to our table and clothing is made for our markets. May we work together so that fair trading becomes natural rather than exceptional. Amen.

Deed for the Day

Make a point of using Fair Trade produce for one meal per day.

ERADICATE EXTREME POVERTY AND HUNGER

Bible Reading

One who is gracious to a poor man lends to the Lord, and He will repay him for his good deed.
(Proverbs 19:17 NAS)

Prayer

Lord, may we forget the new things we want and remember the struggles of our world. May we work each day in our own hearts and those of our neighbors to end hunger, poverty and other preventable vices of our world. Amen.

Deed for the Day

Put down the latte and give just a little bit to the world's poor.

Between nutrition and education. I'll never forget my first day working with children at a school in Tanzania. On my shoulders, I held a boy who suffered from Down Syndrome. He had a nagging cough, which I later found out was the early stages of tuberculosis In my arms, I held two boys, one who suffered disabilities from meningitis earlier in life, and another who was deemed to have mild autism by the history of volunteers who had come before me in this place. These boys, though, were still in school.

Each day, when snack time came around, the evidence of parents choosing education over nutrition was clear. Parents work multiple jobs to send their children to schools, while not being able to afford a sandwich or a clean drink.

I'm struck by the current economic crisis in the USA, a place where the middle-class started lining up at the food banks, dealing with their new struggles. I wonder about others: What about the chronically poor, those who don't have a food bank to turn to? Food is not a luxury; it is a vital piece necessary for human development. No one should go to bed hungry, not the person in the USA, trying to make next month's mortgage, nor the child in Tanzania, trying to make it to the next day of school. **(Ryan D. Smith, Alexandria, Virginia, USA)**

Globalization makes it clear that social responsibility is required not only of governments, but of companies and individuals. All sources must interact in order to reach the MDGs.
(Anna Lindh, Former Swedish Minister for Foreign Affairs)

I have no excuses. Don and his little brother who lived in our small apartment complex had skinny arms and legs but also big stomachs, which I didn't know was an indication that they were not eating enough. One day I was outside eating a sandwich when Don said, "I'm going inside and make me a sandwich, too" and later came out with one slice of bread with sugar on it. "See, I have a sandwich, too," he said.

Later that day I told my mother about Don's sugar sandwich, and she asked me if I had shared my sandwich with him. I told her I hadn't. "I don't think he likes sugar sandwiches," she told me. "I believe it was all they had to eat." This was the first time I realized what being poor can do to a person. Of course I had no idea back then that Don and his brother represent a significant part of the population of this world or what I should do about a hungry child. Well, that was then, but today I have no excuses.

The story of Elijah's encounter with the widow of Zarephath and her son signaled God's concern for the poor, hungry and powerless of our world. God will not allow their suffering to go unnoticed. But note that God addressed Zarephath's need through another person who was willing to act on behalf of God. **(James E. Swanson, Sr., Knoxville, Tennessee, USA)**

(*It is the poorest of the poor - those who spend a large proportion of their income on food - who have been most affected by the increasing prices… But if food prices fall - even substantially - it will not necessarily cancel out these effects. Many households in distress have already sold assets that are difficult to build up, leaving them more vulnerable.* (Kostas Stamoulis, Agricultural and Economics Development Division, UN Food and Agriculture Organization))

ERADICATE EXTREME POVERTY AND HUNGER

Bible Reading

But she said, "As the Lord your God lives, I have nothing baked, only a handful of meal in a jar, and a little oil in a jug; I am now gathering a couple of sticks, so that I may go home and prepare it for myself and my son that we may eat it, and die."

(I Kings 17:12 NRS)

Prayer

My God, once I didn't know, and now that I know help me to act to eliminate these conditions not only for those who are hungry but for my salvation, as well. Amen.

Deed for the Day

Reach out to a hungry child and you will have reached out to the poor, hungry and powerless.

ERADICATE EXTREME POVERTY AND HUNGER

Bible Reading

Carry each other's burdens, and in this way you will fulfill the law of Christ… Therefore, as we have opportunity, let us do good to all people, especially to those who belong to the family of believers.
(Galatians 6:2-10 NIV)

Prayer

Almighty God, source of everything, hear us to consecrate ourselves to serve the poor through our skills and resources. Empower us with our honest purpose and steadfast endeavor to do your will. In Jesus' name we pray, Amen.

Deed for the Day

Provide technical skills and vocational skills in impoverished communities and you will be surprised at the effect on the dignity and standard of living of peoples in the community.

Learned skills, disposable income. Hunger and poverty are two of the problems of developing countries like the Philippines. To help solve this concern, the Northern Cagayan Apayao District (NCAD) United Methodist Women (UMW) is helping to teach women acquire skills in livelihood projects that can help them earn and augment their incomes.

If poor families in the Philippines are given a chance by government and/or civic groups to learn much-needed technical and vocational skills, their status will be lifted and their living standards greatly improved. The northern part of Cagayan has vast resources ready for families to tap and mobilize. Access to technological know-how will help improve the standard of living in this part of the province. Millions of lives can be saved from malnutrition and poverty.

After an actual training conducted by the UMW, many families were enabled with skills on how to market their produce. The additional income they made from these sales helped fund family needs such as schooling of children, medicine and hospitalization, and food. Mothers who became busy with livelihood projects eventually were able to feed their families and hence helped eradicate poverty in their area. **(Various authors, Social Principles Workshop, Northern Philippines Annual Conference of The United Methodist Church, August 2009, Tuguegarao City, Philippines)**

Failure in meeting the MDGs cannot be blamed on the world lacking the resources and the know-how to do so. There is a very wide range of proven policies and interventions which will adapt to national context and will ensure progress.
(Helen Clark, Administrator of the UN Development Program, at 2010 UN High Level meeting on the MDGs)

Feed my sheep. On a recent study tour to China which my wife and I joined, our group visited the Imperial Summer Palace. For 800 years, it was the retreat from the summer heat for emperors.

At the refreshment area, I bought a bag of popcorn for a snack. Then without a word, my wife prodded me to look in the direction of a trash can ten feet away. There, next to the trash can, was a man, perhaps thirty years old, scavenging for food. His t-shirt, drenched with perspiration in the sweltering heat, clung to his back.

I could tell my wife wanted to do something. Unsure that he would take it, I offered the bag of popcorn. He grabbed it with both hands, yelled something with joy, and literally put his face to the bag to eat.

There are millions ravaged by hunger like that man. The Millennium Development Goal on hunger is right for our time. Without exception there's something each one of us can do. Jesus' words "Feed my sheep" are our marching orders. **(Vivencio L. Vinluan, Covina, California, USA)**

More than 30 per cent of children in developing countries – about 600 million – live on less than US $1 a day. Every 3.6 seconds one person dies of starvation. Usually it is a child under the age of five. (unicef.org)

1

ERADICATE EXTREME POVERTY AND HUNGER

Bible Reading

The third time he said to him, "Simon, son of John, do you love me?" Peter was hurt because Jesus asked him the third time, "Do you love me?" He said, "Lord, you know all things; you know that I love you." Jesus said, "Feed my sheep." (John 21: 17 NIV)

Prayer

O God, forgive our blindness to the plight of the hungry among us. Help us look into our hearts to find something to share. Amen.

Deed for the Day

Study carefully the Millennium Development Goals and relate them to Jesus' call to "feed my lambs."

ERADICATE EXTREME POVERTY AND HUNGER

Bible Reading

One who is gracious to a poor man lends to the LORD, and He will repay him for his good deed.
(Proverbs 19:17 NAS)

Prayer

I pray for continued wisdom and guidance and the opportunity to continue to provide pro bono legal assistance to those in need.

Deed for the Day

Do something like I did: sent out the comments from applicants at our Saturday Legal Clinics to the volunteer attorneys and thanked them for their help and support.

Let justice roll down. I have been working for many years with people in poverty who desperately need help with a myriad of legal issues. Recently, local lawyers have begun to provide help to individuals by going to churches and libraries on Saturday mornings to give advice and counsel.

Last Saturday, on my birthday, over 125 applicants came to the library in Memphis for help. They were people who have dropped from middle class to indigent because of the economic situation. These are people who have lost custody of their children, or are about to lose their health care. Eighteen lawyers and five paralegals came to help.

Some of the comments from the applicants were: "I really thank you so much. I am glad I came. The attorneys were so helpful, professional. God Bless!" "Thank you for your free assistance. I truly appreciate you being available to me, Gratefully, LS."

In these difficult times, giving back to others in need is vital. I am grateful to belong to a profession with an ethic of doing pro bono on behalf of the indigent. **(Linda Warren Seely, Jackson, Tennessee, USA)**

Whilst progress has been made, much more remains to be done… As a global citizen we share responsibility for reducing poverty and giving people a better chance at life. (Alexander Downer, Australian Minister of Foreign Affairs)

ACHIEVE UNIVERSAL PRIMARY EDUCATION

Commentary by Jo Anne Murphy

As a young African-American girl raised in the heart of America by parents with very little formal education and equally limited financial means, I know the value of primary education in opening a child's doorway to growth, achievement and eventual contribution to improving the human condition.

We were blessed to live in a small, predominantly white, community that provided excellent public primary education to all, regardless of the fact that my race remained a social barrier throughout my educational journey in Kansas. My parents taught me that I needed to be three times as smart and good as any other student in order to survive and succeed.

I learned to do just that, taking full advantage of that primary school platform to rise through all levels of education with great success. Blessed with scholarships, I was able to attend one of the world's finest institutions of higher education in international relations in Geneva for my ultimate badge of achievement, acknowledging that my primary education foundation enabled me to soar beyond racial and economic barriers to acquire a world-class education.

When it became my turn to give back, in both French West Africa and the USA, I was blessed to bring others' children into my home and give them

MDG 2 – Achieve Universal Primary Education

Target 2.A: *Ensure that, by 2015, children everywhere, boys and girls alike, will be able to complete a full course of primary schooling*

access to a bright future by facilitating their access to education. Today, one of the girls brought to me by her family in Africa from a remote village where they could no longer care for her is now one of the most successful business women in her country, a struggling LDC in West Africa.

Another young girl I helped raise in the USA with my own four children was blessed with receiving an excellent primary education and is now a successful graduate of one of the best universities in her field in the USA. They, like myself, each began with a solid primary education that eventually opened the doors of excellent secondary (Africa) and higher education (USA), leading to a brilliant future for both of them and positive benefits for humanity.

This is reconfirmed daily by NGOs at the grassroots level in Africa, such as AfricAid and the Ethiopian School Readiness Initiative focused on preschool education. The future of our world is irreversibly linked with the quality and extent of primary education now provided to our children – the children of Planet Earth. This makes realizing MDG 2 – the achievement of universal primary education – crucial!

(Jo Anne Murphy, Ph.D., is the Director of Programs with Intergovernmental and Nongovernmental Organizations at the Office of Global Learning of Fairleigh Dickinson University in Teaneck and Madison, New Jersey, USA.)

Commentary by Nguepi Ndongo Donald

I am a 20-year-old Cameroonian studying at the University of Douala, here in Cameroon. I am studying psychology and currently I'm at Level II. I recently founded with the help of some of my young friends

---

What The United Methodist Church says:

"We believe that every person has the right to education. We also believe that the responsibility for education of the young rests with the family, faith communities, and the government. In society, this function can best be fulfilled through public policies that ensure access for all persons to free public elementary and secondary schools and to post-secondary schools of their choice."
(Social Principles ¶ 164. E)

a youth group called Youth for Peace. We aim to promote peace and nonviolence in society and facilitate the integration of youths in the peace process.

While I am already in college, it was at primary school that as children we were taught the value of giving no distinction to sex, being open to society, and learning to adhere to its rules, laws and conventions.

Through primary school, children acquire better social skills, better adaptation to new situations, basic principles that will serve them in later life and many other instances. The primary school is of utmost importance for the proper moral development of girls and boys.

Primary school in Africa, in general, and in Cameroon, in particular, is not always given attention. It is necessary, given the targets of MDG 2, to ensure that all children, both girls and boys, are able to complete primary schooling.

It is our duty to appeal to institutions such as the government, NGOs and associations working for a better education for children to develop methods and strategies to make access to primary schools possible and easier. This can be done by a primary school exempt of any fees, the construction of schools in rural areas, increasing the teaching staff and infrastructure, and rewarding best students.

(Nguepi Ndongo Donald is a college student at the University of Douala in Cameroon training to be a psychologist. On the side, he works with other young people in a youth group they call Youth for Peace.)

"As a teacher in public schools for the past 18 years, I am in great appreciation of the ministry of local churches to schools. I have seen the difference that church partnerships make in the life of children and in the overall functioning of schools." (**JoLisa Hoover**, http://www.umc-gbcs.org/site/apps/nlnet/content3.aspx?c=frLJK2PKLqF&b=2952519&ct=8654563&notoc=1)

2

ACHIEVE UNIVERSAL PRIMARY EDUCATION

Bible Reading

All they asked was that we should continue to remember the poor, the very thing I was eager to do.
(Galatians 2:10 NIV)

Prayer

Almighty God, inspired by the life and ministry of your son Jesus Christ, continue to challenge us to be the living representatives of your love, truth, justice and peace wherever we are. Amen.

Deed for the Day

Sponsor a student's transportation or meal allowance today. Walk the extra mile, do it for a week or even for a month.

Inspired to be an inspiration. I was born in Tondo, in the northwestern side of Manila in the Philippines. People are scared and ashamed of my home-town supposedly because of filth, violence and extreme poverty. Such an image is, sadly, reinforced by media. The horrifying numbers of Filipinos below the poverty line just keep increasing. Born to a poor family myself, I promised that I will never be forever part of the statistics.

I kept my promise. The journey was not easy, though. Having been blessed, it is time to give back and share just as much what God has and continues to shower upon me and my family. I learned that whatever your status in life, God calls us to become living vessels of God's wonderful love to a world needful of it.

Realizing how important education is, I have been an avid supporter of our Church's scholarship foundation. In our neighborhood, I have also been sponsoring the daily transportation and meal allowances of three students – one in elementary, high school, and college. The amount is meager, the most being just a little over one US dollar (no more than 50 Philippine pesos). Their faces glow every time they receive their allowances. The joy and satisfaction that those smiles give me is beyond description.

God has been good to me. Inspired, it is now time to reach out to others and touch their lives. **(Ronald Paz Caraig, Manila, Philippines)**

The Philippines is racing against time. It is struggling to meet the Millennium Development Goals by 2015… Indicator one (for MDG 2) which is to bring the net enrollment ratio in primary education to a full 100 percent by 2015 is difficult to achieve because as of 2007 … the net enrollment ratio in primary education, is still at 84.8 percent, the government said.
(Iris Cecilia Gonzales, Philippine Star, 24 May 2010)

Make primary education viable. I recently visited a United Methodist orphanage just outside Uganda. The school began as a place for orphaned children. Their parents had either died of AIDS or getting killed attempting to cross over the border from the Democratic Republic of the Congo. Several of the children I met now live with AIDS themselves. As soon as we arrived all fifty of the primary school children gathered outside to sing hymns of hospitality to us. They gestured with their eyes, hands and hearts, ever so gently and ever so warmly a welcome to us adult strangers. The schoolhouse consisted of one room cement blocks on which the children sat attentively, willingly, expectantly. Dignity exuded from all of the children.

These little children, whose names I had yet to learn, had so much to teach me about what it means to be a responsible adult. My mind wandered back to my own children, ages five and nine, as the children sang and followed their teacher's lessons that day. My children attend a primary school in Washington, DC. The school aims to be a model for science-based education. It is located in between a strip bar and a liquor store. Parents and teachers try very hard to make sure children are safe from random gang violence outside of the school.

The schools in Kampala and where my children go were both built on a foundation of tolerance, respect and dignity for children. Teachers and students are valued as means to an education of the mind and soul. St. Paul says it's time to grow up, but it's never time to grow cynical. God neither wants us to wallow in ignorance nor expects us to do the impossible. Universal primary school education is a reasonable and viable goal if the community of nations infuses resources to it. **(Neal Christie, Washington, District of Columbia, USA)**

If world leaders decide to (meet the Millennium Development Goals), I think it can be done by 2015...The question is, is there a political will to make this investment? (Thoraya Ahmed Obaid, Former Executive Director, UN Population Fund)

ACHIEVE UNIVERSAL PRIMARY EDUCATION

Bible Reading

When I was a child, I spoke like a child, I thought like a child, I reasoned like a child; when I became an adult, I put an end to childish ways. For now we see in a mirror, dimly, but then we will see face to face. Now I know only in part; then I will know fully, even as I have been fully known.
(Corinthians 13:11-13 NRSV)

Prayer

God, thank you for parenting us to grow in curiosity, kindness, knowledge, and wisdom. Your care raises us up to be responsible adults, doing what is needful, just and good. Help us to work with you to provide universal primary school education for all, that all may come to a full knowledge for you. Amen.

Deed for the Day

Connect with children in the Global South who are learning to advocate for themselves in the midst of war, disease, hunger.

ACHIEVE UNIVERSAL PRIMARY EDUCATION

Bible Reading

Therefore, I urge you, brothers and sisters, in view of God's mercy, to offer your bodies as a living sacrifice, holy and pleasing to God—this is your true and proper worship. 2 Do not conform to the pattern of this world, but be transformed by the renewing of your mind. Then you will be able to test and approve what God's will is—his good, pleasing and perfect will.
(Romans 12: 1-2 NIV)

Prayer

Merciful God, thank you for you have called us and chosen us to be your own people and serve you so that your name may be glorified amongst the humanity. Grant us the strength, courage and wisdom to continue serving you in newness of spirit though Jesus Christ our Lord and savior. Amen!

Deed for the Day

Donate your services and your resources for humanitarian causes and help send children and youths to school.

Change begins with me! I was ordained as United Methodist Deacon in 2006. That year I was appointed as Youth Minister for my Annual Conference and also worked as National Education Programme Officer with Save the Children in Angola. Working with Save the Children increased my awareness of the challenges the education sector is faced with in my country. It also allowed me to reach out to many people and communities and help them pursue a better quality of life through access to education.

"Rewrite the Future" was the main project under the education area in Save the Children at that time of my work with this organization. "Rewrite the Future" offered hope and helped change people's hopeless future, turning that future into a brighter one, and thus rewriting their life stories such that their poverty and sufferings were alleviated. The same way when God's grace reaches out to us and saves us, God no longer remembers our past sins and sinful life.

Being part of Save the Children's team in Angola was such a blessing to me. It gave me the opportunity to respond to God's call in my life and live up to my vocation serving God by serving others. Besides, as Angolan Methodist Christians we have a slogan that expresses one of our strong convictions and that shapes our way of living expressed in the following words: "If you do not live to serve then you are of no use to live!" What a pleasure and joy it is to serve others and impact lives by setting people free to help others in alleviating misery and poverty. **(Mário Gerson Monteiro da Costa, Luanda, Angola)**

Yes, many people lift themselves out of poverty on their own. Yes, the school of hard knocks has many famous graduates who have struggled and succeeded. But how much better it would be to give every boy and girl the opportunity to make the most of themselves. (Ban Ki-moon UN Secretary-General)

Hope and joy of education. Become an advocate for change. When I was 17, my youth group and I went on a service trip to the Philippines. As part of our trip, we visited a few schools, one of which was located in the midst of abject poverty. Part of the school's courtyard was flooded with murky, greenish liquid. Like the courtyard, the classrooms would flood several times a year, preventing students from attending classes. When the moldy, mildewed classrooms were not flooded, they would be crowded with 60 to 70 children, studying without class sets of text books in the sweltering heat.

Despite terrible conditions such as these, the children valued their education so much that they were eager to be at school, finding joy in learning and hope for the future. Many other children in the Philippines, however, do not have access to the hope and joy education can bring, for poverty forces them to struggle for survival, to work or beg instead of attend school.

I will never forget the schoolchildren I met that day and one of their teachers who asked me what my church and I would do to improve the children's situation. His question invites us all to become advocates for children, seeking to change the social systems that deny them their right to a fulfilling education. **(Ashita Eleanko, USA)**

Bible Reading

"Blessed are the poor in spirit, for theirs is the kingdom of heaven. Blessed are those who mourn, for they will be comforted. Blessed are the meek, for they will inherit the earth." (Matthew 5: 3-5 NIV)

Prayer

God of knowledge and truth, help us to educate one another about the difficulties that humans face every day. Help us to be your hands and feet to spread your word and love to all your children. Be with us as we kindly share your knowledge and try to bring all the young children to prosperity. Grant that as we spread the fruit of knowledge we remember that you are the source of all truth. Amen.

Deed for the Day

Donate used textbooks to organizations that help with primary education.

Until equal numbers of girls and boys are in school, it will be impossible to build the knowledge necessary to eradicate poverty and hunger, combat disease and ensure environmental sustainability. And millions of children and women will continue to die needlessly, placing the rest of the development agenda at risk. (UNICEF/MDG/Education)

2

ACHIEVE UNIVERSAL PRIMARY EDUCATION

Bible Reading

He told them another parable: "The kingdom of heaven is like yeast that a woman took and mixed in with three measures of flour until all of it was leavened." (Matthew. 13:33 NRSV)

Prayer

O most gracious God, the one who encourages us to learn and grow and enlarge our hearts, help us to share out of our wealth and experience. Help us to listen to the poor and cooperate with them in bringing the "good news" of knowledge and training to the children and youths. Amen.

Deed for the Day

Research all of the international Advance Specials of The United Methodist Church and support those who are working creatively in schools.

I nvesting in creative local solutions. We were welcomed into the two large rooms of the technical school in Jalapa, Nicaragua, by the teachers and students. In one room, the boys were busy sawing and sanding and so very proud of their work on the wooden coffins. We learned later from the teacher that over the years the boys had had several wood-working projects. It was important to adapt to the local village market – whatever would sell.

In the other room teenage girls were measuring, cutting, pinning and sewing material into dresses and outfits of their own design. The sewing machines were hand pedaled; electricity was scarce and unreliable. Most were able to sell their clothing at local stores or be employed as seamstresses upon graduation.

Keeping students in school is a challenge in this small village in northern Nicaragua. Many start primary school but drop out to help out at home or simply because they don't see the value of an education. These students are part of a program founded by two United Methodist churches which "train" them in carpentry or sewing at no cost, if they stay in school. They spend half the day at school and the other half learning a trade. The teachers are all local. At least one graduate went on to University in Managua. One school program is making a huge difference in the lives of Nicaraguan children and youths and their families! **(Linda Gertenbach, Denver, Colorado, USA)**

The world we seek, where every child can grow to adulthood in health, peace and dignity – in short, a world fit for children – has remained a dream for more years than we can count. (Carol Bellamy, Former Executive Director, UNICEF)

Let them come. One of the many joys of having opportunities to travel is interacting with people, particularly the children. While in the Dominican Republic, I was given the opportunity to visit one of the small villages outside Santiago and help lead a week-long Vacation Bible School for the children. I will never forget the smiles on those children's faces as they ran towards our approaching van driving the dirt road to their village. Buenos dias! Bienvenidos! Good morning! Welcome!

Throughout the week, we shared food, played games, made crafts and connected with my broken Spanish. Maybe those children did not learn much from us during that week. And, it is quite possible that they have forgotten us, but I still remember the enthusiasm with which they participated in every activity.

For those seven hours or so that we were together, their chattering never stopped and their smiles did not fade. They genuinely enjoyed just being around us. I did not know it then, but only later found out that most of them did not have a school to attend; we were school for them. We presented an opportunity that they did not normally have. For that, they were grateful. For that, I am grateful. Unfortunately, they are only a few of the 73 million children of primary school age who are not in school. **(Joseph Kim, Washington, District of Columbia, USA)**

(*The impact the Basungi project [in Congo] has left on the quality of education is reflected through the high attendance rate and school ranking in the area, and the faces of the school children expressing appreciation through giggles and meaningful smiles.* (Marjon Kamara, Head of Africa Bureau, UN High Commissioner for Refugees))

2

ACHIEVE UNIVERSAL PRIMARY EDUCATION

Bible Reading

But Jesus called the children to him and said, "Let the little children come to me, and do not hinder them, for the kingdom of God belongs to such as these." (Luke 18:16 NIV)

Prayer

God of Wisdom, thank you for the faith and the innocence of children. Allow it to be an example for us all. May we, too, yearn for your wisdom and seek your ways. We pray this in the precious name of Jesus Christ. Amen.

Deed for the Day

Consider buying a School-in-a-Box Kit from U.S. Fund for UNICEF (www.unicefUSA.org) and help to educate children.

2

ACHIEVE UNIVERSAL PRIMARY EDUCATION

Bible Reading

The mind of the prudent acquires knowledge, and the ear of the wise seeks knowledge.
(Proverbs 18:15 NASB)

Prayer

Lord, we give you thanks for giving us minds to learn about you and the world you created. Let our hands and feet be those of Christ that we may be inspired to build schools and promote learning among the world's children.
Amen

Deed for the Day

Encourage your church to partner with or raise funds for missionary or service organizations that build primary schools for children in need.

B**eing Christ's hands and feet.** Several years ago, in keeping with Jesus' Great Commission, our ministry had a desire to serve not only our immediate community but other nations as well. Our goal was twofold: to bear witness to the Gospel of Christ and to engage in works of mercy such as building schools. We partnered with a wonderful organization called Hands and Feet Ministries (http://www.handsandfeet.com), an interdenominational nonprofit ministry founded by Roy and Michelle Adams. Their mission is to be Christ's hands and feet to a world in need.

Over the next several years, we have sent volunteers to Mexico on multiple mission trips with Hands and Feet to help build, among other service projects, primary schools for children. Our trips lasted about a week each so our results were limited, but we knew we were just one among many churches working on the same schools. It's difficult to see how we can affect the world for change as individuals, but there is such strength when the church stands together as one body for a common cause.

Universal primary education is a wonderful goal, but how will children learn unless they are taught? And how will teaching happen without schools? As Jesus was a carpenter, so may we build schools with our hands and feet, always remembering our calling as Methodists to spread scriptural holiness throughout the land. **(Mark Kim, New York, New York, USA)**

We cannot tell these children to wait…In countries where conflict, drought, famine, and the HIV epidemic prevail, school fees hit children the hardest. These children need the safe environment, routine and services that schools can provide…he promises of school fee abolition should no longer elude so many countries that are willing to embark on such a bold initiative.
(Cream Wright, UNICEF Education Chief, 2006)

Small but hopeful praying hands. Last March, I participated in a training event for Asian Christian women In Kuala Lumpur, Malaysia. One of the programs I visited was an asylum for children and youths, ranging in age from 4 to 18 years old. I thought they would attend a school building, but instead it was a park, actually more like an empty ground space that turns to mud when it rains. Their parents, who were Christian refugees, had come from Myanmar to Malaysia to find religious freedom. But because the Malaysian government considered them illegal aliens, they did not provide education for their children. The UN refugee program provides four teachers per 400 children and youths.

We spent the morning with the children. The children and youths sat down and studied on the ground. I taught dance and games and shared Bible stories with 4 to 8 year olds. Temperature was hot and humid at over 100 degrees. After three hours with them, my voice was gone. When they received lunch, which we provided, the children prayed with their hands neatly folded. When I saw their small praying hands, all of my tiredness was gone.

Seeing these children, I came to have faith that Jesus Christ will give them a future filled with hope. I also had assurance that for their future God will prepare leaders among them. When I heard that Methodist Women in Malaysia have been supporting education for these children and youths, my sad heart was changed to bright hope. This is their "hope and love in action." MDG Goal 2 is critical to fulfill if we are going to see a brighter future for children and all of us. We are responsible for making it a step closer to reality. **(Myungrae Kim Lee, Oakland Gardens, New York, USA)**

Malaysia has done well in achieving virtual gender parity in access to education for boys and girls. However, women's participation in the labour force has stagnated over the past 25 years at 45–50 per cent. In 2007, women also earned 28 percent less than men, little changed from 1997. (Kamal Malhotra, UN Resident Coordinator, Malaysia, in Preface to Malaysia: The MDG at 2010)

2

ACHIEVE UNIVERSAL PRIMARY EDUCATION

Bible Reading
But Jesus called the children to him And they were bringing children to Him so that He might touch them; but the disciples rebuked them. But when Jesus saw this, He was indignant and said to them, "Permit the children to come to Me; do not hinder them; for the kingdom of God belongs to such as these." (Mark 10:13-14 NASB)

Prayer
Dear God, we resolve to save one dollar each day to feed lunch, to supply school needs, to clothe school children, and give them. Today, we want to practice it in our offerings. In Christ Jesus we pray. Amen.

Deed for the Day
Support programs like providing free lunch to school children, after-school programs, tutoring, kid's leadership training event, Children's Sabbath, and others.

2

ACHIEVE UNIVERSAL PRIMARY EDUCATION

Bible Reading

He established a decree in Jacob, and appointed a law in Israel, which he commanded our ancestors to teach to their children; that the next generation might know them, the children yet unborn, and rise up and tell them to their children, so that they should set their hope in God, and not forget the works of God, but keep his commandments.
(Psalm 78:5-7 NRSV)

Prayer

All praise and thanks to you, merciful God, for adopting us as your own children, for incorporating us into your holy church, and for giving us the ability to share that inheritance with others. Amen.

Deed for the Day

Call your members of Congress or parliament and urge them to support full funding of public education.

Primary **education a keystone.** Many of us who grew up in the United States went through our early school grades believing boys are not supposed to be smart. Only girls got good grades. Much later, we learned that, until quite recently, girls did not have the same opportunities for education as boys. Even today, some cultures deny girls the right to an education.

The larger problem is that today more than 100 million children, both boys and girls, are not in school at all. Nations facing extreme poverty and hunger have few resources to direct to schooling. But as Psalm 78 indicates, without education the people have no future.

Concern for education is not new. In 18th century England, leaders organized Sunday Schools to educate children in poverty. Although many historians credit Robert Rakes with beginning the Sunday School movement in 1780, there were actually many such schools by that time.

These early educators worked to promote salvation by teaching children to read the Bible. But reading gives a general state of empowerment. These educators also increased the well-being of all society as children were able to lift themselves out of the widespread poverty of their time.

In building a society, free and compulsory primary education becomes the keystone that holds up the entire culture. Some believe that countries in poverty cannot afford education. Both rich and poor countries must necessarily work together in supporting the Millennium Development Goal to "achieve universal primary education." **(Robert McClean, Mattoon, Illinois, USA)**

(Those pledges should be engraved on the heart, or at least the desk, of every political leader in every country. Indeed, they should be known throughout every society, so that in each country the people can monitor performance, and hold their leaders to account. (Kofi Annan, Former UN Secretary-General))

Achieving universal primary education a social justice call. From the choosing of his disciples to his treatment of those expelled from society, Jesus' life and actions are a constant reminder that we are all equal in God's eyes. Yet, very little in our world today resembles the egalitarian message that Jesus taught. Instead we find a world of "haves" and "have nots," with not enough being done to close the gap between the two.

When visiting a village in South Africa a few years ago, I spent time at a school where 80 percent of the children were orphans. Their parents had died of HIV/AIDS. Even though these children were racially, ethnically, and in some cases even religiously different from me, I am as responsible for their well-being as I am with my neighbor who lives down the street. I once read a bumper sticker that said, "A gated community…an oxymoron?" This bumper sticker cleverly reminds us that as believers in Jesus Christ we have a responsibility to speak up on behalf of the destitute because we are all part of a larger community created equal in God's eyes.

One of the most practical ways to bridge this gap of "haves" and "have nots" in our community is through the empowering force of education. Achieving universal education, and thus improving literacy rates, not only promotes equality but also a more inclusive and participatory society. Primary education equips children with the necessary tools to better themselves and leads to greater equality in society. **(Wilson Paine, Maryville, Tennessee, USA)**

Work must be intensified to get all children into school, especially those living in rural communities, and eliminate inequalities in education based on gender and ethnicity, and among linguistic and religious minorities. (Sha Zukang, UN Under-Secretary-General for Economic and Social Affairs)

2

ACHIEVE UNIVERSAL PRIMARY EDUCATION

Bible Reading

Speak up for those who cannot speak for themselves, for the rights of all who are destitute. Speak up and judge fairly; defend the rights of the poor and needy. (Proverbs 31: 8-9 NIV)

Prayer

Dear gracious God, please provide me with the strength and courage to speak up on behalf of the poor and destitute. May your word and the teachings of your son, Jesus Christ, guide me as I seek social justice for your entire community, where no child should ever feel inferior. Amen.

Deed for the Day

Find books or magazines that you are willing to give away; ask your pastor to help you find schools outside the US that are in need and ready to receive your donation.

2

ACHIEVE UNIVERSAL PRIMARY EDUCATION

Bible Reading

"Truly I tell you, just as you did it to one of the least of these who are members of my family, you did it to me." (Matthew 25:35-40 NRS)

Prayer

Dear God, whose other name is "Good," help us become more deeply aware as we meet Christ in new and different faces. May we become followers of the way Christ lived his life. Amen.

Deed for the Day

Do something generous to someone beyond your immediate family circle who is in need.

How wide is your world? I remember a few years back when my family from California came to visit us in Honolulu, Hawaii, where I had a local church assignment. We took my sister-in-law and her young daughter to the beach about five minutes away from the parsonage. We watched her run as fast as she could along the beach. We could see her enjoying the thrill of touching the seawater. Moments later, wading through the water up to her ankle and using her palms to scoop some seawater, she exclaimed, "Hey, I got the whole ocean in my palms!"

When we got home late that day, I began reflecting on my niece's words. They kind of illustrate to us how many of us assume we "got the whole ocean in our palms," when actually we are just touching a scoop of it. At times the world we know simply revolves around the people whom we are personally acquainted with. Our pockets and purses are much looser to those close to us.

But the gospel calls us to know and see farther beyond family and close friends. Christ calls us to love even the gentiles–the "outsiders," the "dispossessed," the "poor," the "sinners," the "least." **(Johnny Riingen, San Diego, California, USA)**

Although social integration is not mentioned per se in the MDGs, achievement of these goals is intertwined with the "quest for humane, stable, safe, tolerant and just societies" identified in Copenhagen. (H.E. Mr. Leslie Kojo Christian, Permanent Representative of Ghana)

ACHIEVE UNIVERSAL PRIMARY EDUCATION

A brighter future for our children. In a visit we made to Marag Valley, in Luna, Apayao in Northern Philippines, we saw many children who were in need of basic education but were out of school. We saw their parents needful of livelihood that would earn them a living that could enable them to leap out of poverty and afford to send their children to school.

In the Philippine Constitution, parents are obliged to send their children to have basic education. Public education is available to children from primary to secondary school. Still, poverty and the cost of education are preventing many parents from sending their children to school. Parents who did not go to school could have the tendency to not send their children to school. Even then, education is highly valued in Philippine culture, and parents, if they had the means, will send their children to school.

Jesus grew up well-rounded in wisdom, stature, and in favor with God and humans. We hope our children grow this way, too. Children are part of God's plan of abundant and fulfilled life. Children are God's paragon of entering God's kingdom but cannot be good role models if they are denied education.

Let us intentionally make programs that ensure primary education and even beyond so that our children have a brighter future. **(Various authors, Social Principles Workshop, Northern Philippines Annual Conference of The United Methodist Church, August 2009, Tuguegarao City, Philippines)**

Bible Reading
And Jesus grew in wisdom and stature, and in favor with God and men. (Luke 2:52 NIV)

Prayer
God of little children, grant us your wisdom to do the right things in helping little children to acquire basic education. Amen.

Deed for the Day
Encourage parents to send their children to primary school and beyond. Talk to them about the value of learning.

[T]he proportion of children not going to primary school is still an issue in Asia and the Pacific region...Moreover, there is a particular concern about the gender gap in Southern Asia. Girls are more likely to drop out because of school safety and traveling time. Girls also do not complete school due to early marriage or pregnancy, or because they are needed to work at home.
(UN Economic and Social Commission for Asia and the Pacific)

ACHIEVE UNIVERSAL PRIMARY EDUCATION

Bible Reading

My people are destroyed for lack of knowledge. (Hosea 4:6a NASB)

Prayer

Father, open our eyes to your children that are being trapped in the slavery of ignorance. And help us to build the bridges to ones with resources to the hunger for knowledge. Amen.

Deed for the Day

Read to youths in your family about different children in other cultures and their ability to help other children around the world.

Making hopes and dreams come true. I was in the town of St. Catherine, Jamaica, when I met a young boy on a weekday during the school year. I asked him why he wasn't in school. He told me that his mother had nine children and could not afford to send all of them to school. So only the younger ones went to school – and yet this boy was around ten years old. He said his mother could not afford the tuition for the public school in addition to the cost of transportation, uniforms, books, lunches, etc.

Around the world, many factors prevent children from attending and completing primary education. Some of these factors include malnutrition, inequalities in early childhood care, gender, disabilities, ethnicity, and proximity to conflict zones, to name a few.

Children all over the world have hopes and dreams, but it seems that marginalized children don't have the necessary support for all their hopes and dreams to take shape. **(Kayon Watson, New York, New York, USA)**

(To achieve universal primary education, children everywhere must complete a full cycle of primary schooling. Current statistics show that the world is far from meeting that goal (The United Nations MDG Report, 2011))

PROMOTE GENDER EQUALITY AND EMPOWER WOMEN

Commentary by Jacqueline Sylvie Ndongmo

The MDGs have been successful in creating increased political awareness on development issues. They have enabled solid progress in many countries, especially in the social sectors, but not a similar progress in economic sectors.

The Goal of MDG 3 is to promote gender equality and empower women. The primary focus of the goal is to reduce gender disparity in all levels of education. Additionally under this goal issues of increasing women's access to decent work and participation in political processes are addressed.

The MDG 3, the empowerment of women, is critical to the attainment of all the MDGs, having a potential multiplier effect, transcending the gender issue as such. Focus on MDG 3 is crucial and creation of breakthrough strategies is needed if we are to reenergize and reactivate the MDGs after the crisis, if we are to establish ownership to these goals among a new generation of political leaders, and if we are to accelerate and scale up, based on what we know.

I strongly believe that gender equality and women's empowerment are central for reaching all the other MDGs. For me, MDG 3 is the core to accelerating progress on all the MDGs. It simply pays off to invest in women.

MDG 3 – Promote Gender Equality and Empower Women

Target 3.A: *Eliminate gender disparity in primary and secondary education, preferably by 2005, and in all levels of education no later than 2015*

What The United Methodist Church says:

We affirm women and men to be equal in every aspect of their common life... We affirm the right of women to equal treatment in employment, responsibility, promotion, and compensation.
(Social Principles ¶ 162. F)

The movement to improve the status of women is one of the most profoundly hopeful of our times.... There is increasing awareness that we cannot solve world problems associated with globalization and unequal distribution of resources, population growth, poverty and war so long as the talents and potential of half of the world's people are disregarded and even repressed.
(3445. The Status of Women. The Book of Resolutions of The United Methodist Church, 2008)

Only a joint effort will enhance gender equality and women's empowerment – and thus contribute to achieving all the MDGs. And why me? Because my voice counts.

In terms of political participation, I strongly believe that increasing women's participation and leadership should be a major priority for both the African Women's Decade (2010-2020) and the new agency for women's empowerment: UN Women. This is no coincidence as at both regional and international levels there is renewed emphasis on enhancing women's participation in decision making as a prerequisite for women's empowerment and genuine democracy on the continent. Despite the one increase in women's participation at the regional level, several established democracies like Namibia and Botswana have experienced declines in women's participation in their most recent elections.

For me, it is imperative to maintain continued diligence, and employ mechanisms such as quotas and other affirmative-action measures, while tackling the challenge of campaign financing, poverty, voter education, etc, in order to consolidate the gains made so far.

Noting that rates of retention, completion, and transition to higher levels of education for girls are still low compared to that of boys, there is need to take appropriate measures to address the root causes of gender disparities in school enrolment and retention at all levels of the formal education system in both rural and urban areas, especially those that stem from the family and community context.

I have the strong conviction that no security, peace nor development is possible as long as women and girls will remain slaves of poverty and injustice. Empowerment of women should be a passion for every human being on earth. It pays off.

MDG 3 is seen as a central sustainable approach in addressing the HIV/AIDS menace. Realizing gender equality and empowering women are considered a crucial and effective way to combat, halt and reverse poverty and hunger.

Let's create action for change together: "To Do Something Extra" for women is an important choice. I want the government to recognize that violence against women is a human rights issue and that it must stop. I am committed to showing that it can no longer be justified on the basis of religion, culture or poverty.

Let's act now: There is no time for delay if the world is to achieve the MDGs by 2015. Refrain from rhetoric, asserting that girls' increased access to education comes at the expense of boys' access, and promote gender parity as a win-win strategy for accelerating development in African societies. Commitment by the private sector to strengthen gender aspects in their corporate social responsibility efforts is essential.

I believe people should be able to hold people accountable to the promises they make: a promise to go out and make empowerment of women happen.

(Jacqueline Sylvie Ndongmo is a teacher and an expert in the areas of gender, human rights and peacebuilding. She is based in Douala, Cameroon and serves as the chairperson of the Executive Board of FEMNET, the African Women's Development and Communication Network, headquartered in Nairobi, Kenya.)

If we are to be our most faithful, the Body of Christ should consider and treat all people equally and with dignity, beyond our human bias about gender, race, age, ability, socio-economic status, creed or orientation. (**Garlinda Burton**, http://www.umc-gbcs.org/site/apps/nlnet/content.aspx?c=frLJK2PKLqF&b=7516887&ct=10877237)

PROMOTE GENDER EQUALITY AND EMPOWER WOMEN

Being born a daughter. The Gospel of Matthew describes a woman considered unclean from irregular menses for twelve years who touched Jesus' clothes! In Levitical law, Jesus should have removed himself from the rest of the company to bathe, wash his clothes, and maintain his uncleanness until evening. Instead, Jesus called the woman "daughter," and brought her back into society, into inclusion, and into community.

In contrast, Anju Gautam Yogi, of the Global Press Institute, quotes a 12-year-old Nepali girl saying, "I wish nobody would be born as a daughter." She is confined to a shed that is considered inadequate for the cows. She has no access to the public water source, to nutritious meals, or to public education during her weeks of menses. As a result of this practice of "chaupadi," girls miss a substantial percentage of instruction, including school exams, causing them to repeat years of education and putting them at a disadvantage in furthering their education. Many of these girls, disheartened by their inability to keep up, drop out of school permanently.

My heart goes out to these girls who must be brave and persevere through loneliness, darkness, and shame. These girls are at a disadvantage to benefit from the same education that might provide opportunities for them to transcend ignorance that causes physical and psychological harm to generations of women. Like Jesus, let us assist in bringing these women back into the fold, and into community. **(Susan Aguilar, Laredo, Texas, USA)**

There are millions of women and children who are falling through the gaps because of inequities rooted in gender, economic status, geographical location, education level and social status. Everyone, everywhere has the right to the highest available standard of health. (Fifth Stocktaking Report 2010, UNICEF and UNAIDS, WHO, UNFPA, and UNESCO)

Made well by faith. Jesus' encounters with women never cease to amaze me. One woman's story comes to mind. She has spent all her earnings visiting many doctors but remained ill for twelve years. Having this constant menstrual flow made her unclean in her society. Rejected. Scourged. A non-person. But her desire to be cured was greater than her suffering and discouragement. She did not accept her fate as inevitable. She dared and touched Jesus' cloak, contrary to tradition.

As women we continue being treated as inferior to men, seen as objects to be used and later discarded. Aside from physical and biological processes, women also experience physical and sexual abuse, economic exploitation due to unfair wages compared to their male counterparts, or exclusion in decision-making processes, hence discrimination in the political process.

To those who dared to touch Jesus' cloak, he said to them: Go in peace. You are free of your disease. To women reading this, you too are invited to do the same: touch the cloak of Jesus and you too will be healed and freed. If you are male, touch Jesus' cloak and you too can be a blessed channel for the empowerment of women.

I touched Jesus' cloak more than 20 years ago when I was in my death bed due to a work related incident that affected my health. At that time also, I could no longer hide being a battered wife. But Jesus gave me peace and freed me of my affliction. If he did it for me, he can and wants to do it for every woman on the planet who needs peace, freedom and healing. Spread the word and denounce this injustice until it becomes past history. Gender equality must become a reality. **(María Teresa Santiago Alvarez, Puerto Rico)**

[W]omen are key to human development, poverty eradication, peace and security. Hence, achieving gender equality is not simply a function of MDG 3, but an underlying aspect of all of the MDGs. (Charlotte Bunch, Center for Women's Global Leadership)

Bible Reading

Daughter, your faith has made you well; go in peace and be healed of your disease. (Mark 5:34b ESV)

Prayer

Dear God, don't let the thirst and hunger that I feel for justice become extinguished. Grant me the opportunity to make a difference and make the MDGs a reality because of me and not in spite of me. Amen.

Deed for the Day

Look into the employment policies of your company or church and denounce any practice of gender discrimination.

PROMOTE GENDER EQUALITY AND EMPOWER WOMEN

Bible Reading

Keep falsehood and lies far from me;
give me neither poverty nor riches,
but give me only my daily bread.
(Proverbs 30:8 NIV)

Prayer

God, while food is a basic need for a
human being to live, there are still
many children who dream of food. Help
us to fashion a world where every child
will have a daily nutritious meal, and
perhaps to attend school too, to be fed
with productive thoughts. Make us
your instruments so that by your grace
all are fed. Amen.

Deed for the Day

Encourage your church to write a
letter of appeal to your government
to increase the budget for poverty
alleviation programs, especially those
for food and education.

By God's grace must all be fed. One time, our office went to a peasant village. We organized a fellowship among children whose parents we met when we joined them in front of the Philippine Congress calling for the passage of genuine agrarian reform laws. At the village, we were welcomed by the children. Under the shade of trees, sitting on old rice sacks, the children listened as we led an art session, played games, sang songs, and told stories, all à la Sunday School.

In the art session, we asked the children to trace their hands on a white bond paper and in them write their dreams. Some of them either wrote doctor, teacher, or nurse. Two dreams that caught my attention were by a girl who wanted her parents to own the land they are tilling and by another child who wished to have daily meals.

We had our simple snacks. Most of the children intentionally saved half of their share – either for lunch, or possibly, food for siblings left at home. Each child had their share of the packets we distributed. A girl even returned an extra piece of notebook she found in the packet given out. This trip to a peasant community proved memorable to me. **(Norma P. Dollaga, Quezon City, Philippines)**

No one will deny that education is a basic human right for a decent life and is essential for progressing individuals and societies. This is why so many people invest their money and time in education and why society and government are responsible for securing the right to education. (Eunlim Chi, Professor of Education, Kyung Hee University, Seoul, Korea)

Set apart this dream. 2010 was declared the year of women, but the term woman does not speak directly to the girl child, who can be experiencing sexual violence and abuse at a more vulnerable age. More advocacies must be done on behalf of children, like the girl child. A child is not a child only because of her innocence, but also because of her unbelievable faith.

The Gospel of Mark gives an account about a girl whom to family members was already dead. The father who brought his daughter's death to the attention of Jesus was rebuked by people who thought he was bothering Jesus by raising his concern to the Lord. To this, Jesus said: "Do not fear, only believe…The child is not dead but only sleeping." The girl was raised up by Jesus. Her spirit may have actually waited for the Lord to heal her.

The loss of innocence is traumatic. Those who experience such loss may be left with a feeling of numbness. It is as though they are walking dead when something so precious is taken away from them. To experience that as a child is like having one's childhood stolen.

To the little girl, Jesus said, "Talitha, cum," which is translated "Little girl, get up." Christ had the power to raise the dead to life, and to heal wounds and broken hearts. No girl or child should have to experience such pain. But this is a reality of our time. Even so, it does not have to be the end of a girl's life, innocence, or dreams. Christ calls us to help restore the little ones and help heal their wounds. **(Alvaina Daniels, Baton Rouge, Louisiana, USA)**

Girls worldwide say, "Empowering girls will change our world".
(World Association of Girl Guides and Girl Scouts)

PROMOTE GENDER EQUALITY AND EMPOWER WOMEN

Bible Reading
My little daughter is at the point of death. Come and lay your hands on her, so that she may be made well, and live…
(Mark 5:21-24, 35-43 NRSV)

Prayer
Precious one, as a daughter of God, you are a princess and most holy treasure in God's sight. May the Lord protect and bless you always that you may one day arise and be all that you've dreamed. Amen.

Deed for the Day
Remember the girls in your life and remind them today how beautiful they truly are and greatly beloved of the Lord.

PROMOTE GENDER EQUALITY AND EMPOWER WOMEN

Bible Reading

For I am confident of this very thing, that He who began a good work in you will perfect it until the day of Christ Jesus. (Philippians 1:6 NASV)

Prayer

Oh, Lord, we pray for women and children struggling with poverty and abuse in many parts of the world. Inspire and empower us to find ways to help our sisters help themselves and their families. Amen.

Deed for the Day

Empower women to develop their talents through education and training.

When seeds multiply. In traveling to Guatemala, I had the opportunity to meet leaders of the Evangelical Methodist Church's women's organization. They shared with us their struggle to empower women to bring food to their tables and security to their families. The women agreed to participate in a conference to develop concrete plans to meet these needs. Later that year, I learned that one of the Mayan women, Maria, had presented her dream: The Pigs, Chickens and Vegetable Project. The Volunteers in Mission (VIM) office in Guatemala connected me with Maria's dream, the beginning of an unimaginable friendship with our brothers and sisters in Momostenango.

We learned that alcoholism consumes 90% of the income of the women's husbands. If the women could support their families, it would mean reduced spouse and child abuse. Our team from First UMC, Ocala built pigpens, planted vegetables and held Bible School with over 200 children.

We were blessed to return the following year, on another VIM project. When we visited Maria we learned she had continued to use the Vacation Bible School material with their project's new Children's Street Ministry. She had begun a sewing project and was teaching basket weaving. We saw pictures of the new generation of pigs and more Mayan women who had joined the project. This seed continues to multiply, making a tremendous difference in the lives of women and children in the community. **(Christine Dial, USA)**

Initiatives to promote gender equality must deal openly and vigorously with the issue of partner violence, because women will never be equal in their public lives until they are equal at home. (World Health Organization)

God's equal love for all. Entering college I did not know exactly what I wanted to study so I chose to select any course title that seemed appealing. I chose an introductory women's studies course because I figured since I am a woman I must have some relation to the subject. At the end of the semester I came out of that course with an entirely new outlook on society.

I, a woman, was learning in a university about all the hard-working women around the world who fought for women's rights so that I could be in that classroom and gaining new knowledge. I suddenly got a great sense of pride. I read history and saw how women empowered themselves even in the context of an extremely patriarchal society. Even then, when I look around, I realize we still have a lot of work to do.

Around the world God's word is being manipulated to oppress women. I think about this and do not understand what kind of God is that. I see the beautifully strong and intelligent women in my family and who are my friends and I cannot imagine a God that created them with intentions of oppression. These are my sisters, my mothers, my teachers, my friends and we are inferior to no one. For in God we are all created equal. God is love, equal love. **(Demi Diaz, Germantown, Maryland, USA, with Meredith Duarte, California, USA)**

(*Women in developing countries have the answers to fighting poverty; they just need the support to do it… They do it in an astounding variety of ways – from calling for new laws on violence against women, to setting up small businesses, to ensuring that their daughters go to school* (Lee Webster, UK Campaigns Manager, CARE International))

3

PROMOTE GENDER EQUALITY AND EMPOWER WOMEN

Bible Reading

There is neither male nor female, for you are all one in Christ Jesus. (Galatians 3:28b NASB)

Prayer

Dear God, help us to see the world with your eyes, and help us to make a better world with peace, mercy, and justice. Amen.

Deed for the Day

Tell a woman how important she is in your life, in this world, and with God.

Bible Reading

Is anything too hard for the Lord?
(Gen.18:14 NIV)

Prayer

*Almighty God, may your Holy Spirit
empower us to enable others to partake
in your mission, so that no one will be
left behind in the planning for our day
to day life. May the most vulnerable
ones, women, youth and children,
be given the same right to express
their desires and needs in this male
dominated society. Amen.*

Deed for the Day

*Ask the people in your community or
organization to write down every day
in a notebook or recite: "All human
beings are equal."*

Old rags, beautiful papers. One of God's servants recounted the many visits he has made to a paper factory. And not just any paper, but paper destined to become beautiful editions of precious engravings:

"The entry to the factory is unpleasant. One makes you cross a court where trucks came to pour a whole load of old rags. There were rags of all colors and measurements, and all smelled of sickening odor. Most are dirty that you would have judged them to be destroyed. What of such garbage can one make? At the end of the visit, we are brought to a room where before us were paper samples spread out on walls of glaring white. They are papers made solely from dirty rags but have now been transformed into something beautiful to admire."

The human industry succeeded to make beautiful papers from garbage of dirty rags on which one will print beautiful books that bibliophiles can only acquire for a golden price.

One can admire this result of the human industry, but God can make it even better. Let's not forget God. God can transform each and every one of us, from any level we come, to become new creatures and make use of us – women, men, youths and children – in God's mission. Everything is possible with God.
(Pihaatae Francois, Suva, Fiji)

Whereas recognition of the inherent dignity and of the equal and inalienable rights of all members of the human family is the foundation of freedom, justice and peace in the world. (The Big Seven – Human Rights Conventions & Judicial Declarations, Pacific Regional Rights Resources Team, UNDP, Fiji, 2005)

Greater possibilities for women. What an experience – to be chosen as the bearer of such good news. Mitri Raheb writes in "I am a Palestinian Christian" that to be chosen "will always be a statement of faith…a promise to those…who see themselves as unworthy, weak, and powerless." Mary Magdalene fits this profile perfectly. She is burdened by the loss of a teacher and the weight of powerlessness in the world. It seems appropriate that she is empowered through the return of her teacher. Mary Magdalene's story reveals a truth about our own world: the power of being empowered through our teachers.

In developing societies, women who are educated are increasingly empowered, and they bring this experience into their communities. In developed countries, the equality and empowerment that women have is in part a result of educational opportunities.

Though I have grown up in a highly developed country, I am one of only a few women in my extended family to receive a college degree, and will be only the second woman to begin a graduate degree. The first was my mother. She set a precedent for a generation of women who seek empowerment and equality in the world. The true goal of our world should not only be to ensure primary and secondary education for women and girls, but to ensure that they can live into even greater possibilities. **(Jessica Hawkinson, New York, New York, USA)**

(*The existence of a separate goal on gender equality is the result of decades of advocacy, research and coalition-building by the international women's movement. Its very existence demonstrates that the global community has accepted the centrality of gender equality and women's empowerment to the development paradigm – at least at the rhetorical level.* (UNDP))

PROMOTE GENDER EQUALITY AND EMPOWER WOMEN

Bible Reading

Go to my brothers and say to them, "I am ascending to my Father and your Father, to my God and your God." Mary Magdalene went and announced to the disciples, 'I have seen the lord'; and she told them that he had said these things to her.
(John 20:17-18 NRSV)

Prayer

God of grace and mercy, lift up the weak and powerless as your teachers. Raise their voices so that we might hear and learn of the promise you bring into the world. Teach us, Lord, that we might serve your children and ensure for them life to the fullest. Amen.

Deed for the Day

Work with young people in your church to create a lesson about the MDGs which they can teach during Sunday School.

3

PROMOTE GENDER EQUALITY AND EMPOWER WOMEN

Bible Reading

She touched his cloak…At once Jesus knew that power had gone out of him, so he turned around and asked, "Who touched my clothes?"
(Mark 5:24-34 GNB)

Prayer

Lord, friend and deliverer, we're unseen, except by you who are aware. We ask to draw near your healing presence to be restored, refreshed and given new life. May we foster our love for you by passing on your generous gifts of love and compassion. Amen.

Deed for the Day

Discover more about the world's untouchables and become aware of what a healing touch can do.

Unexpected touch of power. At a retreat, we experienced a dramatic reenactment of the woman who touched Jesus' garment and was healed after 12 years of bleeding. While watching this, I experienced a breathtaking, overwhelming rush of sympathy and a new understanding of the woman and Christ's amazing mercy.

I had been researching today's untouchables in poor countries, learning they are often women who suffer from "obstetric fistula," a medical condition in which a fistula (hole) develops between either the rectum and vagina, or the bladder and vagina. This typically occurs after a difficult childbirth or other severe trauma such as rape, or female genital mutilation. The result of this fistula is an overpowering odor of leaking body fluids. The sufferers of this condition are shunned by everyone as being unclean and are prohibited from food preparation, family interaction and religious rites.

I "saw" Jesus' cloak trailing in the dust and a shaking, emaciated hand reaching out to stroke it, clutch it briefly and be transformed in an unexpected rush of power that healed, cleansed and set its owner free of defilement. Christ turned to question and confront this unexpected call upon his power. He confirmed, blessed and restored the woman's self worth, and somehow, mine. We're all healed by calling upon our Lord's power, and blessed by his kindness and mercy. **(Judy Huff, Union City, California, USA)**

There is no excuse for female genital mutilation to be with us. It is torture. It is inhuman and degrading treatment. It is a real basic human rights abuse and torture. You should see how these girls are excised, mutilated. (Berhane Ras-Work, Director, Inter-African Committee on Traditional Practices Affecting the Health of Women and Children)

Academe and reality on the ground. Poverty and joblessness brought about by a decrepit and unjust social system have driven almost 4,000 Filipinos to leave the country daily. One-third of these are unskilled workers; approximately half of them are women.

Migrants are an exploited lot. The Philippine government rakes in millions on exorbitant fees for a litany of charges. At the workplace, migrants likewise experience abuse ranging from contract violations, sexual abuse and harassment, white slavery, even death in the hands of employers. Women migrant workers are most vulnerable to maltreatment. Where is the church in their plight?

I saw a ray of hope when the Agustin-Smith Annual Lectures (ASAL) was launched at Union Theological Seminary in the Philippines. Patria Agustin-Smith and Paul Smith of New Jersey donated the fund for this program to bring outstanding leaders, preachers, theologians, and feminists to spread God's word, to offer quality education to seminary students, lay and clergy. The fund's memorandum of agreement specifies that the lecturer must be a woman from Asia. Though an academic exercise, ASAL is grounded on concrete pressing issues and realities of God's people such as the migrant issue at hand, especially as they affect the least of them: women, youth and children. **(Aquilino Javier, Jr., Tinley Park, Illinois, USA)**

MDG 3 is central to the achievement of all the other MDGs, yet it has only one target, educational parity. While there is a commitment to track, there are no targets for women's share of wage employment and women's share of representative seats in public decision-making. (UNIFEM, 2009)

3

PROMOTE GENDER EQUALITY AND EMPOWER WOMEN

Bible Reading

On Zion and everywhere in Judah our wives and daughters are being raped.
(Lamentations 5: 11 CIV)

Prayer

O God, make us your instrument for peace, justice, and mercy. Make us learn your ways to right the wrongs in the world. Bless those that have stepped forward to lead us. Amen.

Deed for the Day

Call to encourage and support those that have stepped forward to lead us in the struggle.

3

PROMOTE GENDER EQUALITY AND EMPOWER WOMEN

Bible Reading

God created humanity in God's own image, in the divine image God created them, male and female God created them. (Genesis 1:27 CEB)

Prayer

O Lord, help us to be doers of your word and not hearers only. You require of us to do unto our neighbors that which we want others to do unto us – to treat one another justly. We will truly be your disciples if we obey your commands. Amen.

Deed for the Day

Donate some funds to your favorite charity or church organization for the education of the girl child.

Determining one's own destiny. It is distressing that while the percentage of literate women is at an all-time high, so too is the number of illiterate women. UNESCO estimates that twenty percent of all adults, or 774 million, are not literate. Of those who aren't literate, two-thirds are women. This is ample evidence of the continuing disparity in education between men and women.

Literacy plays an important role in the lives of women. It provides greater opportunities in their communities. In a small rural community in Haiti, I witnessed the plight of an ambitious and industrious grandmother with no formal education who raised 10 children singlehandedly, but her prospects were limited because she could not read and write. The only employment available to her was domestic work where she was usually overworked and underpaid without a union to regulate. Still, she was able to educate all of her children. Today, two are nurses and one is an entrepreneur. Can you imagine how well she could have done given more opportunities?

When women have equal opportunities there is far greater chance of achieving the Millennium Development Goals. Global prosperity and peace can only be achieved when all people are empowered with the ability to determine their own destiny and have access to the tools to provide for themselves and their families. A Chinese proverb says, "Give a person a fish and you feed the person for a day; teach a person to fish and that person eats forever." Imagine that for all women. **(Sophony Lamour, Port-au-Prince, Haiti)**

The education and empowerment of women throughout the world cannot fail to result in a more caring, tolerant, just and peaceful life for all. (Aung San Suu Kyi , General Secretary of the Burmese National League for Democracy and Nobel Peace laureate)

Ending the culture of silence. The culture of silence is very strong among Filipino women. Spanish colonization of the Philippines left imprints of patriarchy. The father as the bread earner is the decision maker and enjoys all the benefits of rest and leisure when at home. "Señor" is his befitting title. The mother is merely a housekeeper. Culture and tradition which started to take shape at an early age has a strong impact on one's perceptions and actions. It cannot be discarded overnight. To date, silence is still held by many women.

In the trainings we conduct in rural Philippine villages called barangays, women articulate their fear to argue with their husbands, a practice considered disrespectful. Even when battered by their philandering husband, they keep silent because it's their "fate." God destined them to be such, we are told. When a daughter is sexually abused by her father, she would be advised by the mother to keep the matter secret because it is a shame to family and the community and a pity to the father if punished by law.

But these scenarios are changing, thanks to education. Enrolment in high school in 1999-2000 recorded more females than males; and more female graduates than males in higher-education courses. Knowing the painful and demoralizing experiences of women makes me all the more insistent to work on justice issues for women, hard it may be. **(Chita Rebollido-Millan, Calasiao, Pangasinan, Philippines)**

Efforts to empower women must address current norms and traditional social customs that legitimize violence against them, as well as legislation and enforcement of laws that discriminate against them."
(World Health Organization)

PROMOTE GENDER EQUALITY AND EMPOWER WOMEN

Bible Reading
There is neither Jew nor Greek, slave nor free, male nor female, for you are all one in Christ Jesus.
(Galatians 3:28 NIV)

Prayer
God, our great Creator, thank you for creating women and men in your image. How just a God you are, creating all of us equal in your sight. Forgive us when at times we feel superior more than others because of our gender, status, race, language, and age. Amen.

Deed for the Day
Extend your hand in any way possible to every woman who is discriminated against because of her gender.

3

PROMOTE GENDER EQUALITY AND EMPOWER WOMEN

No and nothing more. A single, beautiful woman was traveling with a very wealthy client for a major deal and speaking for her company. A few days after, this very rich married man approached her proposing that they engage in a "sexual recreation" together.

The young woman felt harassed but found a way to state firmly to this man: "When I say N-O it means NO! We have a professional working relationship and that's it! Nothing more, nothing beyond!"

The woman stepped up to the plate and whacked the unwelcome proposal! She also brought the matter to her employers, taking into account situations in the workplace where women were placed in uncomfortable, compromising and difficult situations.

The firm took her seriously and re-wrote corporate policies. **(Patria Agustin-Smith, Short Hills, New Jersey, USA)**

The attainment of MDG 3 will require a comprehensive approach to overcome not only violence against women, but also gender-based discrimination in laws and policies, and deeply embedded social and cultural norms that perpetuate gender inequality. (WHO, Addressing Violence Against Women and Achieving the MDGs, www.who.int/gender)

Boy and girl things. Decades ago, there were Filipino children who grew up in a culture that did not give them equal opportunities on account of their gender. Boys were sent to school, while most girls stayed at home to do household chores. In school, boys were seated apart from girls. Boys took Industrial Education while girls took Home Economics. Leadership roles were given to boys. Inheritance too was not divided equally: Only male children were given inheritance.

Some of us were fortunate to grow up in a home where our parents saw the need to give equal opportunities to all their children, boys and girls. Boys eventually experienced doing activities that only girls were previously exposed to and girls got to do what were previously "boy things."

We are glad that the Philippine government has revised its educational system. It has included learning opportunities to learn about gender disparity and how to eliminate it. In the classrooms, there are now more opportunities for both sexes to be equal, enjoying learning experiences together. **(Various authors, Social Principles Workshop, Northern Philippines Annual Conference of The United Methodist Church, August 2009, Tuguegarao City, Philippines)**

The Millennium Development Goals represent a set of simple but powerful objectives that every man and woman in the street, from New York to Nauru, from Abidjan to Antigua, can easily support and understand.
(Louise Frechette, Former UN Deputy Secretary-General, 2003)

PROMOTE GENDER EQUALITY AND EMPOWER WOMEN

Bible Reading

Then God said, "Let us make humankind in our image, according to our likeness; and let them have dominion over the fish of the sea, and over the birds of the air…" So God created humankind in his image, in the image of God he created them, male and female he created them.
(Genesis 1:26-27 NKJV)

Prayer

Our Ever-Equal God, Creator of man and woman, thank You for creating us in your own image. Teach me to remember always that we should treat everyone with respect and dignity. Amen.

Deed for the Day

Work with church agencies and institutions to promote equal opportunities for all genders.

PROMOTE GENDER EQUALITY AND EMPOWER WOMEN

Bible Reading

As she listened with intensity to what was being said, the Master gave her a trusting heart---and she believed!

(Acts 16:14 MSG)

Prayer

God of mighty power and gentle wisdom, help us restore balance to your creation in all ways and places. Where there is gender disparity, let us engender equality. Where limitations diminish, let imaginations empower. Let our minds, hearts and world be renewed by the joy of learning your ways. Amen.

Deed for the Day

Engage someone of another gender or culture in a conversation where each talks uninterrupted for five minutes about how education has shaped her or his life.

A teaching moment for gender equality. By all accounts, Lydia was her own woman. In a short passage in Acts 16, we are introduced to her as someone who deals in expensive purple textiles, heads a large household and ventures out to a public place to pray with other women. When disciples come and join the women and teach them the Gospel, Lydia listens intently and responds in faith. She is baptized along with others of her household and insists the disciples come home with her to enjoy some hospitality.

What does it take to be a "Lydia" – your own woman – in the world today? Certainly economic security and social status added on to proper nutrition, health care and reproductive self-determination. But education is what guarantees access to all of the above.

Education – how we learn to learn – is what shapes who we are and how we fare in the societies and cultures in which we live.

It is hard to know how Lydia may have been educated in her time, but she certainly displays the capacity for learning when the "teaching moment" of faith arrives.

Every girl and woman deserves the right to learn how to learn through educational opportunities and to be empowered to be her own Lydia. That can happen if gender disparity in education is erased at all levels and the "teaching moment" for gender equality finally arrives. **(Jill Wiley, Brockton, Massachusetts, USA)**

(*Our strategy includes women's empowerment. Women must lead the way. Because by empowering women, we empower societies.*
(Ban Ki-moon, UN Secretary-General))

REDUCE CHILD MORTALITY

Commentary by Deva-Marie Beck

Alas! When in the year 2011 about eight million children under the age of five are still dying of preventable causes – every year – I am asking why should we be wondering if this is important?

This is over 21,000 infants and children suffering and dying every day, 365 days a year, every year, forever – unless and until something is done to change this!

I am personally horrified that this is still happening. And, I am equally appalled that these alarming statistics have yet to even reach our traditional media channels.

We all know when one soldier dies of a land-mine explosion in Afghanistan or Iraq.

Why don't we know – or care – that some 21,000 children and babies died today and the same yesterday, and the same tomorrow and the next day?

This intractable tragedy needs lots of prayer, lots of recognition of needs and millions of deeds still to be done.

Meanwhile, we all need to spread the word loud and wide until enough

MDG 4 – Reduce Child Mortality

Target 4.A: *Reduce by two thirds, between 1990 and 2015, the under-five mortality rate*

Children have the rights to food, shelter, clothing, health care, and emotional well-being as do adults, and these rights we affirm as theirs regardless of actions or inactions of their parents or guardians. In particular, children must be protected from economic, physical, emotional, and sexual exploitation and abuse. **(Social Principles ¶ 162. C)**

We should be marching in the streets demanding justice when realizing the horrific reality that each day over 21,000 children die of preventable diseases. **(Linda Bales Todd,** Director, Populations and Women's Advocacy, General Board of Church and Society of The United Methodist Church)

people care enough. I am planning to spend a lot of my time getting the word out any way I can.

I hope you can consider doing the same!

*(**Deva-Marie Beck** holds a **Ph.D.** in Interdisciplinary Nursing Studies and International Health. She is currently International Co-Director of the Nightingale Initiative for Global Health {NIGH}, based in Ottawa, Ontario, Canada. When asked how NIGH took on the MDGs as focus, Beck responded: "During our participation in two Civil Society Development Forums convened in Geneva and New York City in 2009 and 2010, in preparation for the UN Economic and Social Council annual sessions, our team from the NIGH was encouraged to focus on increasing global public awareness about the MDGs. In response, we integrated this request into the celebration of the 2010 International Year of the Nurse and we encouraged nurses to advocate for the achievement of these critical Goals, worldwide.")*

Afast for justice. Fasting is the discipline of denying one's self of something in anticipation of something greater. It could be eating in and giving that money you would have spent, to a food bank. Or, leaving your car at home and giving the earth a breather.

The prophet Isaiah calls for a fast – and regardless of what we fast from, regardless of what we hope to attain – we are encouraged to do it for the benefit of others.

Recently, a layperson returned from the Congo and while in Mulunguishi, a two-year-old girl had come into the clinic and died of malnutrition after only three days.

A child born in a developing country is over 13 times more likely to die within the first five years of life than a child born in an industrialized country. Sub-Saharan Africa accounts for about half the deaths of children under five in the developing world.

This young girl, and thousands more children under five, involuntarily fast every day. These are fasts dictated by their place of birth, poverty and other factors out of their control. This world has not afforded them the chance to flourish in the words of the prophet, as "a watered garden, like a spring of water, whose waters never fail." Isaiah's fast is fitting, "to loose the bonds of injustice, and let the oppressed go free." **(Shalom R. Agtarap, Seattle, Washington, USA)**

(*[F]inding avenues to address unequal power, capacity, and access to resources for the poor and the marginalized is a fundamental challenge to development actors wanting to link poverty reduction to democratic governance and participation.* (Antonio Tujan, Director, IBON International and Chairperson, Reality of Aid.))

REDUCE CHILD MORTALITY

Bible Reading
…and you shall be like a watered garden, like a spring of water, whose waters never fail.
(Isaiah 58:6-12 {11b} ESV)

Prayer
Mothering God, in whom we depend for sustenance and nourishment, mold us into vessels of your justice and grace, that through fasting, we might enable another to live. Correct our ways and help us to care for your children across the world as if they were our own. Amen.

Deed for the Day
Donate nutritious food to a food bank; advocate for food aid that contains proper nourishment for poor families, despite raised food prices.

4

REDUCE CHILD MORTALITY

Bible Reading

[A]nd the leaves of the tree are for the healing of the nations.
(Revelations 22:2c NIV)

Prayer

Dear God, touch the sick, and bring healing; touch me that I too may be a channel of your grace. Amen.

Deed for the Day

Log on to http://www.ministrywith. org/index2.html and check out how you may participate in the Ministry with the Poor campaign of The United Methodist Church.

When **indigenous peoples speak out.** "A week ago, one of the children here died from diarrhea." This was the sad news that greeted me and a team from Manila visiting among the Dumagats in a village up in the Sierra Madre mountains in the Philippines. The news gave us pause. As word got around about our presence in the village, a mother whose little daughter had rashes on her face came to ask for medicine; another came to see if we had any medicine to treat her fever.

Alas, we were unprepared for these requests as all that we had with us were vitamins from UNICEF, and some Aquatabs for making water safe for drinking.

That night we slept without mosquito nets. Later I recalled that there is malaria in this area. I had an acute awareness of the vulnerability of this community which has for centuries been deprived of access to education, health and other social services because they were Dumagats, an indigenous tribe in the Philippines. Dumagats are peace-loving and avoid conflict. But their abhorrence of confrontation has also led settlers from the lowlands to move in and encroach upon their land, forcing them to move farther and farther up the hills where they farm, hunt and live in isolation from the rest of society.

Yet the story does not end there. They are studying about their legal claim to their ancestral land. Their leaders are bravely opposing the proposed building of a dam that would submerge their homes and everything that they hold dear. In the meantime, along with their communal farm, they hope to cultivate an herbal garden. The Dumagats are starting to speak out. **(Rebecca C. Asedillo, New York, New York, USA)**

[A]gencies and bodies of the UN and other inter-governmental organization[must] rethink the concept of development, with the full participation of indigenous peoples in development processes, taking into account the rights of indigenous peoples and the practices of their traditional knowledge.
(Report, Second Session, UN Permanent Forum on Indigenous Issues)

A welcome of clean water. Early in my pastorate, I traveled to Appalachia several times with groups of youths who worked on rehabbing houses in the poorest areas of Kentucky and Tennessee. It was amazing to see young people bond with the families in the area and work hard to improve their homes. Several young women wanted to find the home where they had worked the previous summer installing a well, a source of clean water for the mother and daughter who lived there. We finally found the house; mother and daughter were there and extended us a warm welcome.

The girls in the group renewed what was to my observation a true love relationship. Of course, they asked how the well was working. The mother invited us outside to taste the water. She filled a cup or two, and we passed the cups around the circle. One of the girls in the group, not a particularly churched young woman, looked around the circle, her face alive with realization, and said, "This is just like communion." She got it!

In the sacrament, we participate in the fellowship of God's table where we become so filled with Christ that we live in the Spirit of Christ, feeding the hungry, giving water to those who thirst and welcoming the stranger. The water from that well in Kentucky gave us the living water of Christ that day. **(Ellen A. Brubaker, Grand Rapids, Michigan, USA)**

We all have power. It comes from deep inside each and every one of us. From the way we think and the way we act. A power that can change the world. Today, we are asking you to use yours. (UN Millennium Campaign)

4

REDUCE CHILD MORTALITY

Bible Reading

For I was hungry and you gave me something to eat. I was thirsty and you gave me something to drink. I was a stranger and you invited me in. (Matthew 25: 35 NIV)

Prayer

O, Living God in Christ, may we receive you fully and completely into ourselves that we go forth with great joy to share your passion for justice as we feed your hungry people, give pure water to those who thirst, and welcome all your people, the ones you love. Amen.

Deed for the Day

Do something locally to feed or give water to someone in need. Discover where you might engage in larger acts of justice in the world.

4

REDUCE CHILD MORTALITY

Bible Reading

Then his sister asked her, "Shall I go and call a Hebrew to nurse the baby for you?" "Please do," she answered. So the girl went and brought the baby's own mother. The princess told the woman, "Take this baby and nurse him for me, and I will pay you." So she took the baby and nursed him.
(Exodus 2: 7-9 GNB)

Prayer

God, our parent, source of goodness, through our actions may we work for what is best for your children. Keep us alert to the dangers your children face, especially those that we can change through our determination to consume that which promotes healthy living, and is life enhancing. Amen.

Deed for the Day

Support breastfeeding. Encourage employers to make the workplace breastfeeding-friendly.

Mother's milk is best. Giving birth to our two sons in Papua New Guinea in the 1970s was an exciting time as the newly independent country passed the Baby Feed Supplies Control Act which restricted the sale of baby bottles and prohibited the promotion of baby milk products. Being a firm advocate of breastfeeding, I applauded this decision made to address increased child mortality as a result of the introduction of formula feeding. This law still exists today, and breastfeeding is almost universal. PNG has one of the lowest incidences of diarrhea among children. If every baby were exclusively breastfed for their first six months, an estimated 1.3 million additional lives would be saved and millions more enhanced every year.

In recent years I lived in Southern Africa while breastfeeding again became an issue because of HIV virus transmission. In some poverty-stricken countries, breastfeeding is now thought to be the best method even if you are HIV-positive. The risk of passing the virus is less than 5%, the baby will be healthier, and even an infected baby will take longer to develop AIDS than will a formula-fed baby.

So many lives are saved by a simple, natural method of feeding babies. The valuable immune-building ingredients and antibodies in the mother's milk reduce the vulnerability to diarrhea and pneumonia. As the slogan says, "Breast is best!" **(Janice Clark, Freetown, Sierra Leone, and Rosemary Wass, York, England)**

(Breastfed babies are less likely than formula fed babies to get infections and sickness, and less likely to develop health problems such as asthma, diabetes, obesity and SIDS [sudden infant death syndrome]. To breastfeed successfully, women need support from their doctors, hospitals, families and communities.)
(Dr. Thomas Farley, New York City Health Commissioner, 2009)

Mother's milk for children. Every day 21,000 children die according to UNICEF. All these deaths can and should be prevented. One of the ways these deaths could be prevented is through breastfeeding. Naturally a mother produces human milk for her child. This milk contains antibodies and vitamins that are much needed for infant growth and development. Breastfeeding is safer for a child by protecting a child from water-born illness from contaminated water that could be mixed with infant formula. Breastfeeding is more cost-efficient and can save a family around 1,000 US dollars a year.

God reveals God's will to little children. In order to truly know God we must save these 21,000 children. Children carry the word of God and it is our duty as Christians to educate, love, and provide support to our allies to save the children. There are several ways to get involved with preventing infant and child mortality. Whether that is getting involved in a clean water campaign for developing nations, educating women and men about the benefits of breastfeeding, or boycotting infant formula companies for the practice of spreading lies to women in developing nations about the dangers of breastfeeding where in reality there are none. **(Cindy R. Heilman, Washington, District of Columbia, USA)**

Revitalizing efforts against pneumonia and diarrhoea, while bolstering nutrition, could save millions of children. (The UN MDG Report, UN, 2010)

REDUCE CHILD MORTALITY

Bible Reading

At that time Jesus said, "I praise you, Father, Lord of heaven and earth, because you have hidden these things from the wise and learned, and revealed them to little children." (Matthew 11:25 NIV)

Prayer

Loving God, Creator of us all, provide us encouragement and strength for advocating for policy change, campaigning for change, and educating women and men about the benefits of breastfeeding. God, please help us to better understand your revelations to little children and learn from them. Amen.

Deed for the Day

Educate yourself on the benefits of breastfeeding for both the mother and child.

4

REDUCE CHILD MORTALITY

Bible Reading

But when she could no longer hide him, she got a basket made of papyrus reeds and waterproofed it with tar and pitch. She put the baby in the basket and laid it among the reeds along the bank of the Nile River.
(Exodus 2:3 NLT)

Prayer

God, only you knows how many lives will be saved by simply placing a bassinet in a safe location. Help us to educate others and be your hands and feet so that no more children are left in dumpsters, but given a chance to grow and serve you. Amen.

Deed for the Day

Learn about the Safe Haven Law in your state. Educate others by posting a flyer in your church, grocery store, laundromat, library, or Student Union.

Safe haven for babies. When my children were little, it seemed every two weeks or so I would read about a newborn being found in the river, a dumpster or a public toilet. A woman in my community started "Baskets for Babies." People concerned with this issue would put a basket by their front door. A list of baskets was in each local drugstore. I put my basket out right away. Every morning my girls would look to see if we got a baby yet. They would be a little disappointed and I would be a little relieved.

Some of my friends thought this was the silliest thing I have ever done. Still, how could I even think that someone would come up on my suburban cul-de-sac, climb the steps to my porch and leave a newborn in my care? I never did get a baby. I did get two dogs in my basket one stormy night, but no baby.

Was this whole exercise in vain? I don't think so. It sent a message to our lawmakers that this is an issue that must be addressed. Several years have passed and now all fifty states of the United States have a Safe Haven Law! Some states have done a great job educating the residents on the law. Others have not. I called my local police department and I'm glad to report they now know the Safe Haven Law! **(Joan Lucarelli, Bethel Park, Pennsylvania, USA)**

The problem of maternal, newborn and child mortality is a crosscutting issue that needs to be addressed jointly by government ministries, NGOs, the private sector and international organisations....All sectors need to play their role.
(Right Honourable Edward Lowassa, Prime Minister of the United Republic of Tanzania)

Living longer but a few days. As a pastor, many people come to me to share their stories. Some are joyful, others painful. Some are stories of hope and some of despair. With each story shared, I found myself connecting with people. Their stories are about human experience and engagement with life.

I could still vividly remember the pain in the eyes of a mother whom I comforted because of the untimely demise of her daughter. The family did everything to save the child's life but to no avail. The child died of dengue (hemorrhagic fever), an infectious tropical disease that is mosquito-borne. Though the family wanted to bring the child to the hospital immediately, it took them several days to raise the needed money for hospital deposit. Many hospitals refuse to admit patients who could not give a down payment. By the time they secured some money, it was too late. Their daughter died. My heart cried with her as she asked me in tears, "Pastor, what is the life expectancy of people? For how long do we cry when children die?"

Her questions led me to look deeper how far we have gone in our campaign to eliminate poverty and to expand global health. I am sure there are countless children out there who faced their untimely death because of lack of medical help. The world needs our compassion and help so that children could enjoy full years of their lives and that no more shall there be in our world an infant that lives but a few days. **(Connie Semy P. Mella, Cavite, Philippines)**

Most child deaths are caused by neonatal conditions and communicable diseases, in particular malaria, acute respiratory infections, diarrhoea and epidemics such as dengue fever, measles or meningitis. (UNDP, MDGs at a Glance, Lao Peoples Democratic Republic)

REDUCE CHILD MORTALITY

Bible Reading

No more shall there be in it an infant that lives but a few days, or an old person who does not live out a lifetime; for one who dies at a hundred years will be considered a youth, and one who falls short of a hundred will be considered accursed.
(Isaiah 65:20 NRS)

Prayer

God our Parent, continue to breathe into us the breath of life so that we too can be life-giving. Make us channels of your grace so that in our concerted effort, we could help alleviate poverty, expand global health and reduce child mortality. In the name of Christ, our healer. Amen.

Deed for the Day

Visit children hospitals or orphanages to let the children feel that they are loved and remembered.

4

REDUCE CHILD MORTALITY

Bible Reading

Let the little children come to me, and do not stop them; for it is to such as these that the kingdom of God belongs.
(Luke 18:16 NRSV)

Prayer

Creator God let me be mindful of all the children in the world who long for good health and clean water. Give them strength, hope, and courage for their journey. Amen.

Deed for the Day

Pick an Advance from www. advancinghope.org and support one of the missionaries or health projects related to The United Methodist Church.

Let the little children come to me. In 2007, half of the world's under-five deaths occurred in Africa, which remains the most difficult place in the world for a child to survive until age five. Going into 2010, Sub-Saharan Africa and Southern Asia together account for the highest rates of child mortality. The 2010 UNICEF global database says that some 8.1 million children died before reaching age five.

Thanks to the health initiatives of UMCOR (United Methodist Committee on Relief) and its emphasis on malaria prevention and safe and clean water. By partnering with our United Methodist bishops from Africa and with agencies, The United Methodist Church is working to address this problem so that all children can come to know a full and productive, healthy, happy life.

Some of our United Methodist missionaries are working in health care in hospitals and community health centers creating a new start in health for many areas that have historically had limited health care. **(Joanne M. Reich, Ashland City, Tennessee, USA)**

While the speed at which under-5 mortality rates are declining improved for 2000 to 2009 compared to the previous decade, the under five deaths are still not decreasing fast enough – especially in sub-Saharan Africa, Southern Asia and Oceania. (U.S. Fund for UNICEF)

Achild made well. Dr. Palmer greeted the ten women in the ward with a breezy "Good morning." Each one was seated on the hospital bed cradling a child and I could read worry and hope on their faces. Each woman had come to the Kissy United Methodist Hospital in Freetown, Sierra Leone, with one purpose and that was to save her child from malaria, diarrhea or pneumonia.

Though easily preventable, these diseases cause fifty percent of deaths in children under the age of five. Dr. Palmer went about her work examining the children and prescribing treatment and tests, always with an encouraging word and a smile. This was her morning routine and she was unfazed.

As I observed her at work I realized that she was making each child well, one at a time. But without preventive measures like bed nets, clean drinking water and immunizations, there was every chance that the child would return in three, six or twelve months with another bout of malaria, pneumonia or diarrhea.

Sierra Leone has one of the worst infant mortality rates in the world, but The United Methodist Church through its clinics, hospitals and community-based health-care programs is saving lives one child at a time. **(Cherian Thomas, New York, New York, USA)**

More than 70 per cent of almost 11 million child deaths every year are attributable to six causes: diarrhoea, malaria, neonatal infection, pneumonia, preterm delivery, or lack of oxygen at birth. These deaths occur mainly in the developing world…And the majority [of these deaths] are preventable. (UNICEF)

4

REDUCE CHILD MORTALITY

Bible Reading
But when Jesus heard it he answered him, saying "Do not be afraid; only believe, and she will be made well.
(Luke 8:50 NKJV)

Prayer
Lord, I pray that you will bless all those around the world who are striving to save children's lives while working with resources that are far from optimum and I pray for the millions of little children who face an uncertain future. Amen.

Deed for the Day
Continue to uphold the church in prayer and do whatever each of us can to reduce child mortality.

4

REDUCE CHILD MORTALITY

Bible Reading

And because the midwives feared God, He gave them families of their own.
(Exodus 1:21 NIV)

Prayer

Healer God and sustainer of life, teach me and help me to be a healing agent, so that your love and care for all expectant mothers shine forth, and that babies are born knowing they have your blessings for a healthy life. Thank you, God, for using me as a channel of your grace. Amen.

Deed for the Day

Set aside a time to meet pregnant women in your community and try to counsel and inform them about healthy pregnancy.

Training birth practitioners. Giving birth is very frightening, especially to those who experience it the first time. It is even more frightening if one is not sure about who is going to help the mother deliver the baby. In many parts of rural Philippines, expectant mothers turn to "hilots" for help. Hilots could be self-taught or trained. Trained hilots are birth practitioners like midwives. They could be trained by government health professionals as is the case in the Philippines. There are those who engage the help of hilots as a matter of choice, while others do so because of the lack of doctors and health professionals in their communities. It could also be the lack of resources to pay for the services of a medical doctor. Poverty and lack of education play a great part in decision-making for the care of expecting mothers.

Home deliveries are common in the Philippines. Unless assisted with trained birth practitioners, these home deliveries may contribute to higher child mortality rates. The absence of skilled birth attendants, poor referral system and inadequate basic and comprehensive emergency obstetric services all contribute to higher deaths at birth. The increase could also be attributed to the high incidence of communicable diseases like pneumonia, septicemia and diarrhea, thereby complicating the health of the expectant mother and endangering the baby in the womb.

Our goal must be to reduce child mortality. Resources should be allotted for the training of birth practitioners in rural areas that women can easily access. **(Various authors, Social Principles Workshop, Northern Philippines Annual Conference of The United Methodist Church, August 2009, Tuguegarao City, Philippines)**

It only costs a few dollars to protect young children from conditions that disable or kill millions each year...The US can provide the leadership that will give mothers and children new hope and opportunity to lead healthy and productive lives.
(Charles MacCormack, President and CEO, Save the Children)

IMPROVE MATERNAL HEALTH

Commentary by Manoj Kurian

Women and men are created in the image of God (Genesis 1:27). Women and men are equally precious to God. But it is an ongoing scandal that more than 350,000 women worldwide die while pregnant or in childbirth each year. Half of these deaths occur in Sub-Saharan Africa and almost all the maternal deaths (99%) occur in developing countries.

How can women lose their lives giving a new life? How can the place of birth and economic status of a woman turn a life-giving process to a death sentence?

Male domination has obviously taken its bitter toll on human society. Unfortunately, religions have also been instrumentalized to reinforce the marginalization and neglect of girls and women in society.

We have to prayerfully and consistently transform this situation. Communities of faith and the leadership have a moral and sacred duty to envision and work for a just world where the integrity, dignity, life and health of every girl and woman is nurtured and upheld in society.

I pray to our Lord for strength, strategy and consistency to accompany and to be in solidarity with women worldwide and for perseverance and tenacity to advocate for and contribute to ensuring that women have access

MDG 5 – Improve Maternal Health

Target 5.A: *Reduce by three quarters the maternal mortality ratio*

Target 5.B: *Achieve universal access to reproductive health*

to health, including reproductive and sexual health.

I also pray for humility and transparency in providing equal opportunities for girls and women and to ensure that our communities are safe spaces for them to flourish and grow; and for openness and seriousness to promote the interpretation of our religious texts to edify all humanity and to overcome oppression and exploitation of girls and women.

(Manoj Kurian is a medical doctor from Malaysia and currently serves as Programme Executive for Health and Healing at the World Council of Churches. The WCC promotes Christian unity in faith, witness and service for a just and peaceful world. An ecumenical fellowship of churches founded in 1948, today the WCC brings together 349 Protestant, Orthodox, Anglican and other churches representing more than 560 million Christians in over 110 countries, and works cooperatively with the Roman Catholic Church. WCC's project on health and healing "supports the churches' work in the field of health and healing with particular emphasis on HIV/AIDS, mental health, and the promotion of reconciliation and the 'healing of memories'." WCC is headquartered in Geneva, Switzerland.)

What The United Methodist Church says:

We therefore encourage our churches and common society to… provide to each pregnant woman accessibility to comprehensive health care and nutrition adequate to ensure healthy children." **(Responsible Parenthood, Resolution #2026, 2008 Book of Resolutions)**

When women can plan their pregnancies, they are more likely to have healthier pregnancies and deliveries. Their children are healthier, too. **(Alice Otieno**, http://www.umc-gbcs.org/site/apps/nlnet/content3.aspx?c=frLJK2PKLqF&b=2952523&ct=8863281&notoc=1**)**

Healing the wounds that bind us. An issue of great concern, but one that is a "sleeper" issue in the United States is obstetric fistula. Now you may be wondering what this is. Obstetric fistula is a medical malady experienced by over 2 million women and girls around the globe. A fistula is a hole, and, in the case of obstetric fistula, it is a hole or holes punctured in the vaginal or anal walls of women due to obstructed births. Most times, the baby dies and the mother is left incontinent, a condition resulting in severe stigma and discrimination. Fistulas can also occur from violent rape and/or other conditions affecting the female reproductive system.

Through the General Board of Church and Society, United Methodists in the United States are learning about this condition and how they can make a difference. Fistulas are repairable, but rarely do poor women in developing countries have access to medical facilities and personnel that can perform the surgery.

In the Gospel of Luke, we find Jesus healing the woman who had been bleeding for years. His healing powers made her whole again. This is what we, as people of faith, want for all women around the globe. Please pray for women suffering from obstetric fistula and do what you can to ensure greater access to medical treatment and rehabilitation. **(Linda Bales Todd, Dayton, Ohio, USA)**

Obstetric fistula was eliminated here in Europe and the United States more than 100 years ago. It's unacceptable that women and girls in developing countries are still suffering from this entirely preventable and treatable condition. (Natalie Imbruglia, Virgin Unite ambassador and spokesperson for the Campaign to End Fistula)

Bible Reading
Then he said to her, "Daughter your faith has healed you. Go in peace." (Luke 8:40-48 NIV)

Prayer
Holy God, sustainer of us all, open our eyes to the plight of women around the globe who struggle to give birth safely and who deal with the stigma of fistula. Pour over them your healing balm and walk with us as we work to create a world where all people have access to medical care and are able to achieve the fullness of life. Amen.

Deed for the Day
Go to www.endfistula.org and make a contribution to the United Nations Population Fund's Campaign to End Fistula.

5

IMPROVE MATERNAL HEALTH

Bible Reading

At that time the disciples came to Jesus, saying, "Who is the greatest in the kingdom of heaven?" And calling to him a child, he put him in the midst of them and said, "Truly, I say to you, unless you turn and become like children, you will never enter the kingdom of heaven.
(Matthew 18: 1-3 ESV)

Prayer

God of hope and love, we ask for eyes to see the needs of those who live beyond our cities and villages. Help us to know what they suffer from that we too may feel their pain and help alleviate it. We pray for all women who prepare to give birth. Amen.

Deed for the Day

Look around your community for young women who are pregnant and who might need some help. See how you can help meet the needs of women who leave the hospital with their infant.

Healthy children, healthier world. When little Harley Paige was brought forth in our church to be baptized, there was an abundance of smiles in our congregation. She brought with her hope to our small, but growing congregation. Not all that long ago the church was facing the real possibility of having to close the doors. Now our church is alive with the voices of youths, children and now a precious baby.

It is a fact that every minute a mother dies in pregnancy and childbirth! What if Harley and her mother had not received proper pre-natal care? What if Harley's mother had been too young and not yet ready to give birth? We cannot ignore the problems of the world merely because we do not see them.

The MDGs promise to improve maternal health. By doing so, every child born will bring smiles to villages and congregations across the world. Children are precious gifts. Mothers everywhere deserve the right to have proper care during their pregnancy so that they can give birth to healthy children. Healthy children are the hope of a healthier world. **(Margie Briggs, Creighton, Missouri, USA)**

Ten years ago, when the 2000 Millennium Declaration outlined the eight MDGs, many women's organizations viewed them as "minimalist development goals"... Since then, reports indicate mixed progress , with the new crises worsening the feminization of poverty and threatening progress in other areas. (Feminist Task Force, Global Call to Action Against Poverty, September 2010)

Offering a ride. On a previous trip to Africa, I encountered a young woman named Nandi, seven months pregnant with her second child. Even in her advanced state of pregnancy, Nandi still carried the heavy responsibility of cooking, cleaning, and working in the family's fields. She became increasingly worried about her baby when she began to suffer abdominal cramping and had not seen a doctor.

Like all women, Nandi was very concerned about the health of her unborn child but had to weigh the cost of seeing a doctor and traveling several miles to the nearest hospital against her everyday responsibilities. The cost was to walk several miles to the nearest medical facility and pay what was equivalent to the family's monthly income to see a doctor. At the end of the day, the lack of resources available to women like Nandi affects not only their own health but the well-being of the entire community.

It is not that Nandi cared less for her unborn child than other women. The fact is that she may no longer have the strength – even just to tug at anyone, anybody that might pass her through the crowd. The fact is that the technological solutions are simple and relatively cheap. The problem is that the vitamins, vaccines, and measuring tapes are not available for people like Nandi. **(Betty Gittens, Barbados)**

Whether in Baltimore or Bangladesh, maternal mortality is the single greatest indicator of the failure of heath systems to provide care to society's poorest and most vulnerable women. (Theresa Shaver, Director, White Ribbon Alliance for Safe Motherhood, Global Secretariat – Washington, D.C. USA)

5

IMPROVE MATERNAL HEALTH

Bible Reading

Then suddenly a woman who has been suffering from hemorrhages for twelve years came up behind Jesus and touched the fringe of his cloak. (Matthew 9:20 NRSV)

Prayer

Compassionate God open our eyes to the suffering of your children. Help us lift up the voices of women and children around the world whose full potential is limited due to illness, poverty, hunger, and violence. Amen.

Deed for the Day

Offer a ride to a pregnant woman so that she can get to a clinic or hospital or health-care facility for prenatal checkup.

IMPROVE MATERNAL HEALTH

Bible Reading

Listen to me, O house of Jacob, all you who remain of the house of Israel, you whom I have upheld since you were conceived, and have carried since your birth. Even to your old age and gray hairs I am he, I am he who will sustain you. I have made you and I will carry you; I will sustain you and I will rescue you.

(Isaiah 46:3-4 NIV)

Prayer

Heavenly Father, Nurturing Mother, thank you for life – of the giver and the unborn gift. Utilize me to ensure wellness of both mother and child – physical, mental, emotional, maternal, social, and spiritual – to enhance their quality of life. Amen.

Deed for the Day

Spread awareness of pregnancy illnesses and prevention methods.

Maternal warfare: the battle and aftereffects. Recently my brother and his wife had a new baby boy. Everyone was excited to receive him even as there were many trials that my sister-in-law faced. All throughout her pregnancy, she was sick and had extreme swelling in her arms, hands, legs, and feet. The swelling was so bad that she could not walk, drive, or work, which put stress on the family. Added to this stress was her constantly going into premature labor.

Many times the doctors had to stop her labor and eventually put her on total bed rest. This brought her much sadness, restlessness, and anxiety with the fact that she could not help. When she finally had the baby, the doctors found out that she had toxemia and this was the source of her swelling.

My brother and my sister-in-law had their new baby, but she still faces permanent health issues. Despite all of this, though, she constantly has the support of our families and her husband and is doing much better. I thank God for the healing that God has done on my sister-in law, because without it, I do not believe mother and baby would be alive today. **(Kimberly Miller, Nashville, Tennessee, USA, with KeTia Harris, Miami, Florida, USA)**

([P]utting in place the health workforce needed for scaling up maternal, newborn and child health services towards universal access is the first and most pressing task. (World Health Report, 2005))

Organizing and funding what women and children need. Results for Goal 5 in the 2010 Progress Chart on the Millennium Development Goals caught my attention. The projections that most areas are not making adequate progress to meet targets on maternal health by 2015 are shocking! Mothers are at risk around the world, and many married women, especially in Sub-Saharan Africa, have difficultly accessing contraception.

When Jesus, using apocalyptic language, was describing the trauma of "last days," he described the vulnerability and despair that women who were expecting and nursing would have experienced. You can imagine how this would have heightened the attention of the disciples who had asked about this. Rather than being surrounded by the community of women and aided by skilled midwives, the women in Jesus' description are alone, vulnerable and terrified.

Perhaps that description was a natural one for Jesus to use. Surely he had heard stories of his own birth. Imagine what Joseph might have shared with the boy about the desperation of needing a place to lodge and attending his wife alone in a strange town. Or think about what Mary might have counseled him, keeping in mind her experience of giving birth in a stable.

Goal 5 addresses our ability to invest in women, ensuring their ability to access what they need to assure their own health and the health of their families, especially infants. This is a dramatic and vulnerable time for women for millennia. We've had increasingly sophisticated technologies available to support women and families in each generation.

Will we, our communities and our nations, organize and fund what we know women and families need? No technological or medical barriers prevent us. Will we choose to act? **(Harriett Jane Olson, New York, New York, USA)**

It's all rhetoric; in terms of commitment and action, you wonder why there is no impact in the lives of ordinary people in Africa…When you look at reality on the ground, a lot still needs to be done….I think that takes political will.
(Bineta Diop, Executive Director and founder of Femmes Africa Solidarité)

5

IMPROVE MATERNAL HEALTH

Bible Reading

Woe to those who are pregnant and to those who are nursing infants in those days! (Matthew 24:19 NRS)

Prayer

Let us pray for midwives around the world, and for the success of every midwife currently in training in the many regions of the world. Amen.

Deed for the Day

Go online and research the needs of midwives in a region of your choice. Organize a group to respond to those needs with funding, technical assistance or advocacy.

IMPROVE MATERNAL HEALTH

5

Bible Reading

Then the master told his servant, 'Go out to the roads and country lanes and make them come in, so that my house will be full.' (Luke 14:23 NIV)

Prayer

God of the least of these, help us to work tirelessly on behalf of the women who are cast away from the table. Help us to live out the words of Isaiah, learn to do good, seek justice, rescue the oppressed, defend the orphan and plead for the widow. Amen

Deed for the Day

Does the pregnant woman you know have nutritious food to eat? Find out, and if not, do something today.

Bring to the table the vulnerable. "That's not fair!" a young girl cried during a simulation exercise around the Millennium Development Goals during the Children's Annual Conference in Nebraska 2009.

Micah Corps, a group of young-adult interns in the conference, was helping children understand the consequences of extreme poverty. Using a game from Church World Service, the children were slowly excluded from the group because of the social and/or economic situation assigned by the game. The girls felt the injustice against women and were not happy being taken out of the circle.

When interns shared that in many parts of the world, women eat only after the men and children have eaten, left weak and malnourished. Because the women become so weak from lack of food, their health is compromised during pregnancy and this leads to extremely high rates of maternal mortality.

The parable of the Great Banquet reminds us that God makes a special effort to bring to the table those who are the most vulnerable.

The Millennium Development Goals intend by the year 2015 to improve maternal health and improve the way women are treated by reducing the rate of maternal mortality by two-thirds.

After playing the game, the children drew picture messages on behalf of the poor that were then delivered to congressional members when the Micah Corps traveled to Washington, D.C. **(Ann Brookshire Sherer-Simpson, Lincoln, Nebraska, USA)**

A jumbo jet crashes, killing all on board. International headlines, major investigations, review of protocols, etc. Yet every day the equivalent of three 747 jets of women die as a result of pregnancy and childbirth, more than 500,000 women a year, and it rarely hits the headlines. (Christine Edwards, Christian Medical Fellowship, in www.cmf.uk.org)

Rising up for justice. Kim was happily married and rejoiced when she found out she was pregnant. Her husband, however, was angry and kicked her out of the house. It wasn't long before she became homeless and arrived at the shelter. I met her one morning, and my life changed.

Alone in a big city, Kim asked me if I would be willing to come to the hospital when it was time to deliver her baby. I gave her my phone number. One night around 2:30 am, I received a phone call. Kim was on her way to the hospital to give birth. After a tumultuous delivery, Kim gave birth to a still-born child. Grief filled her and we cried. Her lingering question was "Why would God do this to me?" Throughout her pregnancy, Kim had no access to pre-natal care. Rejected by her husband, she felt rejected by society and rejected by God. Women like Kim deserve access to pre-natal care. It's easy to forget and stigmatize those who are poor and homeless.

Even Jesus was not immune to stigmatizing the other. But the woman advocated for the dignity of her child and Jesus was convicted. May we, too, be convicted by the story of Kim and the many stories like it. May we rise up and demand justice for all women and children. **(Deanna Stickley-Miner, Columbus, Ohio, USA)**

If we are to make significant progress on meeting these Goals and stay true to the promise [the world made to build a better, fairer world for all] there is no time to lose in putting in place the necessary policies and resources needed to achieve these aims. (Kemal Dervis, former head, UNDP)

IMPROVE MATERNAL HEALTH

Bible Reading

He answered, "It is not fair to take the children's food and throw it to the dogs." She said, "Yes, Lord, yet even the dogs eat the crumbs that fall from their masters' table"... And her daughter was healed instantly.
(Matthew 15:21-28 NRSV)

Prayer

God of life, empower us to value all humans. Open our eyes to see the invisible and scorned. Open our ears to hear the wailing of mothers who birth death instead of life. Loosen our tongues to speak truth to power, demanding dignity and access to maternal care. Amen.

Deed for the Day

Write a letter to your senators encouraging them to support improved access to maternal health. Invite two others to join you.

5

IMPROVE MATERNAL HEALTH

Bible Reading

As she was about to die, the women attending her said to her, 'Do not be afraid, for you have borne a son.' But she did not answer or give heed.
(1 Samuel 4:20 NRS)

Prayer

Creator God, you desire health and well-being for all of your children. Empower us to work for healthy mothers, healthy children, and healthy families around the world. Amen.

Deed for the Day

Write a note of encouragement to a pregnant woman you know.

Healthy mothers have healthy babies. For women in developing countries, motherhood can be dangerous. Every minute a woman in Sub-Saharan Africa dies from complications during pregnancy or childbirth. Nearly all of the annual 536,000 maternal deaths worldwide occur in the developing world. Worldwide there are more than 200 million women who would like to avoid pregnancy but lack a family-planning method.

Investing in family planning reduces unintended pregnancy and increases health. When a woman delays pregnancy at least two years after the birth of her previous child, she is much more likely to have a healthy pregnancy and birth. Likewise the risk of infant mortality is much lower. Healthy mothers have healthy babies.

By empowering women and men to make healthy decisions about how to space their children and determine their family size, family planning helps people create healthier lives for themselves and for their children. **(Katey Zeh, Brunswick, Georgia, USA)**

The death of a mother deprives a child, a family, a community and ultimately a country of one of its most valuable sources of health, happiness and prosperity. (Douglas Alexander, Secretary of State for International Development for the United Kingdom)

COMBAT HIV/AIDS, MALARIA AND OTHER DISEASES

Commentary by Mira Shiva

Majority of our people, especially women and children, get afflicted with communicable diseases. Not just malaria and tuberculosis (TB) but many others which do not even exist in the minds of those who do not see the victims of these diseases.

In the late 1970s and decades following that, I saw the pain and suffering of mothers holding their sick babies and watching their lives ebb away in places in my country India like Madhya Pradesh from which Chattisgarh has been carved out as a state, Bihar of which Jharkhand as a state has been carved out, and Orissa.

I have seen the pain of so many who, already suffering from malnutrition, also have malaria due to infection from Plasmodium Vivax and Falciparum. Many of them live in malaria-endemic areas. Infection has increasingly become the more virulent Falciparum malaria. Infected women face the reality of miscarriages, still births, low birth-weight babies, worsening of existing anemia, and increasing vulnerability to maternal death.

Incidentally, deaths of pregnant women even in highly endemic areas have been because of Falciparum malaria. These deaths are not counted as maternal deaths and therefore not included in maternal mortality statistics. The management of malaria in pregnancy is different from routine malaria

MDG 6 – Combat HIV/AIDS, Malaria, and Other Diseases

Target 6.A: *Have halted by 2015 and begun to reverse the spread of HIV/AIDS*

Target 6.B: *Achieve, by 2010, universal access to treatment for HIV/AIDS for all those who need it*

Target 6.C: *Have halted by 2015 and begun to reverse the incidence of malaria and other major diseases*

management.

I was treating large numbers of TB patients coming to Landour Community Hospital in Mussoorie in the Himalayan Mountains who were coming from Happy Valley where Tibetan communities were staying. This was amongst tribal communities and workers in coal mine areas. In my work with them, I realized the vulnerability of some sections of our people who had not been exposed to TB infection earlier and had not developed some immunity. These people were vulnerable and when exposed to TB, they succumbed fast unless diagnosed and treated rationally at the earliest.

I have been involved with issues of access to essential medicines at affordable prices, the rational use of these medicines to be effective and prevent emergence of drug resistance, access to simple diagnostic facilities, and the gender dimensions of diseases.

And so I ask: Why is it that women suffering from TB or HIV get dumped while they continue to serve their partners till the end? Still I ask: Why does genitourinary tuberculosis, which can cause infertility, not given due attention in a society where womanhood is equated with motherhood and the motherhood related to birth of a male child but not a baby girl?

Gender equity, social equity, and health equity are concerns that must be addressed together. The high cost of medicines and the health needs of the majority who neither have the purchasing power nor the voice are equally crucial.

We must also be concerned about the victims of inequitable economic growth models – models that erode the very basic determinants of health, like food, water, shelter and livelihoods – and of unjust intellectual property rights regimes, as they blind spot people's needs and focus their research and development agenda and link it with market potential rather than with the medical needs of people.

MDG 6 is important to address because by addressing its targets we too recognize the health priorities of large number of peoples in developing countries where needs of babies and their mothers need priority attention. This can be done effectively with strengthened public health systems. This involves adequately trained and remunerated health personnel who are equipped with the essential medicines, and diagnostic facilities with functioning referral systems to treat complications. The health system must not be privatized so that its services are within reach by all, including the poor, and not just the privileged few.

I have dealt with meningococcal meningitis outbreaks in children in Koraput area in Orissa, with Japanese encephalitis in Uttar Pradesh, with Kalazar leishmaniasis (black fever) in Bihar, with dengue and its more fatal form Dengue Hemorrhagic Fever (DHF), with Chikungunya, another mosquito-linked vector-borne disease which is deeply debilitating but not fatal. I realized that only a strong public health system can really address additional health problems. Knowing about the breeding and biting habits of mosquitoes is as important as the knowledge of medicines and their rational use.

If MDG 6 is addressed comprehensively it would positively affect other MDGs related to maternal and child health. And it needs to be addressed more vigorously because the quantum is unacceptably high in terms of pain, suffering, loss of life, and productivity of people.

It was in Christian Medical College and Hospital in Ludhiana in Punjab, while doing my medical degree post graduation after my MBBS, that I was given a copy of the Alma Ata Charter on Comprehensive Primary Health

God's creation is in crisis. We, the Bishops of The United Methodist Church, cannot remain silent while God's people and God's planet suffer. This beautiful natural world is a loving gift from God, the Creator of all things seen and unseen. God has entrusted its care to all of us, but we have turned our backs on God and on our responsibilities. Our neglect, selfishness, and pride have fostered: pandemic poverty and disease, environmental degradation, and the proliferation of weapons and violence... We all feel saddened by the state of the world, overwhelmed by the scope of these problems, and anxious about the future, but God calls us and equips us to respond... God's spirit is always and everywhere at work in the world fighting poverty, restoring health, renewing creation, and reconciling peoples. (**The Council of Bishops of The United Methodist Church**, The Pastoral Letter – God's Renewed Creation: Call to Hope and Action, 2010)

Care. It came from my teacher and guide, Dr. Betty Cowan, a professor of medicine and community health. The year was 1978.

My shifting from clinical medicine to community health followed, and over time I realized the importance of ensuring public policies at national and international levels along with providing health care to those who needed it. We must prioritize human health concerns in an increasingly unjust world. My work is my meditation.

(Mira Shiva is a medical doctor and a public health physician. She is a member of the Steering Committee of the People's Health Movement which she also founded. Dr. Shiva is coordinator of Initiative for Health and Equity in Society and sits in the governing council of Health Action International Asia Pacific, and serves as the focal point for South Asia of the International People's Health Council.)

The health system must not be privatized so that its services are within reach by all, including the poor, and not just the privileged few.

Welcoming all people. I never dreamed I'd be living out my call to servant ministry in this way: teaching awareness and prevention of HIV/AIDS. In the 1980s, prior to my ordination, I taught middle school science. "AIDS" education was just beginning to make its way into the curriculum. There was so much misinformation about it: transmissions, causes, populations – all generating fear and judgment.

It is more than 20 years later and there have been major advancements in our understanding of HIV/AIDS. But is it enough, and have our hearts opened to welcome those living with HIV/AIDS into our faith communities? As a chaplain in ministry with people living with HIV/AIDS, I too often meet folks who tell me that they feel ostracized by the church because of their disease. This saddens me greatly. Even more, this statement must grieve the heart of God who welcomes all people. Jesus proclaims in the gospel of Luke that he has been sent to proclaim release to the captives, recovery of sight to the blind and freedom for the oppressed.

Our call as people of God is to proclaim this good news to all people and to be actively involved in solving the pandemic of HIV/AIDS in our own communities and in the world. Faith communities are the hands and feet of Christ in the world, with individuals like you and me, playing a part in God's solution. **(Patricia Archer, Wilmington, North Carolina, USA)**

Bible Reading

The Spirit of the Lord is on me, because he has anointed me to preach good news to the poor. He has sent me to proclaim freedom for the prisoners and recovery of sight for the blind, to release the oppressed, to proclaim the year of the Lord's favor.
(Luke 4:18-19 NIV)

Prayer

Gracious God, the problems of the world seem so large and I'm only one person. But you've called me to be part of the solution. Guide me that I may do your will. In the name of the one who brings release and freedom. Amen.

Deed for the Day

Volunteer to participate in an outreach ministry to those living with HIV/AIDS in your community.

(*There is only one path: to pursue the Millennium Development Goals with fresh resolve – confronting violence, bigotry and hatred with the same determination that we attack the causes from which they spring – conflict, ignorance, poverty and disease.*
(Carol Bellamy, Former Executive Director, UNICEF))

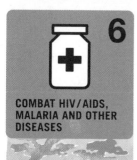

6

COMBAT HIV/AIDS, MALARIA AND OTHER DISEASES

Bible Reading

A man with leprosy came and knelt in front of Jesus, begging to be healed. "If you are willing, you can heal me and make me clean," he said.
(Mark 1:40 NLT)

Prayer

God, who is willing to cleanse, may you grant physical healing and transforming hope to those who stand in need this day, through Jesus the giver of hope. Amen.

Deed for the Day

Be willing to make choices that lead to healing and transformation.

Power greater than disease. It has been 35 years since I visited a leper colony that was sponsored by churches in India. Much in my own life has happened since that time. Many events have caused memories to be formed and forgotten. The memory of the lepers who lived in that colony is one that shall remain with me. I went to the colony expecting to see people whose bodies and spirits were devastated by a horrible disease.

The first part of my expectations was realized as I observed the physical devastation of leprosy. The second part of my expectations was transformed. I expected to find lepers who were sad. Instead, I met people whose spirits were strengthened by a peace that passes all understanding. I expected to find lepers who knew only sadness because of their disease. Instead, I met people who had an inner joy. My expectations were transformed because I was witnessing God at work as I spoke with these lepers. Rather than living in the isolation of their disease, they were strengthened by the hope of their community.

As I listened to the lepers express appreciation to Jesus for the hope they had been given, I encountered a power that was greater than their disease. The strength of MDG 6 is found in the expectant hope that the incidence of disease can be halted and reversed. As I reflect on this goal, I am reminded of the transforming power of those who are willing to believe. **(Marc Brown, Glen Allen, Virginia, USA)**

Health is also an important contributor to several other goals. The significance of the MDGs lies in the linkages between them: they are a mutually reinforcing framework to improve overall human development.
(WHO)

Bringing God's healing to the world. Those of us who call ourselves followers of Jesus must be prepared to take personal responsibility for efforts to end the suffering of all people. It is often said that knowledge is power. Never in my life has that been more evident than during the three months I spent in Tanzania last year, teaching about HIV/AIDS.

I was shocked by some of the questions my teaching partners and I received. Lack of education and the spread of misinformation can quite literally be a death sentence. We did our best to clear up misconceptions and encourage open dialogue. I was filled with hope by the high school students who chose to come back to school during their vacation days to learn how to be peer educators, and was highly impressed by the creativity of the raps and other teaching methods they came up with.

I am very encouraged by the young women and men who will very soon be leaders of their country. But education alone is not enough. Gender equality, consistent access to health care, food security, and infrastructure improvement including road development are essential components to the end of the global HIV/AIDS epidemic. Let us remember that we are the body of Christ that our hands and feet are to do: bring God's healing to the world. **(Natalie Brown, Tucson, Arizona, USA)**

The peoples and nations of the world, acting in concert, have the power to turn back AIDS: to educate our children, protect our young people, end the shameful stigmatization of people living with HIV, and secure the future for all those infected with, and affected, by HIV. We cannot delay.
(Peter Piot, Executive Director, Joint UN Programme on HIV/AIDS)

COMBAT HIV/AIDS, MALARIA AND OTHER DISEASES

Bible Reading

And when He had called His twelve disciples to Him, He gave them power over unclean spirits, to cast them out, and to heal all kinds of sickness and all kinds of disease.
(Matthew 10:1 NKJ)

Prayer

God of all peoples and nations, make us ever mindful of our brothers and sisters throughout the world who suffer from preventable diseases due to unequal distribution of wealth, power, resources, and educational opportunities. Help us to work to correct these injustices. Amen.

Deed for the Day

Encourage churches and schools in your area to incorporate comprehensive HIV/AIDS education. Prayerfully consider contributing to the Global AIDS Fund.

COMBAT HIV/AIDS, MALARIA AND OTHER DISEASES

Bible Reading

He has showed you, O man, what is good; and what does the Lord require of you, but to do justly, and to love mercy, and to walk humbly with your God? (Micah 6:8 AKJV)

Prayer

Lord, disturb my comfort so that I might comfort the disturbed. [Old Haitian Proverb]

Deed for the Day

Don't be afraid to work for justice where you are, just stand up and move out of the ditch.

Mustering courage to alleviate poverty and eradicate diseases. With the world suffering from so many problems, how can my single action make a difference? In the movie "Glory," there is a scene where the men are pinned down in a ditch by their opposition. As they lay there paralyzed by fear, afraid to move forward, scared to defend themselves, their leader decides he must do something. He takes out his sword, faces his men, and charges up out of the ditch. As the men see this they too muster up some courage and move from their paralyzed positions.

It is with this in mind that I envision the church and the communities we serve, many weighed down by poverty and disease. The residents are paralyzed by fear. I believe the pastor is in a perfect position to lead these communities against oppression. The church has to serve as the eyes, ears, and heart of God.

We must work to alleviate poverty and eradicate diseases. We cannot stop or sit idly by as families look to find solutions. Persons must do what they can, however they can. John Wesley said, "Do all the good you can, in all the ways you can, to all the souls you can, in every place you can, at all the times you can, with all the zeal you can, as long as ever you can." **(Joe Connelly, Shreveport, Louisiana, USA)**

It is not in the United Nations that the Millennium Development Goals will be achieved. They have to be achieved in each of its Member States, by the joint efforts of their governments and people.
(Kofi Annan, Former UN Secretary-General)

Touching the afflicted. I stood there as a medical intern staring down at my first patient with AIDS. He had all kinds of tubes, gadgets and monitors strewn around his emaciated body. Thank goodness, I had a white coat, a mask, and another protective covering on my body. I was filled with so much dread that I scurried out of there like a scared cat. But as I tried to make my escape, I saw from the corner of my eye a friend threw herself on him, hugged him, and cried inconsolably at his bedside.

I, however, was so focused on the consequences to myself that I forgot all about my patient. As I took further training in infectious diseases, I learned that the human immunodeficiency virus cannot be spread through casual contact. I now know that HIV/AIDS together with tuberculosis and malaria are three of the world's most devastating diseases.

In some countries the infection rate is so high that one in three people would be HIV positive. In the least developed countries, the cost of taking care of a family member who has AIDS may mean that the rest of the family will have to forego lunch and supper. All of these truths, however, may remain facts in our mind until we really see Jesus extending his hand and touching the afflicted. **(Gary Girao, Quezon City, Philippines, and Hobart, Tasmania, Australia)**

Social protection is particularly relevant to HIV because of its potential to address issues, such as gender inequality, stigma and discrimination, which exacerbate marginalization and vulnerability faced by key populations at higher risk of protection. (Miriam Temin, HIV-Sensitive Social Protection: What Does the Evidence Say, UNICEF, 2010)

6

COMBAT HIV/AIDS, MALARIA AND OTHER DISEASES

Bible Reading

A man with leprosy came to him and begged him on his knees, "If you are willing you can make me clean." Filled with compassion, Jesus reached out his hand and touched the man.
(Mark 1:40-41a, NIV)

Prayer

Lord, help me to love my neighbor just as you have loved me. Amen.

Deed for the Day

Extend a healing touch to someone who is ill today. Let them know that you care and that they are loved.

6

COMBAT HIV/AIDS, MALARIA AND OTHER DISEASES

Bible Reading

For you always have the poor with you; but you do not always have Me.
(Matt 26:11 NASB)

Prayer

O God of compassion, we ask you to open our eyes that we will not only see the poor around us, but will respond the way you want us to: care for them, hear their cries, and listen to their longings. O Holy Spirit, empower our church to be true to her calling to minister to those who are in need. In Christ's name we pray. Amen.

Deed for the Day

Has someone asked for help from you lately? Go back to him or her and learn how you might be of real help.

A church that cares. Ministry with and for the poor strikes my heart the most among the four focus areas of ministry in our church. Jesus Christ preferentially opted for the poor. Jesus ministered to the less fortunate, made sure that the gospel is preached to them (Matt 11:5), and called on the rich to give their possessions to the poor (Matt 19:21). But Jesus warned us that the poor will always be among us (Matt 26:11). Does this mean we may never succeed in eradicating poverty from the face of the earth? This is a challenge, especially because the poor are the majority of the world's population.

In the Baguio Episcopal Area we have two Persons-in-Mission doing ministry with and for the poor. We have a ministry focused on organizing and empowering cooperatives and livelihood projects, teaching the poor in the community to earn a living and live decent lives. Another ministry is focused on extending health services to the poor in far-flung areas, through what we call MODELLE-V, which includes medical, optical, dental, evangelism, legal, livelihood, employment and veterinary services. These ministries involve compassion and justice which are Wesleyan and biblical imperatives.

It is my prayer that our church in the Philippines will get more serious in reaching out to the poor, very much like the ministry of the "United Methodist Church for All People" in Ohio which I was privileged to visit. This local church welcomes everyone, especially the poor, homeless, black, white, gay, and many others. They gather and worship as one family who truly cares for each other, and works for the transformation of society. **(Rodolfo A. Juan, Baguio City, Philippines)**

Working for justice is messier and far less rewarding than charity…But we have little choice….It is a fundamental requirement of our faith. (David Hilfiker, The Limits of Charity, from The Other Side Online, 2000)

Overcoming stigma, empowering women. Women in many parts of the world are at high risk of HIV due to biological and cultural factors. And despite large numbers of HIV-positive people, HIV remains a highly stigmatized topic in many societies where it is prevalent. However, when discussing testing in self-help groups, women admit to a persistent barrier to accessing these services: They do not feel comfortable going to government testing sites, even when it is free, because of the stigma surrounding testing.

Women say that they do not want to go because people will see them and know they are going to test for HIV. HIV is still highly stigmatized in societies, and having HIV or even needing to test for HIV is considered a sign that a person is engaging in immoral behavior. This is a great barrier to reducing the spread of HIV. Testing and knowledge about status is a proven method of reducing HIV transmission. One community program fighting stigma around HIV in Pondicherry, India, has identified a solution: making testing and services home-based. Prime Trust for Social Transformation is raising funds to have a mobile testing van which can bring testing directly to the women in marginalized communities.

There is much more progress needed in different parts of the world. In Sub-Saharan Africa, disparities in knowledge about HIV prevention among women and men are linked to gender, household wealth and place of residence. Gender disparities in awareness about HIV/AIDS can only be mitigated with greater emphasis on working with marginalized women in rural areas. **(Sung-ok Lee, New York, New York, USA)**

In countries where HIV transmission occurs predominantly through heterosexual sex, as is now increasingly the case everywhere, women are more likely than men to be infected. Gender relations and gender inequalities play a major role in this context of the spread of HIV/AIDS.
(UNFPA, in www.unfpa.org.br/lacodm/arquivos/mdg6.pdf)

6

COMBAT HIV/AIDS, MALARIA AND OTHER DISEASES

Bible Reading
And He said to him, "Stand up and go; your faith has made you well."
(Luke 17:11-19 NASB)

Prayer
Lord, we pray for the empowerment of HIV-positive women, and for greater access to education, testing and treatment for women with low or no income. May they experience your Kingdom on earth as it is in heaven. Amen.

Deed for the Day
Volunteer at a local HIV/AIDS organization. Be a voice in helping to end the stigma that is associated with HIV/AIDS.

COMBAT HIV/AIDS, MALARIA AND OTHER DISEASES

6

Bible Reading

Come to me, all you who are weary and burdened, and I will give you rest.
(Matthew 11:28 NIV)

Prayer

God, we thank you for the rest that you continue to assure us of. May we be your hands and feet that we may go and serve your children in need. We pray for wisdom and guidance as we aim to be like Christ and do as he did. Amen.

Deed for the Day

Become educated and involved with the Global Health Initiative of The United Methodist Church.

Making medical care accessible. In 2006, I had the amazing opportunity to travel to Mongolia with a team of United Methodists. While there, we visited the capital, Ulaanbaatar, and spent time with two United Methodist churches and a medical ministry operated by The United Methodist Church. What a joy to worship and fellowship with the Mongolian churches!

Ulaanbaatar is a heavily populated area with half of Mongolia's two million people living there. Like many urban cities, Ulaanbaatar faces social issues of growing poverty and hunger. While many mission teams have gone to Mongolia to try to address the increasing health concerns, there is a deeper issue. One of the biggest problems with Mongolia, and Ulaanbaatar in particular, is infrastructure, specifically transportation methods and road conditions. To address health issues and combat diseases, treatment and basic health services must be readily available.

Fortunately, there are efforts to address this need. Working together with one of the local Mongolian congregations, the United Methodist Korean churches built a medical center that is more easily accessible for the people. While road conditions are still poor, by building where more people can come, more people are able to be treated and the ministry is able to be more effective. Praise be to God who continues to work with us and through us so that more people can be treated! **(Eunchun Timothy Kim, Milan, Ohio, USA)**

[N]ational budgets are such key elements in good governance that will achieve the MDGs. Budgets are more than technical or bureaucratic allocations of resources; they are moral and ethical statements of priorities.
(Peter Henriot, Jesuit Centre for Theological Reflection, Lusaka , MDGs and Good Governance, www.africafiles.org)

COMBAT HIV/AIDS, MALARIA AND OTHER DISEASES

A ddressing isolation and marginalization. Poverty in countries like the Philippines where I live is not only because its economy is weak and poorly run but that its people, its best economic assets, are in reality greatly deprived and hence marginalized. When my friend got afflicted with tuberculosis (TB) she was dreadfully isolated and discriminated by society. My heart bled for she suffered social mistreatment.

The reading from Mark 2:1-5 clearly shows us how the few good persons opened the roof and lowered the afflicted one to Jesus. Those times when the afflicted are isolated – shunned and avoided by peers and friends – we should persist, at all cost, to redress that isolation. Our lack of understanding and ignorance should be addressed.

Reaching out to educate people bound with fear and ignorance liberates them from isolation. When I brought my friend to a pulmonologist for treatment, I discovered that awareness of TB's character and its curability by antibiotics is the answer. Massive information dissemination is needed to address the illness as much as the menacing ignorance about it.

May we be the few good persons who will open the roof and lower the afflicted ones to Jesus. **(Gladys P. Mangiduyos, Cabanatuan City, Philippines)**

Bible Reading

[W]hen Jesus again entered Capernaum, the people heard that he had come home…. Some men came, bringing to him a paralytic, carried by four of them. …they made an opening in the roof above Jesus and, after digging through it, lowered the mat the paralyzed man was lying on. When Jesus saw their faith, he said to the paralytic, "Son, your sins are forgiven. (Mark 2:1-5 NIV)

Prayer

Gracious parent God, empower us to give life its deepest meaning so that we may bring the ill and afflicted to Jesus so they may have access to life and its abundance. Amen.

Deed for the Day

Reach out to a person and hold his or her hand. Talk about actualizing liberation from the pit of isolation and deprivation.

(*Community TB care projects have shown how people and communities can undertake some essential TB control tasks. These networks can mobilize civil societies and also ensure political support and long-term sustainability for TB control programmes.*)
(WHO. Tuberculosis. Fact Sheet No. 104. November 2010)

COMBAT HIV/AIDS, MALARIA AND OTHER DISEASES

6

Bible Reading

Is there no balm in Gilead? Is there no physician there? Why then is not the health of the daughter of my people recovered? (Jeremiah 8:22 ASV)

Prayer

Our loving God, give us courage and wisdom to help our sisters and brothers confront their own fears, and inspire them to share their own special journey so others will be empowered to lead healthier and better lives. Amen.

Deed for the Day

Send a special get-well card with a note of encouragement to someone battling with a disease.

Liberating others from their fears. My friend Gloria was diagnosed with breast cancer a few years ago. Her journey included surgery, rounds of chemo treatments and weeks of radiation. At the time she found out, she told me how much scarier it was just thinking of how to break the news to husband, Ben, and daughter, Melanie. As Filipino mothers are wont to do, they'd rather keep it to themselves, preferring to suffer in silence, afraid to shatter the world around them.

"But I was wrong," she recalls. Melanie's reaction was "more powerful than any cure that was out there or still to be discovered." This time, in a remarkable role reversal, the daughter takes over: "Mom, don't worry, you will get through this. It's something we will all go through together." It's at that moment, Gloria says, when the healing began.

Gloria had already lost her hair by the time she stopped by a holiday party hosted by her co-workers. Not having seen her for months, her co-workers weren't quite sure what to expect until she walked up to the stage, took off her wig and waved it with a triumphant smile. "You go, girl!" the crowd rose to its feet and cheered. She just liberated them from their own fears.

Until then, many in our community only heard about other women with similar afflictions in whispers and hushed conversations. "It's not a death sentence as it used to be," Gloria says. "Cancer is now a rapidly curable disease so I am very optimistic I will be good as new." **(Jonathan Melegrito, Kensington, Maryland, USA)**

Strengthen the health workforce. Fund the MDGs. And embrace the right to health, unleashing its potential to help achieve the health MDGs — and health for all.
(Eric A. Friedman, Physicians for Human Rights, June 24, 2010)

Overcoming indifference, combating diseases. An African proverb suggests "statistics are numbers without tears." The staggering global statistics of the persons infected and affected by HIV/AIDS, malaria, tuberculosis, and other serious diseases sometimes prompts despair rather than hope, paralysis rather than action. But knowing the names of persons and envisioning their faces can help us overcome indifference.

Recently I visited a child-headed household in India. Having lost both parents to AIDS, Siva, a malnourished 15-year-old, works ten hours a day in a poultry farm cleaning eggs with a formaldehyde solution. His 12-year-old sister, Gomathi, suffers from tuberculosis, but does the cooking and cleaning and leaves for school by seven in the morning, daily. Together they care for their HIV-positive brother, Murugan.

Wherever the compassionate Jesus went, he was "curing every disease and every sickness," never stigmatizing or asking how people became infected. He repeatedly called his disciples to the same task, reminding them "the harvest is plentiful, but the laborers are few."

Halting and reversing the spread of HIV/AIDS, malaria, TB, and other diseases by 2015 requires the engagement of every person as well as governments and non-governmental organizations. Christians are called to join with other persons of faith and goodwill in combating these diseases.

Our calling is to support and advocate for persons infected and affected through programs of awareness, education, research, prevention, care and treatment. **(Donald E. Messer, Centennial, Colorado, USA)**

Today, on World AIDS Day, we're proud to support the work of The Global Fund to Fight HIV/AIDS, Malaria, and Tuberculosis. The Global Fund is an innovative global public-private partnership which raises and disburses funds to prevent and treat HIV/AIDS, tuberculosis and malaria. (Meril Cullinan, Nothing But Nets, 1 December 2010)

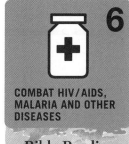

6

COMBAT HIV/AIDS, MALARIA AND OTHER DISEASES

Bible Reading
Then Jesus went about all the cities and villages, teaching in their synagogues, and proclaiming the good news of the kingdom and curing every disease and every sickness. When he saw the crowds, he had compassion for them, because they were harassed and helpless, like sheep without a shepherd. (Matthew 9:35-36 NRSV)

Prayer
O God of compassion, deepen our empathy and help us to stand in solidarity with the suffering. Move us from apathy to advocacy and action. Amen.

Deed for the Day
Choose an organization combating malaria, HIV/AIDS, tuberculosis or other diseases and make a personal financial contribution.

COMBAT HIV/AIDS, MALARIA AND OTHER DISEASES

6

Bible Reading

God is our shelter and strength, always ready to help in times of trouble. (Psalm 46:1 GNB)

Prayer

Dear God, give us the strength to live with the weights laid upon us, wisdom in our speaking or in our silence, gentleness in our actions and peace within our hearts and souls. Amen.

Deed for the Day

Call someone living with HIV/AIDS and offer to take them a meal.

A burden too heavy. It was 5:30 in the evening in December of 1988 when our world fell apart. Our middle son, Fred, had just called to tell us he had AIDS. Four months later our oldest son, Tim, wrote to us saying he, too, had the AIDS virus. What should we do? To whom should we confide? What kind of coping skills did we possess to deal with having two of our three sons die?

When we finally began to share our sorrow with friends and family over a year later we were flooded with calls, cards and visits. We should have been aware the church would know how to care for us – that is the church's calling.

Tim succumbed to this dreaded disease in December of 1990 and Fred took his last breath in September of 1991. In nine months we lost two sons and there stood the church people among us: solid in their compassion and faith. They encouraged us with the promise of the resurrection. They inspired us with hope. They gave us the assurance that we could survive the hard days that were to come. God's presence was made known to us throughout our journey by way of our church family. **(Etta Mae Mutti, Kansas City, Missouri, USA)**

There is evidence that core interventions to prevent infections among adolescents and young people can be effective when used as part of a combination prevention approach that includes behavioural, biomedical and structural components. (Opportunity in Crisis, UNAIDS, June 2011)

Candles and prayers. Every year seminary students in Kansas City invite the community to participate in World AIDS Day events. At dusk on the eve of the day of remembrance, students gather at a busy intersection with posters and candles. The flickering lights catch the eyes of drivers and they respond in different ways. Some pass by without turning their heads, just as they pass by homeless persons asking for help. Some slow down and read the signs. Some stop and talk with the students, take information flyers and express appreciation. Some stop long enough to pray and promise to pass the word to others.

The next day folks gather in the chapel to sing, learn from one another, and make commitments to work for an AIDS-free world. Sometimes speakers may be persons living with AIDS. They may tell what it is like to suffer with an incurable illness, to be stigmatized and ostracized, and about caring persons who have helped them through this hard journey. Another person may share about engagement in a project in Africa that offers support to orphan children and provides a clinic for testing and access to treatment. This person may bring resources to educate those who would like to work to end the spread of HIV.

Those who gather year after year raise awareness and evoke a response from the community. Like a candle burning in the dark, the light radiates in a way that makes a difference. **(Fritz Mutti, Kansas City, Missouri, USA)**

Although social integration is not mentioned per se in the MDGs, achievement of these goals is intertwined with the "quest for humane, stable, safe, tolerant and just societies" identified in Copenhagen. (H.E. Mr. Leslie Kojo Christian, Permanent Representative of Ghana to the UN)

COMBAT HIV/AIDS, MALARIA AND OTHER DISEASES

Bible Reading

No one after lighting a lamp puts it under the bushel basket, but on the lampstand, and it gives light to all in the house. In the same way, let your light shine before others, so that they may see your good works and give glory to your Father in heaven. (Matthew 5:15-16 NRS)

Prayer

Let our lights shine so that the denial, stigma and suffering of HIV/AIDS is overcome in the world. Amen.

Deed for the Day

Write a note of encouragement to someone who is living with HIV/AIDS.

6

COMBAT HIV/AIDS, MALARIA AND OTHER DISEASES

Bible Reading

For freedom Christ has set us free. Stand firm, therefore, and do not submit again to a yoke of slavery (Galatians 5:1 NRSV)

Prayer

Our gracious and parent God, we uphold in our prayers the "Morong 43" health workers and families in the Philippines. Strengthen their spirit, keep them safe, heal the wounds in their heart, and bless them in their search for justice. In Christ's name we pray. Amen

Deed for the Day

Share my story to members of your church. Invite them to sign the petition on this website: http://www.ipetitions. com/petition/free_all_political_ prisoners/#sign_petition

Healing wounds of injustice and poverty. I am a niece of one of the 43 health workers illegally arrested on 6 February 2010 in Morong, Rizal, Philippines. My uncle, Dr. Alexis Montes, was falsely accused by the Philippine military of being a member of the New People's Army, an armed rebel group in the Philippines. At the time of their arrest, the health workers were undergoing a First Respondents Training to equip community health workers with skills to handle medical emergencies due to natural calamities and disasters.

Dr. Alexis Montes is a 62-year-old licensed medical doctor with almost 40 years of his life spent visiting poor rural villages, organizing medical missions, and sharing his live-saving gift to the people. He has tirelessly devoted his service as lay leader to the healing ministry of the United Church of Christ in the Philippines.

Community health workers like my uncle and his 42 co-workers are both hope and lifeline to many poor people. As doctors, nurses, midwives and community health workers, their oath committed them to save lives by providing health care to anyone, at all times, and in any place. Such help is needed in the Philippines where half of the population has no access to basic health care. Forty percent cannot afford basic medicines even to treat simple colds. Ten women die every day due to childbirth-related complications.

We are angered by the physical torture and mental anguish they suffered. But we continue to heal from the wounds of this injustice, even as most of them have now been released, after 10 months of illegal detention. **(Necta Montes Rocas, Quezon City, Philippines)**

(There is near unanimity today that part of the human resource response in low-income settings should include salaried and well-trained community health workers to dispense knowledge, medicines, and contraceptives within the households and to support the linkages of households with facilities-based care. (Jeffrey Sachs, Special Advisor to UN Secretaries-General on the MDGs, 18 September 2010))

ENSURE ENVIRONMENTAL SUSTAINABILITY

Commentary by Ann Marie Braudis

Part of the early development of humanity was awakening to awareness of the future.

As humanity sharpened its sense of the future, it universally developed a sense of hope for a better future for its offspring. Everywhere touching stories are told of parents who sacrifice for their children's future.

This basic human characteristic continues to evolve. Today it takes the form of a pull toward thinking as a species for the well-being of whole generations of future children. Unfolding alongside of this is the knowledge that the well-being of future generations will be dependent on a healthy and flourishing Planet Earth.

However, as is well documented, the health of the planet is degraded. Therefore, two great pieces of work need to be undertaken. The first is to prevent further depletion of natural resources. The second is to restore what has been damaged so that nature may flourish again and all Earth's children may be healthy and have what they need to live a dignified life.

Going forward, all development projects need to be planned and implemented in such a way that they respect and enhance nature. This is the path of sustainability, the sign of which is justice for the entire Earth

MDG 7 – Ensure Environmental Sustainability

Target 7.A: *Integrate the principles of sustainable development into country policies and programmes and reverse the loss of environmental resources*

Target 7.B: *Reduce biodiversity loss, achieving, by 2010, a significant reduction in the rate of loss*

Target 7.C: *Halve, by 2015, the proportion of the population without sustainable access to safe drinking water and basic sanitation*

Target 7.D: *By 2020, to have achieved a significant improvement in the lives of at least 100 million slum dwellers*

What The United Methodist Church says:

All creation is the Lord's, and we are responsible for the ways in which we use and abuse it. Water, air, soil, minerals, energy resources, plants, animal life, and space are to be valued and conserved because they are God's creation and not solely because they are useful to human beings. (**Social Principles ¶ 160. I**)

The continued pattern of environmental racism represents a serious challenge to the conscience of all Christians. We therefore ask all our local churches, conferences, and general agencies to join with other religious bodies and groups in actions to end this form of racism. (**1025: Environmental Racism. The Book of Resolutions of The United Methodist Church, 2008**)

community.

For many years I was privileged to accompany the Ibaloy and Kankanay Indigenous Peoples in their homeland in the northern mountains of the Philippines. It was a period of ruthless assault against the environment by large-scale gold-mining corporations and logging companies that left the mountains bare and hollowed-out, the land unproductive, and the water contaminated.

As the people struggled against these overwhelming forces, their only motto was, "Remember the children," referring to the children of tomorrow. I find this to be the perfect slogan for the global campaign for realizing MDG 7, a crucial work of justice.

(Ann Marie Braudis, MM, Ph.D., is associate for the integrity of creation for the Maryknoll Office for Global Concerns and serves as Maryknoll NGO representative at the United Nations. Ann previously served in the Philippines as director of the Maryknoll Ecological Sanctuary in Baguio, and as professor at the Asian Social Institute in Manila.)

Commentary by David G. Hallman

Is it important to us to live in a healthy world and for our grandchildren to have clean water to drink?

There is a powerful self-interest reason for caring about effective implementation of MDG 7 on environmental sustainability. Without assertive action to address the causes of ecological degradation, the quality of life of our and future generations will be imperiled.

But caring about the well-being of God's creation is not just about us and our families. It is also about our neighbor.

We are called, in love and solidarity, to care for the well-being of those most vulnerable to threats such as climate change, biodiversity loss, and pollution.

And in reading the Gospel in today's context, that neighbor in need includes non-human species as well as our human brothers and sisters.

Life, in all its healthy abundance, is possible for all. But we must act to participate in God's mission to bring that about.

(David G. Hallman formerly coordinated and now acts as an advisor of the Programme on Climate Change of the World Council of Churches.)

By virtue of the fact that we exist as living, breathing human beings, we have a relationship with the earth because we were created out of it. And, we have a relationship with God because God is our very breath of life. (**Rev. Pat Watkins**, http://www.umc-gbcs.org/site/apps/nlnet/content3.aspx?c=frLJK2PKLqF&b=2952531&ct=9110167&notoc=1)

7

ENSURE ENVIRONMENTAL SUSTAINABILITY

Bible Reading

Jesus said: "I came that they may have life, and have it abundantly."
(John 10:10b ESV)

Prayer

Creator God, gracias for your love and kindness. I commit to live to manifest the abundant life, to fulfill the Lord's prayer: Thy will be done on earth as it is in heaven. Amen.

Deed for the Day

Study and share information about WCC Justice, Peace and Integrity of Creation, the 1992 Treaty on Environmental Education for Sustainable Societies and Global Responsibility, and the 2010 Declaration of the Rights of Mother Earth

What we plant we reap. What is going on with climate change? Terrible natural disasters, happening all at the same time on the planet. Impoverished communities, a large percentage of the world, are suffering increased starvation, poverty, and death. In Haiti, Guatemala and El Salvador, we are experiencing in our daily life more frequent and intense floods, drought, and other calamities. The environment, just as the people, are being destroyed and exploited. As children, mom and dad taught us to take care of Mother Earth. Today, we must address climate change and crises in food, energy, finance and economy as a human rights imperative.

I am blessed to have been a part of global processes like the drafting in 1991 of the World Council of Churches covenant called Justice, Peace and the Integrity of Creation, prior to the Earth Summit in Rio de Janeiro. In 1992, I was part of the civil society worldwide process to concretize at the Earth Summit the multilingual, multicultural "Treaty for Environmental Education for Sustainable Societies and Global Responsibility," now used widely and part of the Brazilian public educational system.

In El Salvador we are working on culture of peace. We have an ecological house, a permaculture farm, a Free University, and a folk-arts museum for planetary and global citizenship. The Global Call Against Poverty, including the call against hunger, is also part of our efforts to make the kingdom of God here on Earth possible. Let us live peacefully with Mother Earth. **(Marta Benavides, Sta Ana, El Salvador)**

Civil society participation must be central to assessing progress on the MDGs and most importantly to achieving them. (The World We Want 2015. Open Letter to UN Secretary-General Ban Ki-moon)

Divine or "the vine" inspiration? The earthwide crises we now experience are words starting with letter F: food, fuel (energy), feeds, fertilizer, forest, fish, fertility (population), finance, floods, famine and even crisis of family and faith. These are interrelated and one condition leads to another. A response to one can alleviate the others. These affect individuals, families, communities, peoples and nations and the whole humanity.

Natural disasters like flood and drought, or human-caused disasters, such as mining and agri-business incursion, have increasingly displaced indigenous peoples from their ancestral domains, exposing them to hunger, malnutrition and disease. But with their natural resources and simple, traditional technology and management, the Aytas (Philippine aboriginal peoples) can be self-sufficient and self-reliant in their food supply. The choice of the variety of vertical, vine vegetables as basic food crops could provide them sustainable food sources. Such crawler, clinger, climber crops as sweet potato, turnip, winged bean, stringed bean, flat bean, lima bean, winter melon, sweet gourd, bottle gourd, squash, bitter melon, chayote, and passion fruit are high-nutrient foods rich in protein, vitamins and minerals.

Most of us associate the vine with grape growing in vineyards. However, there is much variety of vines in tropical countries. And they could be tapped to produce much-needed food. Paul Wolf, a United Methodist pastor from Kansas with wife, Peck Kam, visited the Philippines. After learning the above initiatives, Paul remarked: Is this "divine" or "the vine" inspiration? **(Jose Pepito Manansala Cunanan, Quezon City, Philippines)**

Environmental harm from human activity is another borderless issue affecting the global economy with respect to which human rights claims are made. (Stephen P. Marks, The Sustainable Development and Human Rights Nexus, at CoNGO CSDF 2008)

7

ENSURE ENVIRONMENTAL SUSTAINABILITY

Bible Reading
Jesus said "I am the true vine, and my Father is the gardener... I am the vine; you are the branches. If a man remains in me and I in him, he will bear much fruit..."
(John 15:1, 5. ERV)

Prayer
Dear God, we thank you that you are a gardener and understand our needs for food, health and livelihood. May we share this to others who are hungry that they may grow their daily food. Amen.

Deed for the Day
Dig a one-cubic-meter hole and fill it with leaves, grass, and organic waste and make compost. Use the hole and plant seeds of vine vegetables and make a simple trellis for the crops to cling and climb.

ENSURE ENVIRONMENTAL SUSTAINABILITY

Bible Reading

Hear the word of the Lord, O people of Israel; against the inhabitants of the land. There is no faithfulness or loyalty, and no knowledge of God in the land...Therefore the land mourns, and all who live in it languish; together with the wild animals and the birds of the air, even the fish of the sea are perishing. (Hosea 4:1-3 NRSV)

Prayer

Dear God, as we continue to progress in this world, I pray that you may give us the opportunity and knowledge to realize how we can make this world better without destroying the land on which we live and make our living. Amen.

Deed for the Day

Read up on what organizations are doing and get a healthy understanding on their effects to the land they are working on.

Using land, sustainably. To "achieve significant improvement in lives of at least 100 million slum dwellers, by 2020" and to "reduce by half the proportion of people without sustainable access to safe drinking water," are two goals aimed to ensure environmental sustainability.

These are ideas that must be conceived properly without resorting to means that involve coercion. These goals deserve to be achieved for the sake of sustainability in our communities.

It is a travesty that I see loss of environmental resources within U.S. soil through aggressive land acquisition by business enterprises for commercial purposes. Coming from a city, I have personally seen land being appropriated for business development, like retail stores, parking lots, etc. I believe these are not necessities.

Providing good transportation to places where these enterprises are already available will avoid using land for commercial purposes. Those instances where coercive force has been used to secure these lands prove unnecessary and uncalled for. We must continually examine the ways we can use land and its resources sustainably and not to deplete the resources it provides. **(Christopher de Pano, Whittier, California, USA)**

Redoubled efforts will be needed to improve the lives of the growing numbers of urban poor in cities and metropolises across the developing world. (The UN MDG Report, 2010)

The interconnectedness of life. We need to take into account the Bible's affirmation that the earth belongs to God, not to humans (Psalm 24:1). Human beings are created in the image of God and commanded to have "dominion" over the earth and all creatures. But this command carries responsibility of caring for the whole of creation. It is a dominion to image God in creation, to care and protect and not to dominate and abuse.

The central biblical message built into this command for humanity to have dominion calls for respect, love, and care for God's good creation. This is a call to exercise wise guardianship rather than a license for exploitation.

Coexistence is the basic form of life in this universe, the coexistence and interdependence of all created beings. This relation extends beyond the circle of human life. Human beings exist with animals, with the soil, sun, water, and all forms of life that they produce.

God is creator of a world whose inhabitants are intrinsically and profoundly interdependent. This interconnectedness of life is a mark of the universe we now live in. **(Pihaatae Francois, Suva, Fiji)**

As a ten-year-old, I used to look at the sea with awe, at the seemingly endless supply of fish that I could harvest... now when I look at it, I wonder how far into the new millennium we will be before it overwhelms our coasts. What is there to celebrate about a new millennium if the northern group of the Cook Islands, or the many islands of Kiribati, Tokelau, Tuvalu, the Federated States of Micronesia and the Marshall Islands are about to disappear beneath the ocean? (Tamari'i Tutangata, Former Director of South Pacific Regional Environmental Programme, 2000)

7

ENSURE ENVIRONMENTAL SUSTAINABILITY

Bible Reading
The earth is the Lord's, and everything in it, the world, and all who live in it.
(Psalm 24:1 NIV)

Prayer
God, forgive our selfishness in regards to your Holy creation. Open our eyes and mind in order to value all creatures that exist in our world and to show respect to them. Kill in us the desire of consuming more and more instead producing. Amen.

Deed for the Day
Ask the people to re-read and meditate on the Genesis stories of creation.

7

ENSURE ENVIRONMENTAL SUSTAINABILITY

Bible Reading

Where were you when I laid the foundation of the earth? Tell me, if you have understanding. Who determined its measurements – surely you know! (Job 38:4-5 ESV*)*

Prayer

Creator God, open our eyes and ears to the damage we have been causing the earth. Remove our arrogance and indifference and instill in us awe for the majesty of your creation that we might begin living more reverent and sustainable lives. Amen.

Deed for the Day

Lower the carbon footprint of your church and yourself. Find out how at www.greenfaith.org and www. theregenerationproject.org.

Treating **earth with reverence.** I once heard environmentalist Bill McKibben point out that God's longest discourse recorded in the Bible occurs in response to Job's insistent demand for an explanation of his terrible circumstances. Rather than answer Job's pleas of innocence, however, God talks about the intricacies of creation to point out Job's arrogance and lack of understanding: "Where were you when I laid the foundation of the earth?"

We too have been acting with the arrogance of Job. We have been treating the earth with reckless abandon. We have been extracting resources and burning fossil fuels at ever-increasing rates. Unfortunately, we are beginning to see the effects of such actions: stronger and more frequent extreme weather events, damage to corral reefs and forests, to name just a few. We can make guesses about what all these changes will mean, but the reality is that we have a limited understanding of the astounding complexity of creation. We, like Job, do not really understand.

God's response to Job should be a warning to us today as we consider the urgency of issues like environmental sustainability and climate change. Not only does it reinforce our lack of understanding of creation's complexities, it also reminds us of God's intimate connection to all of creation. Perhaps we should begin treating the earth with a reverence that reflects that intimate connection. **(Jay Godfrey, New York, New York, USA)**

The environment might just be the pillar upon which all the goals and hence a more sustainable development may well fall or stand. And the environment is not a luxury only affordable when all other issues have been resolved. It is, as stated, the red ribbon running around. (Environment Times)

Water as compassion and justice. Four years ago I was visiting Kibera, an enormous slum that is home to about a quarter of the four million inhabitants of Nairobi, Kenya. Following the dirt-littered alleys we were taking in the bustling life: people walking, cooking, meeting, and selling on the streets. At the same time we were trying to avoid stepping into the open sewers. One minute we would pass wild dumps of waste and "flying toilets" and the next we would see food being prepared on the street, often covered with flies. Adults and children were carrying heavy containers of water home.

Overlooking this vast expanse of tin-roofed shanty houses and rivulets of waste water in the other direction was a thick green lawn with a water course running through it and a golf course.

It is a striking symbol of the injustice that marks today's water crisis. Almost 900 million people do not have basic access to the life-saving 20 liters of daily clean water. The reasons are not simply water scarcity and lack of financial resources. Rather, the needs of marginalized communities are often not given priority. The United Nations reported in 2006 that Kibera's water supply was further restricted in favor of other residential areas in Nairobi.

Water and sanitation have implications for all MDGs and efforts in this area must be expressions of both compassion and concern for justice. **(Maike Gorsboth, Geneva, Switzerland)**

If the tables were turned, and one of us lived in a shanty town, we wouldn't say that the Goals should be scaled back. Our daily lives would show us that each of the Millennium Development Goals is critically important.
(Asha-Rose Migiro, UN Deputy Secretary-General)

ENSURE ENVIRONMENTAL SUSTAINABILITY

Bible Reading
Defend the cause of the weak and fatherless; maintain the rights of the poor and oppressed.
(Psalm 82:3 NIV)

Prayer
God, thank you for water that gives life to all creation. May the water we use every day be a reminder to us of your covenant with us humans and all living things on Earth. Help me to use your gift respectfully, to share it freely, and to protect the rights of the many who are without clean water. Amen.

Deed for the Day
Experience not eating meat for a day. A vegetarian diet uses about 3,000 liters (800 gallons) of water less, daily, because the production of meat requires a lot of water. Learn more at www.waterfootprint.org.

7

ENSURE ENVIRONMENTAL SUSTAINABILITY

Bible Reading

Is it not enough for you to drink clear water? Must you also muddy the rest with your feet?
(Ezekiel 34:18 NIV)

Prayer

Creator God, we give thanks for your sacred gift of water. We confess that we have not been faithful stewards of your good creation and today renew our commitment to caring for the earth and all your children. Amen.

Deed for the Day

Host a community dialogue with your elected officials to examine water issues in your area.

Proclaiming enough. Although water covers roughly two-thirds of the earth's surface, more than 80 countries – 40 percent of the world's population – suffer serious water shortages. By 2025, two-thirds of our brothers and sisters will be facing water stress. Every year, two million children die because of lack of access to basic water and sanitation.

Despite the vast quantity of water on this planet, less than .01 percent is usable by humans. But the real culprits are our rampant consumption and constant despoiling of God's creation. We have the technology and resources to provide sustainable access to safe water supplies, yet we continue to turn a blind eye to the suffering of our global neighbors, believing that our affluence can protect us from our own unsustainable behaviors.

At the 2002 World Summit on Sustainable Development in Johannesburg, South Africa, I participated in the Global People's March. We began in Alexandra, where residents lived in makeshift housing without running water. We ended a few short miles away at a site of the UN conference in a convention center attached to a luxury shopping mall where water flowed freely in decorative fountains and pools. Those interconnected and starkly contrasting images – the result of human choices – left me wondering how much suffering we must witness before we proclaim "enough!" and take action to ensure that all God's children have enough. **(John S. Hill, Washington, District of Columbia, USA)**

The question is whether [government] financing interventions address the needs and priorities of those most vulnerable to climate change. (Gender and Climate Change Finance. Heinrich Böll Stiftung and Women's Environment and Development Organization. November 2008)

The hope of ever-flowing streams. Water is the common thread in the fabric of life. Water is essential, indispensable, and life-giving. It's hard to think of an aspect of life that doesn't involve water. Images of water flow throughout the Scriptures: the deep waters of creation, waters of chaos with the flood, women at wells, parting seas, and baptisms in flowing rivers.

A familiar and frequently quoted biblical verse embedded with water is Amos 5:24, "But let justice roll down like waters, and righteousness like an ever flowing stream." In this passage, the vigorous use of water imagery appears in Amos' vision for justice and righteousness as both cleansing and constant. However, more than one billion people worldwide do not have access to clean water and water-related diseases are the leading cause of death in the world, taking the lives of 6,000 people a day.

Amos paid close attention to the roots of injustice in his prosperous context. As people in today's world, we need to hear the call of God and see with real clarity water-related injustices. Amos challenging the status quo was risky, but justice should roll down like waters and righteousness like an ever-flowing steam. If justice were to come like a mighty waterfall, what consumption practices might get washed away? If righteousness were to come like an ever-flowing stream, what environmental habits should we sustain? **(Rebekah Cypert Krevens, Allen, Texas, USA)**

(*Climate change places new and additional burdens on people in developing countries. These new challenges must be addressed with additional resources if the fight against climate change and the eradication of poverty are to reinforce rather than undermine one another. (Deadline 2015. CIDSE Background Paper on the MDGs. July 2010.)*)

7

ENSURE ENVIRONMENTAL SUSTAINABILITY

Bible Reading
But let justice roll down like waters, and righteousness like an ever flowing stream. (Amos 5:24 ESV)

Prayer
God, creator of us all, we lift up to you all those who thirst. Equip us to work together to let justice roll down like waters and lead us to your ever-flowing streams. Amen.

Deed for the Day
After every time you use water today, tell someone else about the lack of clean drinking water.

7

ENSURE ENVIRONMENTAL SUSTAINABILITY

Bible Reading

A river flows out of Eden to water the garden, and from there it divides and becomes four branches.
(Genesis 2:10 NRSV)

Prayer

God, thank you for all you've given us. While we who live in abundance can choose to overlook how much we have, may we not do so. As we drink freely today, let us be mindful of those throughout the world who are denied a cup of cold water. Amen.

Deed for the Day

Inform someone else today that we have many brothers and sisters who, because of someone else's greed, have inadequate water to meet their daily needs.

A **right and not a privilege.** Have you ever been denied something you thought you deserved? How did that make you feel? On a cold, windy day recently, a construction barrel blew out in front of my car. My choice was to hit the barrel or swerve into another car. I chose the barrel. The construction company that owned the barrel denied responsibility. I was angry! I deserve to be reimbursed for my expenses for the repairs. I was denied a just outcome. Wow! You can see what a privileged position I come from. Maybe you are in such a position, too. So let's get real. Some folks have life-sustaining necessities denied them.

In this Scripture passage, a river flows out of Eden, dividing into four branches. This river was of God's good creation, one intended to flow into the four corners of the Earth, bringing life-giving water to all of creation. According to the UN MDG Report 2008, "1.6 billion people live in areas of economic water scarcity, where human, institutional, and financial capital limit access to water, even though water in nature is available locally to meet human demands." How dare that happen!

God created with the intention that all should be able to partake, and here we learn that some are unjustly denied. Having safe water to drink is a basic need. It's a right, not a privilege. **(Jane D. McCarthy, Willow Grove, Pennsylvania, USA)**

Globally, around 2.4 million deaths could be prevented annually if everyone practiced appropriate hygiene and had good, reliable sanitation and drinking water. (Jamie Bartram, Ph.D., and Sandy Cairncross, Ph.D., in Public Library of Science Medicine , November 16, 2010)

Warning calls, not punishment. The Philippines was lashed not too long ago with strings of typhoons – Ondoy, Pepeng, Ramil and Santino. Ondoy poured the heaviest rains in 40 years in the country, claimed almost a thousand lives, forced evacuation of around a hundred thousand people, and destroyed countless crops and infrastructures. My family was not spared. Water crept swiftly into the house and our cars and office furniture were submerged in water as we squeezed into the house's seventh floor. What mattered then was life. Thank God we were safe.

During those dark days aggravated by electricity shut down, I realized that the devastations we experienced were people-caused. We have not been good stewards of God's creations. Trees are cut, forests are denuded and illegal logging is practiced. Solid wastes, especially plastic, are not managed well, blocking sewerage systems and causing deaths of rivers. Poor people with shanty houses along rivers and mountains were blamed. Yet, corruption in the government is denying people their basic needs and social services. Worst, they were caught unprepared when this calamity sprang.

Many people claim that the distressing effects of typhoons were acts of God. But it could never be because our God is loving and compassionate. God must have sent these warning calls but not to punish God's people. God only longs that this beautiful creation of Mother Earth be given the best care. **(Chita Rebollido-Millan, Calasiao, Pangasinan, Philippines)**

Just as we have mobilized to fight climate change, let us this year mobilize to achieve the Millennium Development Goals. (Ban Ki-moon, UN Secretary-General)

7

ENSURE ENVIRONMENTAL SUSTAINABILITY

Bible Reading
The earth is the LORD's, and everything in it, the world, and all who live in it; for he founded it upon the seas and established it upon the waters. (Psalm 24: 1-2 NIV)

Prayer
Thank you God for your gift of Mother Earth. We are ashamed that we have to learn the lesson the harder way. May we not wait for other typhoons in order to change our carelessness and abusiveness to our environment. Help us to be the best stewards we can ever be. Amen.

Deed for the Day
All peoples should do something, great or small, to save Mother Earth. It's 'better late than never.'

7

ENSURE ENVIRONMENTAL SUSTAINABILITY

Bible Reading

How good and pleasant it is when God's people live together in unity! For there the Lord bestows his blessing, even life forevermore.
(Psalm 133:1+3b NIV)

Prayer

O God, you created humanity with the goal that we live together in peace. Give us your Holy Spirit to open our hearts and minds to recognize each other as brothers and sisters. Help us to find ways to work together for all creation. Amen.

Deed for the Day

Write a letter to your country's ambassador to the UN and tell him or her the story of the two donkeys.

Finding a common solution. I am sitting in the big Assembly Hall of the United Nations Office in Geneva. As Alternate Representative to the United Nations for the General Board of Church and Society, my place is in the balcony. But downstairs in the hall are the 193 member-state delegates gathered to discuss how the right to education for all can be fulfilled.

What a variety of people! What a variety of problems and opinions even. Can they find a solution? If they will find one, will the different states agree, and will they implement the solution?

In this moment the story of the two donkeys crosses my mind. The two donkeys were bound together with a rope. Two haycocks were nearby. Each donkey tried to get to a haycock. Although each of them was very hungry, no one could feed, because each donkey pulled in his own direction. The rope was too short for both of them to have a haycock at the same time. Suddenly they were aware, when they feed together on one haycock first and then work on the other next, they would satisfy their hunger.

Back with my mind in the meeting, I decided to go downstairs during the break and try to tell this little story to one or two delegates. Perhaps this could help to find a common solution. **(Martin Roth, Olten, Switzerland)**

(Enormous progress has been made toward meeting the MDGs, and we must recognize, celebrate and support these achievements....But much more remains to be done. If we are to meet the ambitious objectives we have set, historic leaps in human development will be needed. (The United States Strategy for Meeting the MDGs, September 2010))

Assuming responsibility for nature. On the occasion of his 62nd birthday in January 2007, the governor Sinjo Harry Sarundayang of North Sulawesi province, where I live, invited thousands of people to gather on a damaged beach. After a short worship service, he then invited everybody to take mangrove seeds and plant them along the beach. People were encouraged by their leader to assume responsibility for their share in destroying nature.

During the Executive Committee meeting in October 2007 in Trinidad and Tobago of the World Alliance of Reformed Churches, the local organizing committee gave us a tour of the beach. In a small boat we went through the mangrove jungle observing and enjoying a beautiful part of the Caribbean islands!

Two years later, in May 2009, the World Ocean Conference and the Coral Triangle Initiative summits were launched in Manado, the capital of North Sulawesi. With the strong support of the governor, who convinced the Indonesian government, including President Susilo Bambang Yudoyono, and the United Nations, the Manado Ocean Declaration was produced, showing how to handle and manage coastal and marine ecosystems. This was later brought to the UN Conference on Climate Change in Copenhagen, in December 2009. Now I keep in mind and pray for the replanting of mangrove trees that have been maintaining and sustaining our environment and the earth. **(Richard A.D. Siwu, Tomohon, North Sulawesi, Indonesia)**

(*For the sake of the planet, the biodiversity science community has to create a way to get organised to advise governments to halt the potentially catastrophic loss of species.* (Robert Watson, Intergovernmental Panel on Climate Change))

ENSURE ENVIRONMENTAL SUSTAINABILITY

Bible Reading
The Earth and everything on it belong to the Lord. The world and its people belong to him. The Lord placed it all on the oceans and rivers.
(Psalm 24:1-20 CEV)

Prayer
God, Creator and Sustainer of the earth and everything on it, grant us wisdom that we may participate in your redeeming work to sustain the integrity of your creation. Grant us courage in taking care of our environment for the eternity of your creation. Amen.

Deed for the Day
Control ourselves to not throw out rubbish wherever we want to, be an example and encourage people how to care more for the environment.

7

ENSURE ENVIRONMENTAL SUSTAINABILITY

Bible Reading

I have set before you life and death, blessing and cursing; therefore choose life, that both you and your descendents may live.
(Deuteronomy 30:19-20 NKJV)

Prayer

Holy and Gracious God, you are all around us, in every flower, rock and planet. May we honor the way you've made this earth, and choose life, each and every day. Amen.

Deed for the Day

Determine one thing you will commit to change to ensure environmental sustainability, to protect the created order from our misuse. Act for life.

Acting without my consent. I watched open mouthed as NASA, the U.S. National Aeronautics and Space Agency, bombed the moon on October 9, 2009. The U.S. justification for the act was that we might find evidence of water deep under the moon's surface. At this rather removed NASA announcer counting down to "impact," I spontaneously yelled out loud: "What are you doing? How could you do this without my and our consent, dialogue, understanding, debate?" To bomb the moon, penetrating it at 6,000 miles per hour, seemed an overtly horrific and violent act, and it got under my skin. You see, women have a spiritual and physical connection with the moon. How could this happen without a national ethical debate and conversation?

When will we stop? When will we begin to see the natural world – the air, water, rock, soil, moon – as something sacred rather than just pillage, abuse, bomb, siphon, alter, or pave over, to protect our own rather misguided sense of development and advancement? If what we have is enough for such an act after a devastating economic crisis, leaving thousands of families without housing, can't we use that plenty to do something else? This act reportedly cost the U.S. taxpayer 79 million dollars. Imagine using the US$79 million to help people in this country non-violently gather rainwater, so that we can save water we need for the sake of life here and now.

I don't get it. When will "because we can, we do" be checked by a dialogue about ethics, theology, rights, anthropology, sustainable development, and self-control of our excess? **(Kathleen Stone, New York, New York, USA)**

(At the top of the agenda is the climate change problem, which will have to be regarded as an opportunity to develop more efficient 'green' technologies and make the structural changes needed that will contribute to sustainable growth.
(Sha Zukang, UN Under-Secretary-General for Economic and Social Affairs))

Public witness and responsible stewardship. Sanchez Mira, a northeastern town in the province of Cagayan, north of the Philippines, is very rich in natural resources. Sometime in 2005, a group of Taiwanese businessmen and some Filipino political leaders attempted to quarry along the seashores in order to extract mines. But people in the community, religious leaders and the municipal mayor, Napoleon Sacramed, who is a United Methodist, barricaded the area for a period of three weeks. These people took turns in protecting the place. Day and night they guarded the seashores. Residents living near the affected places were very vigilant in protecting their natural environment.

This act of concern was an expression of their deep care for their environmental resources. Hence, the quarrying did not succeed. The Taiwanese businessmen left the place, leaving behind their heavy equipment. Sigh of relief, joy and hope dawned in the hearts of the people of Sanchez Mira, Cagayan. Glory to God for the Cagayanos who made public their witness to the beauty of God's creation and exhibited responsible stewardship of the natural environment. **(Various authors, Social Principles Workshop, Northern Philippines Annual Conference of The United Methodist Church, August 2009, Tuguegarao City, Philippines)**

The MDGs are a major international challenge, but also a basis for re-affirming our linkages with the environment and natural resources as key assets for our livelihoods. (Edmund Barrow, R.J. Fisher, Lucy Emerton, and Andrew Ingles, European Tropical Forest Research Network)

7

ENSURE ENVIRONMENTAL SUSTAINABILITY

Bible Reading
The Earth is the Lord's, and everything in it, the world, and all who live in it; for He founded it upon the seas and established it upon the waters. (Psalm 24:1-2 NIV)

Prayer
Dear God our heavenly Father, we thank you for giving us a beautiful world to enjoy and take care of. Help us to continue to protect and sustain the beauty of the earth. Bless our Mother Earth. Amen.

Deed for the Day
Include in your Sunday School discussion how you are protecting your natural environment and God's sustainable creation.

ENSURE ENVIRONMENTAL SUSTAINABILITY

Bible Reading

How many are your works, O Lord! In wisdom you made them all; the earth is full of your creatures. There is the sea, vast and spacious, teeming with creatures beyond number – living things both large and small.

(Psalm 104:24-25 NIV)

Prayer

God of all creation, thank you for surprising introductions to creatures we did not even imagine. Thank you for plants and animals both delicate and immense. Help us live in ways that allow all creatures to continue, that we might delight in their goodness together. Amen.

Deed for the Day

Learn about species that are endangered in your area, and the threats to survival. Share what you learn with someone else.

Being surprised and awe-inspired. This summer, I spent time in California's Sierra Nevada Mountains, camping and visiting lakes inaccessible by car or a day's hike, remote worlds hidden by geography even in a populous US state. There, at a very high and beautiful lake, I was startled by the plopping sound of frogs jumping into the clear blue waters as I walked past. I don't know why their presence surprised me. I suppose because I associate frogs with marshy lowlands.

The mountain yellow-legged frogs I encountered are one of a number of species that have adapted to the particular and difficult high-mountain environment. Their survival, though, is threatened by other species introduced to these lakes for recreational fishing. In our ignorance, our human decisions have disrupted an intricate and carefully balanced system.

As I read the Psalms, and hear them describe the incredible, awe-inspiring, bountiful creatures in God's world, I think of these High Sierra frogs. I marvel that I hadn't been able to imagine their existence, and give thanks for their beauty. For the many creatures and plants we don't even know of yet, I give thanks to God. **(Molly Vetter, San Diego, California, USA)**

We are the first generation with the resources, knowledge and political commitment to end extreme poverty. We cannot miss the opportunity to do so.
(UN Millennium Campaign)

Shaping foreign policy to address poverty. I did not want to go to Nicaragua, but somehow felt compelled to make the trip. After all, I had read much about the strife between the Contras and Sandinistas. I knew the history of this small country and how US foreign policy had often been on the side of the elite, participating in repression and violence. I did not want to face these realities in three dimensions. But the prompting of the Holy Spirit would not cease. My partner and I packed our bags and joined a Christian group to see with our own eyes the situation for our Christian sisters and brothers.

The contrast of our air-conditioned bus taking us through the streets of Managua and the slums we walked through was not lost on us. As we approached shanties, built with whatever could be found, I had to remind myself that this was not a movie set. These children were not "extras" in a scene. This was the reality of their lives, trying to survive in cramped metal, cardboard huts.

That was in 1988. Today, we have an incredible opportunity to shape our foreign policy in ways that address the desperate needs of the poor through the support of the Millennium Development Goals, which include improving the lives of at least 100 million slum dwellers by 2020. **(Carol Windrum, Omaha, Nebraska, USA)**

Investing in the poor and most vulnerable must be part of our solution to the economic crisis. The Millennium Development Goals alone will not be enough to lift them out of poverty.
(Asha-Rose Migiro, UN Deputy Secretary-General)

ENSURE ENVIRONMENTAL SUSTAINABILITY

Bible Reading

Everyone will find rest beneath their own fig trees or grape vines, and they will live in peace. (Micah 4: 4 CEV)

Prayer

God, forgive the "haves" of the world from living in comfort and privilege. Open our eyes to sisters and brothers who live each day in desperate poverty. Instill in us your vision to advocate for a beloved community where all will experience adequate housing, clean water, and proper sanitation. Amen.

Deed for the Day

Download a copy of Making Poverty History by Church World Service (www.churchworldservcie.org) and request that your pastor finds ways to use this resource in your church.

7

ENSURE ENVIRONMENTAL SUSTAINABILITY

Bible Reading

God spoke: "Let us make human beings in our image, make them reflecting our nature so they can be responsible for the fish in the sea, the birds in the air, the cattle, And, yes, Earth itself, and every animal that moves on the face of Earth." …God looked over everything he had made; it was so good, so very good! It was evening, it was morning.
(Genesis 1:26-28 MSG)

Prayer

God, forgive us for not reflecting your nature nor being responsible for all that you have entrusted to us. Teach us to love this world as you love it. In Jesus' name, Amen.

Deed for the Day

Eat or drink something that you really enjoy. Give thanks to God for it. Imagine never tasting it again.

Enjoying God's creation. Growing up I spent many formative summers in Japan during the height of its economic boom and development. Every time I returned to Tokyo from San Francisco, everything was new. New buildings replacing old. Train ticket agents replaced by vending machines. Wanting to develop quickly, Japan discarded at a frightening pace things like perfectly usable TVs and microwaves – thrown away in favor of the newest and best.

My perception? That new is good, old is bad. I was taught technology and science will make things better, and resources are unlimited. I still struggle to be liberated from this triumphant consumerism. Resources are limited, and I appreciate more the beauty of using things as long as I can. We hold the responsibility to steward the resources around us so that they will be around in perpetuity.

When creation is destroyed, we lose our joy. Imagine neither seeing your favorite landscape, nor smelling the fragrance of a flower you love, nor tasting your favorite dish, nor hearing your favorite birds chirp outside your home, nor feeling the softness of your favorite piece of clothing.

When creation is destroyed, God also loses glory and the ability to enjoy creation. May this not happen on our watch! Let us go forth to serve this world as those who love our Lord and Savior Jesus Christ! **(Andrew Yamamoto, Grand Rapids, Michigan, USA)**

It would be accurate at one level to say you cannot be a Christian if you are not an environmentalist. God is the ultimate environmentalist, going to the point of dying on behalf of all parts of the environment. (Tony Campolo, Professor Emeritus of Sociology, Eastern University, Pennsylvania)

A GLOBAL PARTNERSHIP FOR DEVELOPMENT

Commentary by John L. McCullough

I was stunned to receive an email from a colleague in rural Kenya. He lived in a village without electricity or running water. Technology has advanced in the developing world, but not quickly enough.

There is no special formula for how development takes place, but there is a moral obligation. MDG 8 is essential to ending poverty and securing peace.

No one and certainly no nation should be left behind. The obligations of debt relief, competitive trade, and technology are equally shared by the developed and developing world. This is not a task for the next millennium; it is one that must be completed now. While glad to hear from my friend, sadly he is an exception to the rule. I worry about the countless others who still cannot.

Church World Service believes that partnership and working at solutions begins at the grassroots. The poor and vulnerable are not deficient of ideas but of sufficient resources. So CWS utilizes a community organizing methodology that is intensely indigenous.

This ethos of regularly engaging people to discern both vision and appropriate strategies is instructive to the MDG process, and critical towards relieving the vulnerability of so many people to poverty.

MDG 8 – Develop a Global Partnership for Development

Target 8.A: *Develop further an open, rule-based, predictable, non-discriminatory trading and financial system*

Target 8.B: *Address the special needs of least developed countries*

Target 8.C: *Address the special needs of landlocked developing countries and small island developing States*

Target 8.D: *Deal comprehensively with the debt problems of developing countries*

Target 8.E: *In cooperation with pharmaceutical companies, provide access to affordable essential drugs in developing countries*

Target 8.F: *In cooperation with the private sector, make available benefits of new technologies, especially information and communications*

Delineating between crisis and chronic conditions, either way, durable solutions that benefit entire communities must be the end goal. When we fail to recognize this, by default we contribute to a burgeoning gap between the rich and the poor; development for some, but certainly not for others.

(John L. McCullough is the Executive Director and Chief Executive Officer of CWS {www.churchworldservice.org}, a global faith-based humanitarian and development organization with headquarters in New York, NY. Together with partners around the world, CWS builds interfaith and intercultural coalitions focused on eradicating hunger and poverty in conjunction with promoting peace and justice. Its program work supports sustainable grassroots development, humanitarian response, and durable solutions for refugees and the displaced. CWS devotes enormous energy to building and sustaining partnerships that drive toward solutions at the grassroots. CWS has positioned itself to build global connections and understanding through the lens of food and food security. CWS programming integrates key aspects directly associated to food and nutrition security, such as access to clean water, maternal and child health initiatives, and agricultural extension; integrating food and nutrition security also applies indirectly in other CWS core programming areas: humanitarian response and refugee work.)

What The United Methodist Church says:

The United Methodist Church must participate in building communities that prioritize the eradication of poverty and the elimination of hunger; the ending of wars and the resolution of conflicts; and the overcoming of ignorance, curing of diseases, and healing of enmities. **(Globalization and its Impact on Human Dignity and Human Rights, Resolution #6025, 2008 Book of Resolutions)**

When we partner with communities, rather than doing work on their behalf, we empower them to take responsibility for their own well-being. **(Beatrice Gbanga,** http://www.umc-gbcs.org/site/apps/nlnet/content3.aspx?c=frLJK2PKLqF&b=2952667&ct=9352781&notoc=1)

Building the new Creation: I'm often asked if I have a favorite biblical text that points me to the MDGs.

In the Greek and Latin texts of the Book of Daniel, there is a song attributed to the three men thrown into the fiery furnace by Nebuchadnezzar. In the Episcopal and Roman Catholic traditions, the canticle, called Benidicite, is read at Morning Prayer. "Glorify the Lord, all you works of the Lord," it begins, "Praise him and highly exalt him forever."

On it goes for more than 20 verses, calling for praise of God from the moon and the stars, the rain and the dew, mountains and hills, beasts of the wild, and men and women everywhere. Each phrase ends the same way: "Praise him and highly exalt him forever."

How does this point to the MDGs? The Benedicite presents a picture of creation – all creation – in perfect harmony with itself and its maker. The realms of nature, all living beings, and humanity itself are freed from every want or need, concerned only with singing praise to the One who created them.

It's a picture of a world that has achieved the MDGs, and of the global harmony and partnership to which Goal 8 challenges us. **(Alexander D. Baumgarten, Washington, District of Columbia, USA)**

To approach the MDGs as basic human rights implies linking poverty eradication with enhancing equity and social integration…In times of unprecedented crisis, courage to be bold and innovative is required from leaders. (Social Watch, Statement on the 2010 UN Summit, Dar-es-Salaam, April 2010)

A GLOBAL PARTNERSHIP FOR DEVELOPMENT

Bible Reading

Glorify the Lord, all you works of the Lord; praise him and highly exalt him forever. (Daniel 3:52 RCB)

Prayer

Heavenly Father, whose blessed Son came not to be served but to serve: Bless all who give themselves to the service of others; that with wisdom, patience, and courage, they may minister in his name to the suffering and the needy; through Christ our Lord. Amen.

Deed for the Day

Visit your denomination's website and join its public-policy network, uniting with others advocating for achievement of the MDGs.

8

A GLOBAL PARTNERSHIP FOR DEVELOPMENT

Bible Reading

Now to each one the manifestation of the Spirit is given for the common good… to another speaking in different kinds of tongue, and to still another the interpretation of tongues.
(1 Corinthians 12:7-10 NIV)

Prayer

Spirit of all languages, let our words, actions, and partnerships serve the common good of constructing a world where jewelry means hope for a better life. Each one with a different gift, we are stronger when joined together in fairness and justice. Bless the path.
Amen.

Deed for the Day

Make a consumer choice respecting the global interconnection and responsibility you have with the person who produced your purchase.

Partnering for fair trade. Peggy arrived in Lima, Peru, with limited Spanish but unlimited energy for partnership. She courageously accepted the challenge to work with a group of silver jewelry artisans for a month with the Bridge of Hope Fair Trade Program, an element of the Joining Hands Network of Peru, program of the Presbyterian Church (USA). The Group Munay Rumi welcomed Peggy and me and we visited the artisan group every morning for a month.

As Peggy and the artisans spoke to each other, I translated. After a few days, however, Peggy and the artisans approached each other without translation. While they couldn't communicate with words, I saw them speaking the language of jewelry. With Peggy's accompaniment, Munay Rumi developed 25 new pieces of jewelry. In the fair trade store where she volunteers, the pieces sold within a week and regular clients made orders.

With Peggy's partnership, each artisan developed design and finishing techniques, as well as confidence and creativity. Together, they generated money to buy new tools, improve their workspace, and start savings to fulfill their dream to have their own jewelry business.

Thanks to her experience, Peggy advocates fair trade and encourages friends to partner with Fair Trade artisan groups in Peru. Perhaps they don't understand the words, but they do speak the same language of justice, development, and hope. **(Alexandra Buck, Lima, Peru)**

The reference to lessons learnt, particularly the issue of supporting community-led strategies is also of paramount importance in the achievement of the MDGs. The emphasis on expanding the human rights framework by emphasizing on the right to development is also a step in the right direction.
(Archbishop Njongonkulu Ndungane, former Primate, Anglican Church of Southern Africa)

Aid for the people. After attending a conference on the MDGs during my study abroad experience in Ireland, I learned the tremendous difference in policy and especially in reputation in the international community between Irish Aid and its American equivalent USAID. Although the United States donates millions of dollars to developing countries every year, the amount is in fact a tiny percentage of its Gross Domestic Product (GDP). Ireland, a much smaller country with a much lower GDP, sends less actual money but it is a much higher percentage of the GDP.

To me this is glaringly alarming that as America, the richest and most powerful country in the world, it should surely be able to give more money to those living without access to life's most basic necessities that so many of us take for granted. The amount of money sent is less significant. With reports of money filtering through corrupt governments or private corporations, there needs to be more done to make sure the aid actually makes it to the people.

The recipient people need to learn how to use wisely and sustainably the aid money and food that they receive. In this way, both the international community and the domestic governments are responsible to actively engage in this global partnership so that we may see a better future for all. **(Rebecca Burkhart, Wingdale, New York, USA)**

Our common purpose must be to build a global alliance – a global partnership – a truly lasting political consensus to achieve the MDGs on time. This is truly the greatest gift that we could give to humanity. (Sheikha Haya Rashed Al Khalifa of Bahrain, The Public-Private Foundation MDG Award Recipient)

Bible Reading

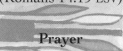

So then let us pursue what makes for peace and for mutual upbuilding. (Romans 14:19 ESV)

Prayer

Dear God, please allow the boundaries between countries and differences between peoples to be blurred so that they may work together in unity to help those that are suffering from poverty and hunger. Let us understand that we are all connected and cooperation is of utmost importance. Amen.

Deed for the Day

Inform someone unfamiliar with the MDGs about the need for a Global Partnership and tell them where to research the topic.

8

A GLOBAL PARTNERSHIP FOR DEVELOPMENT

Changing individuals and systems. I had mixed feelings when I watched on YouTube Efren Peñaflorida, a 28-year old Filipino social worker and teacher, receive the CNN Hero of the Year award. Chosen in an online vote among 9,000 nominees around the world, Efren is known for his pioneering "pushcart classrooms." Every Saturday he and his volunteers set out for the slums, loading into their pushcarts books and visual aids that they use to help poor children learn.

Efren is a classic case of someone sharing his gift with the less fortunate. But I worry that his powerful and inspiring story may be spun in a way that overshadows the very reality that he seeks to address in his own way, the massive poverty in a country that has all the ingredients to become an economically prosperous nation.

To me, Efren's success serves as an indictment of the policy environment that neglects people's basic needs. Policy makers, under the tutelage of multilateral agencies like the International Monetary Fund, prefer to honor massive debts misused by corrupt administrations instead of renegotiating these so that more resources could go to investment in people like health care and education.

For Efren's efforts to be truly enabling, we must complement them with our own efforts to connect his story with the larger picture, by helping to enable others to change not just oppressive individuals, but also systems. **(Haniel R. Garibay, Manila, Philippines)**

(*Evaluate existing policies on aid and beyond to ensure that they do not contradict or undermine this overarching commitment to development. This should be done through an inclusive and participatory process…* (Civil Society Voices for Better Aid, Statement to the UN Development Cooperation Forum, 29-30 June 2010))

G od shows no partiality. I was born in Texas as were my first three daughters. My youngest was born in Alaska while I served as a mission pastor in the territory and state from 1955 to 1966. Following the death of their beloved mother, we moved to New York City where I served as an NGO Representative at the Methodist Office for the UN from 1966 to 1971. My daughters found themselves in the 2% to 3% of white students in their Manhattan schools.

So why was I surprised when one day my four daughters surrounded me as I was reading and asked if I remembered preaching a sermon on "God shows no partiality"? Turned out that was a prelude to meeting black and Haitian boyfriends. In my 80s, I am now a happy grandfather and great-grandfather with many descendants who resemble our current handsome and intelligent first family!

And I am still reading books by perceptive writers like Antonio Juhasz, John Perkins, Robert Wright, and theologians like Jeorg Rieger to understand more about why we still have more poor and starving people than ever. As Pogo said years ago, we have met the enemy, and he is us. **(Richard K. Heacock, Jr, Fairbanks, Alaska, USA)**

Working with indigenous peoples on the MDGs also requires a culturally sensitive approach, based on respect for and inclusion of their world-views, perspectives and experiences, as well as their concepts of development.
(The Secretariat of the UN Permanent Forum on Indigenous Issues)

8

A GLOBAL PARTNERSHIP FOR DEVELOPMENT

Bible Reading

Then Peter began to speak: "I now realize how true it is that God does not show favoritism but accepts men from every nation who fear him and do what is right." While Peter was still speaking these words, the Holy Spirit came on all who heard the message.
(Acts 10:34-35, 44 NIV)

Prayer

Enlighten me O Fount of All Wisdom, that I may learn all I need to learn in order to effectively join with all those who seek to resist the imperial racist exploitation of global resources and markets which continues to perpetrate poverty and genocide. Amen.

Deed for the Day

I will send a generous contribution to my favorite organizations working to end all wars for the control of oil, and other global resources and markets.

A GLOBAL PARTNERSHIP FOR DEVELOPMENT

Bible Reading

When Jesus saw her, he called her forward and said to her, "Woman, you are set free from your infirmity.
(Luke 13:12 TNIV)

Prayer

Dear Lord, bless the work of the General Board and Annual Conference Boards of Church and Society – that they may continue to fulfill their mandates for peace with justice. Amen.

Deed for the Day

Do something today that alleviates someone's poverty or heals someone's illness.

What a mandate! I am 80 years old. You may know women or men older than I. We are all living longer lives than we used to be able to do. I am constantly reminding myself to stand up as tall as I can or just "straighten up!" As I shrink, others get taller. It is harder to look someone in the eye than it used to be – especially for very tall persons. Persons in wheelchairs have this problem. Little children have this problem. That is why we generally bend down so they don't have to crane their necks to see our faces.

Imagine what it took for this bent-over woman to make her way into the synagogue to see Jesus. Not only did Jesus see her, he called her to come over to the men's side of the sanctuary and to come to him. He touched and healed her. She praised God as Jesus was belittled by his opponents.

To keep today's "bent-overs" essentially in bondage and generally out of our sight, we let them stay mired in poverty, under educated, in poor health, enduring abusive situations, in perpetual war, violence, and discrimination.

The General Board of Church and Society and our Conference Boards of Church and Society are always stretching out their necks to get others to look us in the face and listen to stories of hope achieved, darkness turned to light, children loved, women and families protected, and even sight restored to the blind. What a mandate! **(Betty Henderson, Brookfield, Wisconsin, USA)**

The world possesses the resources and knowledge to ensure that even the poorest countries, and others held back by disease, geographic isolation or civil strife, can be empowered to achieve the MDGs.
(Ban Ki-moon, UN Secretary-General)

Don't ignore this epidemic. Human trafficking is one of the world's dirtiest and best-kept secrets. It is difficult to measure the extent of this hidden trade, but UN statistics estimate that two to four million people are trafficked across international borders every year, and millions more are exploited within their own countries.

I am spending the summer working on human trafficking issues for IOM in Tajikistan. I feel blessed to be working with the inspiring staff here who continually give themselves to this cause no matter how many trafficking horror stories they encounter. Tajikistan is the poorest state in Central Asia and one in two households has sent a family member abroad in hopes that they can send much-needed remittances back home. Some, however, have found more sinister ways to earn their keep, taking advantage of the most vulnerable labor migrants by trafficking them abroad for sexual exploitation, domestic servitude, and slave labor in sweatshops, construction, agriculture and more.

There are more slaves today than at any other time in human history. It is tempting to ignore this epidemic. After all, if there were no demand for cheap goods or the services often provided by trafficking victims, such as sex work, the criminals behind trafficking would have no reason to continue exploiting their victims. **(Anne Johnson, Minocqua, Wisconsin, USA)**

The world we seek, where every child can grow to adulthood in health, peace and dignity – in short, a world fit for children – has remained a dream for more years than we can count.
(Carol Bellamy, Former Executive Director, UNICEF)

8

A GLOBAL PARTNERSHIP FOR DEVELOPMENT

Bible Reading

Although we are of the same flesh and blood as our countrymen and though our children are as good as theirs, yet we have to subject our sons and daughters to slavery.
(Nehemiah 5:5 NIV)

Prayer

God, our protector and source of hope, help us to remember that wealth is often simply the flip side of poverty and exploitation elsewhere in the world. Give us the strength to recognize our lives are inextricably tied with those struggling to find freedom from trafficking. Amen.

Deed for the Day

Examine the way your consumption decisions may help to fuel demand for the exploitation of the world's most vulnerable workers.

Bible Reading

For I was hungry and you gave me no food, I was thirsty and you gave me no drink, I was a stranger and you did not welcome me, naked and you did not clothe me, sick and in prison and you did not visit me.
(Matthew 25:42-43 ESV)

Prayer

Lord God we know that you are all powerful and through you all things are possible. Let not our hearts be hardened. Allow us to see the despair among us. Reveal your plan for us as we move to help your people, our brothers, sisters, sons and daughters. Amen.

Deed for the Day

Research groups that interest you that you can become a part of to allow you to share your gifts and help others.

Partnerships are the way. God charges us to share our resources and see that everyone is cared for. As a child I remember walking to the local food bank with my mother to get groceries. As I grew older I started to understand what a gift it was to get food from somewhere when we had none, and the hearts of giving that were behind each can of creamed corn – a personal favorite. Still moved by this years later, I ran a food drive and delivered huge quantities of donations to the same food bank that I had gone to as a child.

Someone's generosity had helped instill in me a spirit of giving. The community coming together as a whole not only fed my mother and me, but also birthed a continuing lifestyle trend. This was only possible because the government, town, community people, friends, and volunteers at the bank worked together for the benefit of those in need. I could not have collected all the food I did without others' help.

There are many things we cannot do alone; partnerships are the way to help the big number of people needing assistance. But connections between people do not spontaneously surface. We must take the initiative to meet others, and the time to nurture relationships that they may grow strong. **(Casey R. Laggan, Madison, New Jersey, USA)**

Voluntary action and volunteers add great value and will be indispensable in meeting the MDG target. And indeed, each of us should make that personal decision to get engaged. (Mark Malloch Brown, Former UNDP Administrator)

I am my brother's keeper. Why is there so much suffering in the world? Why do so many go to bed hungry every day, many of them dying for lack of food? Why does a few have so much more than they need, but use and abuse, even waste, just because they can? The answer can be both easy and difficult.

We can start by examining what God's intention for us has always been. God is a God of community and wants us to live in community. What does that look like? I believe it means being each other's keeper. Unlike Cain who asked "Am I my brother's keeper?" We need to state and believe "I am my brother's keeper."

As we live in community our concern should not be selfish but selfless, creatively looking for ways to share with each other as opposed to ways in which we can take advantage of one another. We should not allow ourselves to fall victims to greed and war in order to get what we want. We should not be satisfied until each one of us can have not only a decent place to live in but also afford decent meals for ourselves and our families. It is only then that we can each truly say, "I am my brother's keeper" **(Dahlia Leigh, Freetown, Sierra Leone)**

The number of Internet users continues to expand. However, penetration levels in the developing world remain relatively low, at 21 per cent by end-2010, compared to 72 per cent in the developed regions. Globally, two out of three people are not using the Internet.
(The MDG Report 2011, United Nations, New York)

A GLOBAL PARTNERSHIP FOR DEVELOPMENT

Bible Reading
Then the LORD said to Cain, "Where is Abel your brother?" He said, "I do not know; am I my brother's keeper?"
(Genesis 4:9 ESV)

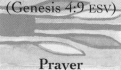

Prayer
Lord God who created each one of us to live in community, help us to live lives that reflect the love you have for each one of us by the way we take care of your word and each other. Amen.

Deed for the Day
Take time each day to tell a total stranger how happy you are to meet him or her.

A GLOBAL PARTNERSHIP FOR DEVELOPMENT

8

Bible Reading

Commit your way to the LORD; trust in him and he will act. He will make your vindication shine like the light, and the justice of your cause like the noonday. (Psalm 37:5-6 NRS)

Prayer

LORD, in this broken world, help me to continue to hope in You and to believe that I, too, can make a difference. Amen.

Deed for the Day

No act of love is too small to do good. A smile or word of encouragement can have far-reaching effects. We do not toil alone.

Making difference in a broken world. When I look on the world I often feel overwhelmed by the injustice I see around me and I wonder how I, as one person, could possibly make a difference.

I see pain and hunger. I hear the cries of the homeless, the orphaned, the destitute and the disenfranchised. I fall to my knees and I pray for hope and for change. I am only one person. I only have my two hands and feet. Then I remember I also have a heart that feels both pain and joy. And I have a mouth that gives voice to injustice.

My hands touch the hands of others and my feet can carry me where God calls. I am not alone. I follow those who came before me and I lead those who will come after. This knowledge of an ever-living community gives me hope that change is possible even in this broken world. **(Gheeta S. Smith, Salt Lake City, Utah, USA)**

An estimated 1.1 billion people in urban areas and 723 million people in rural areas gained access to an improved drinking water source over the period 1990-2008. Eastern Asia registered the largest gains in drinking water coverage—from 69 per cent in 1990 to 86 per cent in 2008. Sub-Saharan Africa nearly doubled the number of people using an improved drinking water source—from 252 million in 1990 to 492 million in 2008.
(Sha Zukang, UN Under-Secretary-General for Social and Economic Affairs, in The MDG Report 2011)

Partnership bears fruit for all. After completing 30 years working with Ford Motor Company, I became a part time development consultant for the United Methodist Committee on Relief (UMCOR). I eventually served on the world-wide planning group for the College of Agriculture and Natural Resources of the United Methodist-related Africa University in Zimbabwe. After all my life experiences, I was ready to develop plans for increased food productivity.

While I would be in Africa part time, I spent time mostly in Zimbabwe. I incorporated officers of the Zimbabwe Department of Agriculture, a committee of local farm owners and businesses, plus officers of the United Methodist Annual Conferences. We developed plans for a major United Methodist Mission farm (Nyadire) which could also be adjusted for other mission farms in Zimbabwe and Southern Africa. Coordination with United Methodist bishops ensured the continuity of my work even when I left.

I was successful in developing the Mission Statement and the curriculum requirements for the College of Agriculture and Natural Resources on whose basis the US Agency for International Development (USAID) was encouraged to pay for the total cost of the college.

Including my efforts, a major policy statement for the Africa University was changed. From a proposed start of a maximum of 1,000 students, all to be financed by United Methodist Annual Conferences, a maximum of 2,000 students was approved for Phase 1. The approval came on the guarantee that African countries would support most of the students enrolled at Africa University rather than students going to Europe or the United States. With more students approved, all architectural plans had to be changed to accommodate future expansion.

The partnership and cooperation of many people bore fruit for all of those involved in the ministry of Africa University. I was blessed to have been a part of it.
(Harold S. Stanton, Birmingham, Michigan, USA)

The MDGs were never meant to be a one-way street -- something that rich countries do for poor ones. Quite the contrary: our long-standing work for development in general has always been based on global solidarity...
(Ban Ki-moon, UN Secretary-General)

8

A GLOBAL PARTNERSHIP FOR DEVELOPMENT

Bible Reading
The Spirit of the Lord is upon me, because he has anointed me to set at liberty those who are oppressed.
(Luke 4: 18 ESV)

Prayer
Dear God, we are always your servants and all things are possible for asking in your name. We are forever thankful. Amen.

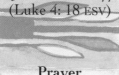

Deed for the Day
Think big, work hard. The power of working with others helps energize all.

8

A GLOBAL PARTNERSHIP FOR DEVELOPMENT

Bible Reading

My dear friends, pay attention. God has given a lot of faith to the poor people in this world. He has also promised them a share in his kingdom that he will give to everyone who loves him. (James 2:5 CEV)

Prayer

Heavenly father, thank you for all the many blessings that you have rain down on us and strengthen us that we may share these blessings to the needy and seek nothing in return. May your grace reign among mankind, this we ask I Christ our Lord Jesus. Amen.

Deed for the Day

Give something to those that needy without expecting anything in return.

From brokenness to normalcy. Growing up as a child in Mount Barclay, Montserrado County in Liberia, life was so amazing and worth living. My daddy had one of the largest sugar cane plantations in Montserrado County. He worked for the government.

I was born in 1987. I experienced only two-plus years of peace when in 1990 the Samuel K. Doe regime plunged my country and the Liberian people into a deadly devastating 14 years of civil war. Atrocities, unjust and repressive practices, including suppression of press freedom were committed.

My family lost everything to the war.

The consequences of war rule the lives of Liberians today: child soldiers, sexually abused women, poverty, crimes, inaccessible judiciary system, fragile peace, economic deprivation, and unemployment. But I never gave up hope that one day peace will be restored. And then a new government was elected and inaugurated. A plan to reopen multilateral partnership was launched with various stakeholders across the country. With limited resources, high unemployment, and insurmountable demands from the citizens, the fragile security of a weak system made us strive even more for recovery and hope for a new day.

When society herself shall see children and former child soldiers like precious jewelry, and when we shall exchange our sorry lot and pain with mercy, that is when my country will be free. This is my story, my pain, and my belief. **(Jeremiah Swen, Liberia, Africa, with Mote Houma, West Valley City, Utah, USA)**

> *Local governments and regional authorities have a very important role to lay in the development of sound local governance, which will be a key accelerator to achieve the MDGs.* (Councilor Berry Vrbanovic, Federation of Canadian Municipalities, 15 June 2010)

Prayer and change. Jesus often engaged in high holy moments. These transformative moments impacted his life and ministry because Jesus connected with God. We can also connect with God by praying to Him. Often, during prayer moments, God will move us to examine ourselves and encourage us to establish a relationship with Him and others.

One day, a Pharisee and a tax collector went to pray. The Pharisee prayed with flattering words while the tax collector prayed from his heart. He also made a movement from where he stood to where his heart was. As a result, the tax collector's prayer helped him to discover his inner self. I call his revelation a prayer movement.

Another example would have to be one of the UN's responses to the economic situation in the developing world. As one of its response, it created a development goal that calls for the formation of a global partnership. I am sure that when the UN created this goal, MDG 8, its members formed a relationship with our Creator and others to implement a movement from their hearts.

Prayer moments and movements help us to implement changes in our lives.
(Sinnathamby Thevanesan, Snyder, New York, USA)

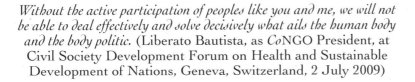

Without the active participation of peoples like you and me, we will not be able to deal effectively and solve decisively what ails the human body and the body politic. (Liberato Bautista, as CoNGO President, at Civil Society Development Forum on Health and Sustainable Development of Nations, Geneva, Switzerland, 2 July 2009)

A GLOBAL PARTNERSHIP FOR DEVELOPMENT

Bible Reading
For everyone who exalts himself will be humbled, and he who humbles himself will be exalted.
(Luke 18:14 NIV)

Prayer
Most gracious God, teach us to see ourselves honestly who we are; transform us and make us what we are not and instead to be like the Christ who loves and serves and cares for all. Amen!

Deed for the Day
Choose one of the MDG goals and dedicate one day to pray for its success.

8

A GLOBAL PARTNERSHIP FOR DEVELOPMENT

Bible Reading

*This plan which God will complete...
is to bring all creation together,
everything in heaven and on earth,
with Christ as head.*
(Ephesians 1:9-10 GNB)

Prayer

*Lord God, help us to change the world
with the gospel values of neighborly
love and justice in our relationships.
Amen.*

Deed for the Day

*We must share resources and never
forget to help those in need.*

Collective accountability. Today I see two great plans unfolding in our world. Under one plan, the global economy is rendering national laws and borders meaningless. Goods and services are moving around the world answering only to supply and demand. The unjust rules of finance and trade that regulate the markets work only for the benefit of the owners of capital, not the poor and vulnerable.

But there is another plan: God's plan to bring everything in all creation together with Christ. Many Christians believe the church is called to be a partner with God engaged in bringing about the kind of development where people, especially the poor, matter more than material things.

I am from Fiji, a group of over 300 islands with a population of 800,000. About half are indigenous Fijians, mainly Methodists, and others are made up of largely Hindu Indian origin. In a globalized world, Fiji may seem unimportant. Many Pacific Islanders feel powerless in the face of a global economy that does not benefit the weak and vulnerable. But Fijians also realize that the sustainability of their communities and their development efforts can only be achieved through just and participatory partnerships among themselves and other stakeholders.

In God's plan, economic relations flow from God's freely given gifts and are shared without reserve. If one small nation suffers we all suffer. When the weak ones are not heard, and relegated to the margins of the global economy, discontentment rises and pretty soon they protest their situation. We have a collective accountability to one another as people created in God's image.
(Akuila Yabaki, Fiji)

*Rather than retreat, now is the time to accelerate progress towards the MDGs
and to strengthen the global partnership for development. If the global
community responds constructively to the crisis, the goals can still be achieved.*
(Ban Ki-moon, UN Secretary-General,
in Millennium Development Goals Report 2009)

The documents in this resource section are the work of many people in government and in non-governmental and civil society organizations. The civil society organizations that crafted the texts included here come from a number of religious, faith- and ethics-based groups that are active at the UN.

The 189 high-level representatives of UN Member States, including Heads of State and Government who adopted at the UN Millennium General Assembly in September 2000 the UN Millennium Declaration, recognized that they have "a collective responsibility to uphold the principles of human dignity, equality and equity at the global level," and as leaders they have "a duty . . . to all the world's people, especially the most vulnerable and, in particular, the children of the world, to whom the future belongs." Government leaders promised in this Millennium Declaration to free people from extreme poverty and a multiplicity of other deprivations. This promise became the pledge now known as the MDGs. The text of the MDGs and their specific targets are found next to the introductory commentaries to each of the goals in the devotionals section of this book.

The focus on development and poverty eradication is but one of the Declaration's eight sections. All the eight sections of the Millennium Declaration are constitutive of the understanding of the MDGs. The focus on development and poverty eradication is but one of the Declaration's eight sections. The other seven sections include peace, security and disarmament; protecting our common environment; human rights, democracy and good governance; protecting the vulnerable; meeting the special needs of Africa; and strengthening the United Nations.

The Outcome Documents and the Action Points included in this section came out of the Civil Society Development Forums (CSDF) that were convened in New York, Geneva and Vienna by the Conference of Non-Governmental Organizations in Consultative Relationship with the United Nations (CoNGO). I had the privilege to preside over these forums between 2008 and 2010 as the CoNGO president.

Resources

CoNGO members and representatives of other NGOs produced from these Forums outcome documents, action points, and conclusions and recommendations. These documents were very intentional in reviewing the MDGs. They were included in this collection with the hope that they too help illuminate the necessity and urgency, indeed the nexus, of social justice and sustainable development.

At the CSDF in Geneva, Switzerland, in 2009, representatives of a cross-section of civil society from many parts of the world said: "Attaining the MDGs by 2015 is in greater jeopardy ever since their promulgation by the leaders of the world nine years ago. The combined threats of the failure to achieve the MDGs, which are cross-sectoral goals, the current paralysis in foreign assistance policies, and the misallocation of national budgets to favor non-productive and military activities are likely to harm the delicate interrelationship between the pursuit of human rights and poverty eradication, global public health and development, and gender equality and the empowerment of women."

That was 2009. In the 2011 CSDF in Geneva, civil society representatives were more emphatic: "The 2015 deadline for achieving the MDGs is perilously close, and while many significant gains have been registered, there are alarming gaps in many sectors and many geographical areas…There is time – but only to close just some of the gaps….Civil society will not relax on commitments and initiatives. But it is plain and undisputed that the primary responsibility rests with governments, from whom we expect renewed political courage, revitalized political determination, and enlightened political budgetary decisions."

The importance of locating the MDGs in the provision of other global public goods such as human rights, peace, sustainable development, and disarmament is not always visible even among ardent MDG supporters. It is the assertion of this book that a greater understanding of the relevance and the urgency of the MDGs, including the misgivings of some about these goals, is crucial. The inclusion of the UN Millennium Declaration and the CSDF Outcome Documents and Action Points in this book will, I hope, contribute to that greater understanding.

It is also my hope that in reading every section of this book you will get a sense of how the MDGs echo the prophet Micah's exhortation to do justice, to love mercy and to walk humbly with our God (Micah 6:8), and through the meditations and devotionals demonstrate what it means to have a living faith sustained by prayer and moved by action. (**Liberato C. Bautista**)

The importance of locating the MDGs in the provision of other global public goods such as human rights, peace, sustainable development, and disarmament is not always visible even among ardent MDG supporters.

United Nations Millennium Declaration

Resolution adopted by the General Assembly (A/55/L..2)

The General Assembly adopts the following Declaration:

United Nations Millennium Declaration

I. Values and principles

1.   We, Heads of State and Government, have gathered at United Nations Headquarters in New York from 6 to 8 September 2000, at the dawn of a new millennium, to reaffirm our faith in the Organization and its Charter as indispensable foundations of a more peaceful, prosperous and just world.

2.   We recognize that, in addition to our separate responsibilities to our individual societies, we have a collective responsibility to uphold the principles of human dignity, equality and equity at the global level. As leaders we have a duty therefore to all the world's people, especially the most vulnerable and, in particular, the children of the world, to whom the future belongs.

3.   We reaffirm our commitment to the purposes and principles of the Charter of the United Nations, which have proved timeless and universal. Indeed, their relevance and capacity to inspire have increased, as nations and peoples have become increasingly interconnected and interdependent.

4.   We are determined to establish a just and lasting peace all over the world in accordance with the purposes and principles of the Charter. We rededicate ourselves to support all efforts to uphold the sovereign equality of all States, respect for their territorial integrity and political independence, resolution of disputes by peaceful means and in conformity with the principles of justice and international law, the right to self-determination of peoples which remain under colonial domination and foreign occupation, non-interference in the internal affairs of States, respect for human rights and fundamental freedoms, respect for

United Nations
Millennium Declaration

the equal rights of all without distinction as to race, sex, language or religion and international cooperation in solving international problems of an economic, social, cultural or humanitarian character.

5.   We believe that the central challenge we face today is to ensure that globalization becomes a positive force for all the world's people. For while globalization offers great opportunities, at present its benefits are very unevenly shared, while its costs are unevenly distributed. We recognize that developing countries and countries with economies in transition face special difficulties in responding to this central challenge. Thus, only through broad and sustained efforts to create a shared future, based upon our common humanity in all its diversity, can globalization be made fully inclusive and equitable. These efforts must include policies and measures, at the global level, which correspond to the needs of developing countries and economies in transition and are formulated and implemented with their effective participation.

6.   We consider certain fundamental values to be essential to international relations in the twenty-first century. These include:

- Freedom. Men and women have the right to live their lives and raise their children in dignity, free from hunger and from the fear of violence, oppression or injustice. Democratic and participatory governance based on the will of the people best assures these rights.
- Equality. No individual and no nation must be denied the opportunity to benefit from development. The equal rights and opportunities of women and men must be assured.
- Solidarity. Global challenges must be managed in a way that distributes the costs and burdens fairly in accordance with basic principles of equity and social justice. Those who suffer or who benefit least deserve help from those who benefit most.
- Tolerance. Human beings must respect one other, in all their diversity of belief, culture and language. Differences within and between societies should be neither feared nor repressed, but cherished as a precious asset of humanity. A culture of peace and dialogue among all civilizations should be actively promoted.
- Respect for nature. Prudence must be shown in the management of all living species and natural resources, in accordance with the precepts of sustainable development. Only in this way can the immeasurable riches provided to us by nature be preserved and passed on to our descendants. The current unsustainable patterns of production and consumption must be changed in the interest of our

[W]hile globalization offers great opportunities, at present its benefits are very unevenly shared, while its cost are unevenly distributed.

future welfare and that of our descendants.

- Shared responsibility. Responsibility for managing worldwide economic and social development, as well as threats to international peace and security, must be shared among the nations of the world and should be exercised multilaterally. As the most universal and most representative organization in the world, the United Nations must play the central role.

7.   In order to translate these shared values into actions, we have identified key objectives to which we assign special significance.

II. Peace, security and disarmament

8.   We will spare no effort to free our peoples from the scourge of war, whether within or between States, which has claimed more than five million lives in the past decade. We will also seek to eliminate the dangers posed by weapons of mass destruction.

9.   We resolve therefore:

- To strengthen respect for the rule of law in international as in national affairs and, in particular, to ensure compliance by Member States with the decisions of the International Court of Justice, in compliance with the Charter of the United Nations, in cases to which they are parties.
- To make the United Nations more effective in maintaining peace and security by giving it the resources and tools it needs for conflict prevention, peaceful resolution of disputes, peacekeeping, post-conflict peace-building and reconstruction. In this context, we take note of the report of the Panel on United Nations Peace Operations and request the General Assembly to consider its recommendations expeditiously.
- To strengthen cooperation between the United Nations and regional organizations, in accordance with the provisions of Chapter VIII of the Charter.
- To ensure the implementation, by States Parties, of treaties in areas such as arms control and disarmament and of international humanitarian law and human rights law, and call upon all States to consider signing and ratifying the Rome Statute of the International Criminal Court.
- To take concerted action against international terrorism, and to accede as soon as possible to all the relevant international conventions.
- To redouble our efforts to implement our commitment to counter the world drug problem.

[O]nly through broad and sustained efforts to create a shared future, based upon our common humanity in all its diversity, can globalization be made fully inclusive and equitable.

- To intensify our efforts to fight transnational crime in all its dimensions, including trafficking as well as smuggling in human beings and money laundering.
- To minimize the adverse effects of United Nations economic sanctions on innocent populations, to subject such sanctions regimes to regular reviews and to eliminate the adverse effects of sanctions on third parties.
- To strive for the elimination of weapons of mass destruction, particularly nuclear weapons, and to keep all options open for achieving this aim, including the possibility of convening an international conference to identify ways of eliminating nuclear dangers.
- To take concerted action to end illicit traffic in small arms and light weapons, especially by making arms transfers more transparent and supporting regional disarmament measures, taking account of all the recommendations of the forthcoming United Nations Conference on Illicit Trade in Small Arms and Light Weapons.
- To call on all States to consider acceding to the Convention on the Prohibition of the Use, Stockpiling, Production and Transfer of Anti-personnel Mines and on Their Destruction, as well as the amended mines protocol to the Convention on conventional weapons.

10.   We urge Member States to observe the Olympic Truce, individually and collectively, now and in the future, and to support the International Olympic Committee in its efforts to promote peace and human understanding through sport and the Olympic Ideal.

III. Development and poverty eradication

11.   We will spare no effort to free our fellow men, women and children from the abject and dehumanizing conditions of extreme poverty, to which more than a billion of them are currently subjected. We are committed to making the right to development a reality for everyone and to freeing the entire human race from want.

12.   We resolve therefore to create an environment – at the national and global levels alike – which is conducive to development and to the elimination of poverty.

13.   Success in meeting these objectives depends, inter alia, on good governance within each country. It also depends on good governance at the international level and on transparency in the financial, monetary and trading systems. We are committed to an open, equitable, rule-based, predictable and non-

No individual and no nation must be denied the opportunity to benefit from development.

discriminatory multilateral trading and financial system.

14. We are concerned about the obstacles developing countries face in mobilizing the resources needed to finance their sustained development. We will therefore make every effort to ensure the success of the High-level International and Intergovernmental Event on Financing for Development, to be held in 2001.

15. We also undertake to address the special needs of the least developed countries. In this context, we welcome the Third United Nations Conference on the Least Developed Countries to be held in May 2001 and will endeavour to ensure its success. We call on the industrialized countries:

- To adopt, preferably by the time of that Conference, a policy of duty- and quota-free access for essentially all exports from the least developed countries;
- To implement the enhanced programme of debt relief for the heavily indebted poor countries without further delay and to agree to cancel all official bilateral debts of those countries in return for their making demonstrable commitments to poverty reduction; and
- To grant more generous development assistance, especially to countries that are genuinely making an effort to apply their resources to poverty reduction.

16. We are also determined to deal comprehensively and effectively with the debt problems of low- and middle-income developing countries, through various national and international measures designed to make their debt sustainable in the long term.

17. We also resolve to address the special needs of small island developing States, by implementing the Barbados Programme of Action and the outcome of the twenty-second special session of the General Assembly rapidly and in full. We urge the international community to ensure that, in the development of a vulnerability index, the special needs of small island developing States are taken into account.

18. We recognize the special needs and problems of the landlocked developing countries, and urge both bilateral and multilateral donors to increase financial and technical assistance to this group of countries to meet their special development needs and to help them overcome the impediments of geography by improving their transit transport systems.

19. We resolve further:

Responsibility for managing worldwide economic and social development, as well as threats to international peace and security, must be shared among the nations of the world and should be exercised multilaterally.

- To halve, by the year 2015, the proportion of the world's people whose income is less than one dollar a day and the proportion of people who suffer from hunger and, by the same date, to halve the proportion of people who are unable to reach or to afford safe drinking water.
- To ensure that, by the same date, children everywhere, boys and girls alike, will be able to complete a full course of primary schooling and that girls and boys will have equal access to all levels of education.
- By the same date, to have reduced maternal mortality by three quarters, and under-five child mortality by two thirds, of their current rates.
- To have, by then, halted, and begun to reverse, the spread of HIV/AIDS, the scourge of malaria and other major diseases that afflict humanity.
- To provide special assistance to children orphaned by HIV/AIDS.
- By 2020, to have achieved a significant improvement in the lives of at least 100 million slum dwellers as proposed in the "Cities Without Slums" initiative.

20.   We also resolve:
- To promote gender equality and the empowerment of women as effective ways to combat poverty, hunger and disease and to stimulate development that is truly sustainable.
- To develop and implement strategies that give young people everywhere a real chance to find decent and productive work.
- To encourage the pharmaceutical industry to make essential drugs more widely available and affordable by all who need them in developing countries.
- To develop strong partnerships with the private sector and with civil society organizations in pursuit of development and poverty eradication.
- To ensure that the benefits of new technologies, especially information and communication technologies, in conformity with recommendations contained in the ECOSOC 2000 Ministerial Declaration, are available to all.

IV. Protecting our common environment

21.   We must spare no effort to free all of humanity, and above all our children and grandchildren, from the threat of living on a planet irredeemably spoilt by human activities, and whose resources would no

We will spare no effort to free our peoples from the scourge of war, whether within or between States, which has claimed more than 5 million lives in the past decade.

longer be sufficient for their needs.

22.   We reaffirm our support for the principles of sustainable development, including those set out in Agenda 21, agreed upon at the United Nations Conference on Environment and Development.

23.   We resolve therefore to adopt in all our environmental actions a new ethic of conservation and stewardship and, as first steps, we resolve:

- To make every effort to ensure the entry into force of the Kyoto Protocol, preferably by the tenth anniversary of the United Nations Conference on Environment and Development in 2002, and to embark on the required reduction in emissions of greenhouse gases.
- To intensify our collective efforts for the management, conservation and sustainable development of all types of forests.
- To press for the full implementation of the Convention on Biological Diversity and the Convention to Combat Desertification in those Countries Experiencing Serious Drought and/or Desertification, particularly in Africa.
- To stop the unsustainable exploitation of water resources by developing water management strategies at the regional, national and local levels, which promote both equitable access and adequate supplies.
- To intensify cooperation to reduce the number and effects of natural and man-made disasters.
- To ensure free access to information on the human genome sequence.

V. Human rights, democracy and good governance

24.   We will spare no effort to promote democracy and strengthen the rule of law, as well as respect for all internationally recognized human rights and fundamental freedoms, including the right to development.

25.   We resolve therefore:
- To respect fully and uphold the Universal Declaration of Human Rights.
- To strive for the full protection and promotion in all our countries of civil, political, economic, social and cultural rights for all.
- To strengthen the capacity of all our countries to implement the principles and practices of democracy and respect for human rights, including minority rights.

We are committed to an open, equitable, rule-based, predictable and non-discriminatory multi-lateral trading and financial system.

- To combat all forms of violence against women and to implement the Convention on the Elimination of All Forms of Discrimination against Women.
- To take measures to ensure respect for and protection of the human rights of migrants, migrant workers and their families, to eliminate the increasing acts of racism and xenophobia in many societies and to promote greater harmony and tolerance in all societies.
- To work collectively for more inclusive political processes, allowing genuine participation by all citizens in all our countries.
- To ensure the freedom of the media to perform their essential role and the right of the public to have access to information.

VI. Protecting the vulnerable

26.   We will spare no effort to ensure that children and all civilian populations that suffer disproportionately the consequences of natural disasters, genocide, armed conflicts and other humanitarian emergencies are given every assistance and protection so that they can resume normal life as soon as possible.
We resolve therefore:

- To expand and strengthen the protection of civilians in complex emergencies, in conformity with international humanitarian law.
- To strengthen international cooperation, including burden sharing in, and the coordination of humanitarian assistance to, countries hosting refugees and to help all refugees and displaced persons to return voluntarily to their homes, in safety and dignity and to be smoothly reintegrated into their societies.
- To encourage the ratification and full implementation of the Convention on the Rights of the Child and its optional protocols on the involvement of children in armed conflict and on the sale of children, child prostitution and child pornography.

VII. Meeting the special needs of Africa

27.   We will support the consolidation of democracy in Africa and assist Africans in their struggle for lasting peace, poverty eradication and sustainable development, thereby bringing Africa into the mainstream of the world economy.

We call on the industrialized countries to implement the enhanced programme of debt relief for the heavily indebted poor countries without further delay.

28.   We resolve therefore:
- To give full support to the political and institutional structures of emerging democracies in Africa.
- To encourage and sustain regional and subregional mechanisms for preventing conflict and promoting political stability, and to ensure a reliable flow of resources for peacekeeping operations on the continent.
- To take special measures to address the challenges of poverty eradication and sustainable development in Africa, including debt cancellation, improved market access, enhanced Official Development Assistance and increased flows of Foreign Direct Investment, as well as transfers of technology.
- To help Africa build up its capacity to tackle the spread of the HIV/AIDS pandemic and other infectious diseases.

VIII. Strengthening the United Nations

29.   We will spare no effort to make the United Nations a more effective instrument for pursuing all of these priorities: the fight for development for all the peoples of the world, the fight against poverty, ignorance and disease; the fight against injustice; the fight against violence, terror and crime; and the fight against the degradation and destruction of our common home.

30.   We resolve therefore:
- To reaffirm the central position of the General Assembly as the chief deliberative, policy-making and representative organ of the United Nations, and to enable it to play that role effectively.
- To intensify our efforts to achieve a comprehensive reform of the Security Council in all its aspects.
- To strengthen further the Economic and Social Council, building on its recent achievements, to help it fulfil the role ascribed to it in the Charter.
- To strengthen the International Court of Justice, in order to ensure justice and the rule of law in international affairs.
- To encourage regular consultations and coordination among the principal organs of the United Nations in pursuit of their functions.
- To ensure that the Organization is provided on a timely and predictable basis with the resources it

[M]ake the United Nations a more effective instrument for pursuing the fight for development for all the peoples of the world, the fight against poverty, ignorance and disease.

needs to carry out its mandates.

• To urge the Secretariat to make the best use of those resources, in accordance with clear rules and procedures agreed by the General Assembly, in the interests of all Member States, by adopting the best management practices and technologies available and by concentrating on those tasks that reflect the agreed priorities of Member States.

• To promote adherence to the Convention on the Safety of United Nations and Associated Personnel.

• To ensure greater policy coherence and better cooperation between the United Nations, its agencies, the Bretton Woods Institutions and the World Trade Organization, as well as other multilateral bodies, with a view to achieving a fully coordinated approach to the problems of peace and development.

• To strengthen further cooperation between the United Nations and national parliaments through their world organization, the Inter-Parliamentary Union, in various fields, including peace and security, economic and social development, international law and human rights and democracy and gender issues.

• To give greater opportunities to the private sector, non-governmental organizations and civil society, in general, to contribute to the realization of the Organization's goals and programmes.

31.   We request the General Assembly to review on a regular basis the progress made in implementing the provisions of this Declaration, and ask the Secretary-General to issue periodic reports for consideration by the General Assembly and as a basis for further action.

32.   We solemnly reaffirm, on this historic occasion, that the United Nations is the indispensable common house of the entire human family, through which we will seek to realize our universal aspirations for peace, cooperation and development. We therefore pledge our unstinting support for these common objectives and our determination to achieve them.

8th plenary meeting
8 September 2000

[T]he United Nations in the indispensable common house of the entire human family, through which we will seek to realize our universal aspirations for peace, cooperation and development.

Civil Society's Essential Role in Achieving Education for All

1. Representatives of member organizations of the Conference of Non-Governmental Organizations in Consultative Relationship with the United Nations (*Co*NGO) and other civil society groups met in Geneva [on June 29 and 30 and July 1, 2011] for the Civil Society Development Forum (CSDF) 2011 Main Component, in preparation for the UN Economic and Social Council (ECOSOC) Annual Ministerial Review (AMR) taking place on July 4-8, 2011. The 2011 AMR is dealing with "Implementing the internationally agreed goals and commitments in regard to education," and the CSDF focused on "Civil society's essential role in achieving education for all." *Co*NGO has organized such pre-ECOSOC Fora during the past decade.

2. The CSDF received warm messages of encouragement and partnership from the UN Department of Economic and Social Affairs (UN DESA) and the United Nations Office at Geneva (UNOG). The discussions were led off and inspired by excellent statements from:

- Manjit Dosanjh, International Federation of University Women and Guild of Service
- Bob Harris, Education International, and former President of *Co*NGO
- Jason Scorza, International Association of University Presidents and Fairleigh Dickinson University
- Eunlim Chi, Kyung Hee University
- Meena Kadhimi, Bahrain Women Association for Human Development
- Addaia Marrades and Margarita Serra Mestre, Intervida
- Liberato Bautista, General Board of Church and Society of The United

Outcome Document

Methodist Church, and former President of *Co*NGO
- Royston Flude, CMDC-SPOC (Self-Sustaining Peoples, Organizations and Communities)
- Ilona Graenitz, former *Co*NGO Vice President, on behalf of the *Co*NGO Vienna community.

3.   The CSDF met in plenary and in four working groups: 1) Education for development; 2) Education and decent work; 3) Young girls and women; and 4) Vulnerable and minority groups. The following outcomes are submitted to the attention of the Annual Ministerial Review and all participants in the ECOSOC Session, to call attention to some deep concerns and issues to which civil society attaches importance. The Outcome Document is also a work-paper for the wider civil society as it pursues on a daily, weekly and year-round basis its multiple advocacy and operational roles to achieve the implementation of international and national goals and commitments in regard to education.

4.   Education For All and the Millennium Development Goals (MDGs) relating to education were at the core of the deliberations at the CSDF, it being frequently underscored that the MDGs are interlinked and mutually reinforcing. The 2015 deadline for achieving the MDGs is perilously close, and while many significant gains have been registered, there are alarming gaps in many sectors and many geographical areas. The urgent plea – the urgent demand – of civil society is that governments fully live up to the promises they have made through adopting the MDGs. There is time – but only just to close some of the gaps – and thousands of civil society organizations internationally and throughout the world are working with governments and communities to ensure that people's needs and aspirations are met in education as in all other sectors. Civil society will not relax on commitments and initiatives. But it is plain and undisputed that the primary responsibility rests with governments, from whom we expect renewed political courage, revitalized political determination, and enlightened political budgetary decisions. Achieving the MDGs in education and all other areas is not solely a matter of financial resources, but without the commitment of additional finance the gaps will not be closed. Achieving the MDGs in regard to education does not only concern Ministries of Education but also Ministries of Finance (for budgets, including teachers' salaries and training allocations), and Ministries of Infrastructure/Equipment (for school and teacher-training buildings, roads in rural areas, investment in information technologies).

5.   Achieving education and other MDGs is a high policy matter that must be on the agendas of Cabinet Meetings, prepared in depth by inter-ministerial Cabinet Committees. In short, the firm commitments

We need to broaden the notion of education away from the concept that the foremost purpose of education is to train children to be competitive in a changing world: this is grossly inadequate.

made by Heads of State and Government in adopting the Millennium Declaration, followed by the MDGs and relevant international Conventions and other legal instruments need to be unfailingly implemented down the governmental chain of authority. Local governments are also part of that chain and need to be brought fully into the consultative and implementation processes, most particularly when they have devolved authority in the areas of taxation and investment. Civil society is frequently in close proximity to local government and will often be a natural and competent partner for translating MDG commitments, through solidarity, down to the local level.

6. The nexus that joins education and development is critical and must be clarified: what kind of education and what kind of development are we aspiring to? We need to broaden the notion of education away from the concept that the foremost purpose of education is to train children to be competitive in a changing world: this is grossly inadequate. Education involves appreciation of life and preparation for living in community, taking into account local and global solidarity and diversity of cultures. Education takes place not only in formal education systems, but throughout every part of daily life and the entire life cycle. We need a holistic approach to education, with curriculum including teaching literacy, numeracy, sciences, philosophy, arts, as well as the development of core values, virtues, and meta-consciousness. Education must not focus on the achievement, even prescription, of a specific model of "development", but contribute to the transition to a sustainable development that is relevant to peoples and appropriate to their communities. Curriculum provides the framework for teaching; sustainable development provides the environment for lifelong learning.

7. MDG and Education for All targets are often construed and trumpeted in statistical terms. But statistics only tell part of the story, and may indeed often conceal the drama of the true story. Primary education enrolments may go up – which is naturally positive – but there may be inequalities in access as between girls and boys, or between social strata, or between urban and rural areas. In too many countries children, while statistically properly enrolled, may attend school infrequently or haphazardly, when they are required by their families to also be breadwinners many days per month or even per week. Governments are urged to look behind the statistics, to bring to light the types of ambient factors illustrated above, and to ensure that the administrative mechanisms are in place – and are funded – to iron out these inequalities and constraints.

Quality in education cannot be achieved without quality teaching.... Teachers are the bedrock for achieving social cohesion and societal development.

8.   Quantitative indicators do not necessarily reflect quality in education. Education is laying the groundwork for coping and affirming in life (cultural life; economical life; family life; for some, life with disabilities; and life as participatory citizens – including as voters!). It must therefore be based on optimal standards of quality. Quality in education cannot be achieved without quality teaching. There is a need for worldwide additional targeted investment in quality teacher training, both for entrants to the teaching profession and through refresher courses while teachers are in service. Since classes of 50, 80 or more pupils are sadly all too frequent, government policies - notably financial policies – must encourage more university and college graduates to enter the teaching profession. Equally, the remuneration and pension arrangements for the teaching profession must be such as to encourage teachers to stay in it. The teaching profession must be honoured, recognized to be fulfilling, and acknowledged for its irreplaceable role in promoting a tolerant and culturally-conscious society. Teachers are the bedrock for achieving social cohesion and societal development. It is therefore in society's interest – and thus in a government's interest – that the teaching profession be among the nation's financial priorities.

9.   Quality in education also needs to be monitored, both to ensure that standards are maintained and raised, and to contribute to eliminating disparities and inequalities. Assessment theories and procedures are increasingly known and elaborated but need to be much more widely applied. This is one of the areas where governments, local authorities, educational authorities should call upon institutions of higher education and of civil society to bring their research and other expertise to the table, also to achieve greater awareness and accountability. The dimensions of assessment include educational environments, including environments beyond the classroom, learners' cognitive and affective development, and logical interpretation. None of this is a luxury only affordable in high-income societies: it is a contribution to problem-anticipation, to problem-solving, and thereby to quality education.

10.   The internationally agreed goals in regard to education are intimately tied in with internationally agreed goals on women's rights, women's empowerment and gender equality. In still too many areas girls are "at the back of the queue" where inbuilt patriarchal attitudes may see them as unpaid house servants and/or marriage-consignees, thereby implicitly and explicitly denying their dignity, their rights and their potential. Immature marriage and immature pregnancy is just such a denial. Treating girls and women as easy prey for sexual violence is just such a denial. Overturning all such attitudes and practices – and in some places the laws or legal systems that back them up – must remain a

Civil society will not relax on commitments and initiatives. But it is plain and undisputed that the primary responsibility rests with governments...

162

top priority for parliamentarians, governments, educational and economic institutions, and civil society. In too many places humanity is still deprived of the social, economic, cultural, caring contributions of women. Justice cries out for action by all concerned: parliaments, government and judiciaries must not shirk their responsibilities or shrink their commitments in this crucial area. Civil society will not relent in advancing this cause, not least because educated girls and women are the bedrock of humane, healthy and prosperous societies.

11. To achieve the MDGs and Education for All and to implement international and national standards and goals in education, we must always remember that all these targets and aspirations are not ceilings but base floors to build on. Engaged civil society organizations, based on their intensive grass roots experience, call already now on governments to set ambitious goals and targets for the post-2015 period. This will require greater inputs from universities and other institutions of higher education (viz the UN Academic Impact Initiative). The business sector must play an active socially-responsible role. The knowledge and diversity of local communities must be fully brought in. The collective experience of civil society will have to be brought together in innovative ways, avoiding duplication of words and deeds, and seeking explicit harmonization of effort.

12. Culture and education are intertwined concepts. Learning processes reflect and shape cultures, and education must acknowledge, foster and enrich diversity. An education that does not take into account culture and cultural diversity loses its legitimacy. Education must recognize the multiplicity and plurality of narratives of the world's peoples, including narratives of indigenous peoples and their right to their own ways of being, knowing and doing. Indigenous peoples have often suffered from educational systems based on assimilation, cancelling their cosmovisions, their languages and their traditions. The recognition of linguistic, cultural and religious minorities, and the recruitment of teachers belonging to such minorities, should be factored into assessments of the quality of education. We call upon governments to develop culturally appropriate educational mechanisms geared to the elimination of inequalities, especially affecting marginalized and vulnerable groups. Education must be focused to repudiate entrenched negative attitudes, perceptions and practices that maintain stigmatization and marginal status.

13. Education needs to be compatible with sustainable lifestyles and people's need to earn a livelihood

We call upon governments to develop culturally appropriate educational mechanisms geared to the elimination of inequalities, especially affecting marginalized and vulnerable groups.

and to engage in decent work upon completion of their education. People's aspiration is to become contributing and participating members of a developing society, in a world that is becoming increasingly technologically complex. Civil society organizations can and will cooperate with educational systems to target and ensure the availability of resources that enhance youth preparedness for productive employment, including vocational education standards and infrastructures. Entrepreneurship is a skill that can be incubated, provided financial resources are made available.

14.   Civil society recalls the words of the United Nations Secretary-General on the occasion of the MDG Summit: "Our world possesses the knowledge and the resources to achieve the MDGs. Our challenge today is to agree on an action agenda to achieve them." Civil society is an indispensable partner with government in harnessing knowledge and resources, and in implementing the action agenda in the education arena and across all the MDGs. Civil society will hold itself and governments to account for the successful further implementation of all internationally agreed goals and commitments, so that they may become meaningful reality for the peoples of the world.

Entrepreneurship is a skill that can be incubated, provided financial resources are made available.

Women's Human Rights and Development: Inclusion, Participation and Equality

Introduction

1. Representatives of member organizations of the Conference on Non-Governmental Organizations in Consultative Relationship with the United Nations (CoNGO) and other civil society groups convened in New York, 4-5 May 2010, and joined online, for the Civil Society Development Forum (CSDF) 2010 Main Component. We met in preparation for the ECOSOC Annual Ministerial Review that will look into the "internationally agreed development goals, including the Millennium Development Goals, in regard to gender equality and women's empowerment." Within the general theme of women's human rights and development, we discussed critical sub-themes such as inclusion, participation and equality, with the objective of putting forward our conclusions and recommendations for careful consideration and decision by ECOSOC Member States during its June-July session.

2. The keynote presentations addressed the general theme in terms of the causes and consequences of the world economic crisis and its impact on women of all ages. In five workshops, the forum examined the issues in the context of sub-themes: legal and institutional mechanisms – implementation and enforcement; women and sustainable development; women, decent work and migration; gender discrimination – multiple layers and multiple forms; and health and reproductive rights.

3. We gather at a time when the world continues to be trapped in the most complex economic crisis with serious consequences throughout the world in the areas of food, energy, finance and the environment. Unrelenting natural disasters and conflicts in different regions and countries have not only intensified threats to

Outcome Document

the socio-economic foundations and stability of the Global North, but they have also imposed ever greater burdens on the Global South. These events, coupled with the dismal failure to observe human rights and respect gender equality, have obliterated the socio-economic gains achieved over past years. They have devolved most negatively on women and children, in particular girls, whose role and strengths are consistently ignored as demonstrated by the continued deprivation of their access to education, funding and technology, as well as social and health services. Nonetheless, a growing number of reports show that the empowerment of women and improvement of conditions faced by women and girls is key to economic development, democracy and civil rights.

4.   UN Member States and international financial institutions (IFIs) should without delay take into account the conclusions and recommendations of the UN Conference on the World Financial and Economic Crisis and Its Impact on Development held from 24 to 26 June 2009 in New York. Those recommendations remind us of the increasing impoverization of women throughout their life cycle and urge the United Nations system and the IFIs to ensure adherence to the social and economic rights of the vulnerable and marginalized communities, a particular concern being the urgency of effecting a move towards improving the conditions faced by women.

5.   We have observed the 30th Anniversary of the Convention on the Elimination of All Forms of Discrimination against Women (CEDAW) and the 10th Anniversary of its Optional Protocol, the adoption of United Nations Security Council resolutions on women in war and sexual violence in armed conflict, the appointment of a Special Representative of the Secretary-General on sexual violence in armed conflict, and the 15th Anniversary of the Fourth World Conference on Women and the Beijing Platform for Action. Further action should be taken to ensure international treaties and conventions are adopted and implemented in their entirety at the national levels, without reservations or conditions to the detriment of human rights and social justice. Laws that discriminate against women and girls need to be repealed or amended, thus ensuring women's equality in the legal system. Special efforts should be made to enforce the implementation of current laws that protect women and their rights, thereby effectively containing customary laws and social practices based on patriarchal ideology which would otherwise render the legislation declarative and inefficient.

6.   During its 2010 review session, the UN Commission on the Status of Women (CSW) adopted

Gender equality, in addition to being a way to achieve all the MDGs and a key to peace and development, is a major goal in itself...

a political declaration and reaffirmed previously existing commitments to the women of the world, a resolution on women's economic empowerment, and a resolution on strengthening the institutional arrangements of the United Nations system by consolidating the four existing offices focusing on women into a composite whole. Member States must move swiftly to establish the new entity, ensuring that its mandate addresses women's empowerment in all countries; it includes a strategic operational presence at the country level; it is ambitiously and adequately funded with stable and predictable resources; and a strong leader is appointed, who combines global vision with gender equality expertise and experience.

7.   Attainment by 2015 of the Millennium Development Goals (MDGs), which bear significant implications for the advancement of women, is in dire jeopardy owing to the world economic and social crises and an apparent lack of political will. Particularly disturbing is the fact that MDG 5, reduction of the maternal mortality ratio, is the area of least progress among all the MDGs. Gender equality, in addition to being a way to achieve all the MDGs and a key to peace and development, is a major goal in itself. Moreover, although MDG 3 and MDG 5 are gender-specific, all eight goals have clear and interrelated gender dimensions.

8.   In MDG 3, in particular, one target is the elimination of gender disparity in primary and secondary education, preferably by 2005, and at all levels of education by no later than 2015. Achievement is measured in terms of three indicators: ratio of girls to boys in primary, secondary and tertiary education; share of women in wage employment in the non-agricultural sector; and proportion of seats held by women in national parliaments. These indicators constitute measurable yardsticks for the advancement of women. It is contingent upon governments continuing to invest national resources in the three areas, fully realizing that access to quality education for all bears wide implications for women's empowerment and as a result, for the quality of life of society at large.

9.   Violence against women and girls is a major impediment to achieving gender equality. Violence is one of the key factors raising the risks of maternal and infant mortality and causing other diverse women's health issues. The Secretary-General's in-depth study on this issue recognizes that while violence against women varies – in its nature and manifestations – across as well as within societies for different groups of women and girls, and for the same woman/girl at different stages in her lifetime, it remains a universal phenomenon which persists in every country of the world and manifests itself in a variety of forms and

Violence against women and girls is a major impediment to achieving gender equality. Violence is one of the key factors raising the risks of maternal and infant mortality and causing other diverse women's health issues.

different settings. No country is free of domestic violence against women, practiced by their intimate partners. Gender-based violence, including trafficking in women (and, increasingly, girls), has far-reaching consequences for them, their families and society at large; it has a fundamental impact on the development process.

10.   Several decades after the United Nations system first declared their commitment to women's empowerment and women's human rights, structural discrimination against women remains deeply embedded in social systems worldwide. To counter the bias of our inherently patriarchal societies and ensure progress towards true gender equality, promotion of gender awareness through education and public discussion should be of highest priority for governments, civil society, private sector, and mass media. Information about women's contribution women to economic and social development, as well as about the discrimination and human rights violations that women suffer daily, including the manner in which they have overcome and struggled against such discriminations and violations, should be systematically collected and widely disseminated.

11.   In addition, the link between a higher status for women and more caring social and economic policies that support human capacity development – such as universal health care, child care, paid parental leave – needs to be understood and acted upon. A number of studies, including the World Economic Forum's Gender Gap reports, show convincingly that nations with the lowest gender gaps and significant investment in the social and fiscal support for caring policies maintain a generally high quality of life for all and enjoy economic success. Findings of such studies should be widely disseminated as they also show that gender equity is a major factor in determining whether stereotypically 'feminine' qualities and activities, such as caring, care-giving, and non-violence are truly valued – be it in women or men – and the effect it has on social and economic policy.

Legal and institutional mechanisms: implementation and enforcement

12.   Good governance goes hand in hand with respect for the rule of law. Independent and impartial legal and judicial institutions, legal identity, equality before the law, and access to both justice and legal information are building blocks which permit women to enjoy their human rights. The harmonization of national law with international treaties is a significant step towards implementing

[N]ations with the lowest gender gaps and significant investment in the social and fiscal support for caring policies maintain a generally high quality of life for all and enjoy economic success.

the rule of law, and ensuring government accountability for their internationally agreed obligations. Institutional mechanisms, including national machineries, should be a means for women to protect their rights. They serve to implement law reform, monitor enforcement and design social policy. In addition, international criminal law, including the Rome Statute, should be applied when States fail to pass or enforce laws protecting girls and women from systemic and widespread acts that cause great harm, and even death.

13.   Civil society needs to campaign firmly for the ratification of international treaties and conventions and the withdrawal of reservations to the same; the repeal of discriminatory laws against women; the establishment of a special UN mechanism concerning equality before the law; the organization of national consultations relating to law reform; the conduct of gender equality assessments for all legislation; gender sensitivity training for judges, court personnel, legal professionals and law enforcement officers. Civil society actors should also use complaint procedures based on the UN human rights machinery and regional human rights mechanisms to hold governments accountable for their obligations relating to women's human rights. The CEDAW Committee should be adequately funded and resourced so that it can monitor country reports in a timely manner and continue supporting the elaboration of the convention's provisions through drafting additional general recommendations.

14.   Member States should fulfill their obligations as set forth in the United Nations Declaration on the Rights of Indigenous Peoples and take the necessary steps to ensure that these rights are implemented, in particular to ensure the protection of indigenous women and girls. Indigenous women that migrate to cities are particularly vulnerable as they lose the link with their home land, communities and traditions. They become invisible among other migrants. Culturally sensitive policies, legislations and programmes should be elaborated at all levels to ensure the recognition of their interests and rights.

15.   Women's equal participation in parliament and political office is a necessary prerequisite for the recognition of women's human rights by government and other sectors of society. Women's leadership empowers women, enabling them to prioritize their concerns and take decisions on addressing those concerns. The United Nations system and Member States should use temporary special measures called for in CEDAW in order to achieve the measurable target of equal participation. The private sector, particularly corporations, should also use temporary measures to secure the participation of women in positions of leadership and decision-making.

Member States should fulfil their obligations as set forth in the United Nations Declaration on the Rights of Indigenous Peoples and take the necessary steps to ensure that these rights are implemented.

Women and sustainable development

16. **A** holistic approach to sustainable development necessarily integrates environment, economics, and ethics that embrace all life. Women must be recognized as critical agents for successful environmental change. They should be included in the design, implementation, decision-making, and monitoring of climate change and adaptation policy at all levels of government, private sector, civil society and media. Sustainable development should focus on process rather than ready-made solutions. The participation of women is necessary for locating sustainable solutions that would arise from bottom-up processes which embrace the economic, ecological, gender, psychosocial and cultural aspects of development.

17. Responsible consumption coupled with genuine resource redistribution is called for, including global cooperation between producers and consumers to mitigate and control climate change, to increase resource productivity, and to limit resource consumption. Sustainable development goes beyond conserving the environment and resources; it is very much about releasing the potential offered by women to make a lasting contribution to sustaining growth and development based on local resources and knowledge. To this end, measures of economic health must be changed to give visibility and value to the work of caring, traditionally performed by women, in both the market and non-market economic sectors, as support for this work is fundamental to both the economic empowerment of women and human and economic development.

18. While women and girls in developing countries of Asia, Africa, and Latin America produce two thirds of the food, they themselves go hungry and suffer from malnutrition which, in turn, affects infant and maternal mortality rates. Special attention should be paid to rural and peri-urban women who are typically small-scale livestock farmers. Such focus is essential for combating malnutrition and the generation of financial resources for medical care and education for their children. Lack of investment in agriculture and the failure to recognize women's rights to land and inheritance has given rise to chaos in food production in both the Global South and Global North. Instead of learning from and using the potential of sustainable farming practices established by women, we continue to watch even more women become landless and jobless.

19. There can be no further delay in the development, promotion, and introduction of climate-friendly

While women and girls in developing countries of Asia, Africa, and Latin America produce two thirds of the food, they themselves go hungry and suffer from malnutrition which, in turn, affects infant and maternal rates.

and climate-change adaptation technology. New policies and programmes need to aim at pro-poor environmental outcomes that will raise the living standards of the poor and vulnerable, disproportionately represented by women. Innovative financial mechanisms should be introduced to raise significantly financing for the environment and create strong incentives for conservation practices, slum upgrading and affordable housing for the poor, in particular women. Developed countries, which cause eighty percent of climate change and environmental disasters, must respond to the devastating effects that their unsustainable development has on the global scale. They should provide fair financial and technical assistance to the developing countries, whose population are demonstrably most vulnerable to the consequences of climate change. That assistance should be especially channeled towards women and address their particular needs.

20. Achieving just, sustainable, equitable, stable and participatory development, focused on improving living standards and securing well-being and human dignity for all, calls for a mix of value systems that offer an effective response to the problems and challenges posed by living itself, regardless of actual geographic location. Member States should pay special attention to "The Peoples Agreement," an outcome of the World People's Conference on Climate Change and the Rights of Mother Earth held 19-22 April 2010 in Cochabamba, Bolivia, particularly with a view to incorporating the agreement in the preparatory process for and run-up to the upcoming Conference of Parties to the United Nations Framework Convention on Climate Change in Cancun, Mexico.

Women, decent work and migration

21. The International Labour Organization's (ILO) concept of decent work deserves full recognition by Member States. The ILO Global Job Pact states that it is the responsibility of governments to ensure decent work opportunities for women of all ages and to provide social policies and social services. Governments and the private sector should guarantee equal pay for equal work to both women and men. Governments must recognize women's unremunerated work and their contributions to a "caring economy" in their countries and provide fair compensation and assistance for all the care work women perform. Without adequate day-care services, after-school programmes, family leave and financial assistance, women's participation in economic development will remain impeded. Just as critically, for want of such policies, investment in human capacity development may not be sufficient, despite its essentiality

Lack of investment in agriculture and failure to recognize women's rights to land and inheritance has given rise to chaos in food production in both the Global South and Global North.

in the knowledge/information economic era in both human terms and financial terms.

22.   Governments need to analyze the issue of migration in the context of human rights and its social dimensions, rather than exclusively in terms of international markets and economic consequences. Member States should recognize the human rights of migrants and their families, treating them in the same manner as their nationals and including them in social programmes. Bilateral agreements or memoranda of understanding between the countries of origin and recipient countries should be concluded which emphasize the protection of the human rights of migrant workers. Member States should regularly scrutinize recruiting agents and employment contracts for the safeguarding of the rights of migrant workers. This is particularly important when dealing with migrant women who are often employed in the informal economy that is poorly regulated by legislation.

23.   Women migrants include both skilled and unskilled workers. Skilled workers whose qualifications are not recognized in recipient countries frequently end up as domestic workers. Women migrants are more vulnerable to physical violence, including sexual violence and human trafficking. Domestic work exposes women to violence and their being stripped of their rights; their passports are seized; they are denied food and refused access to health services, in addition to working round-the-clock in servitude. South-South migration, primarily from the Asian countries to the Gulf region, poses a serious problem for women. Member States and civil society should fully support an ILO Convention relating to domestic work.

24.   Member States should include discussions relating to migration more frequently in the work of the United Nations system. The participation of civil society, trade unions and the private sector is essential in such fora, significantly the Global Forum on Migration and Development, and the voices of women should be heard in those discussions. Civil society should advocate the ratification of ILO Conventions relating to migrant workers and their families.

25.   Microfinance is recognized as a tool used to reduce poverty, provide credit and financial services to underserved populations, create livelihoods and jobs, and foster community development. The reliability and efficiency of women in managing often scarce finances, especially in times of crisis, have been acknowledged. However, women should not become hostage to perpetual expectations based on the gender division of roles in a patriarchal society. Microfinance is not a goal in itself, but should be considered the

Developed countries, which cause eighty percent of climate change and environmental disasters, must respond to the devastating effects that their unsustainable development has on the global scale.

172

first of many steps leading to equitable and sustainable development. Women play crucial roles at both the micro-economic and macro-economic levels.

Gender discrimination: multiple layers and multiple forms

26. Discrimination against women and girls is grounded in patriarchy and affects them all at many points throughout the life cycle. Women of all ages experience more than one type of discrimination, compounded by such factors as race, social class, age, ethnic identity, disability, sexual orientation, culture, religion, situations of war and natural disaster, and statelessness, including citizenship.

27. Assessment of the impact of disasters and conflict upon women, indigenous peoples and rural populations, the elderly, the displaced, and youth should be carried out to ensure their needs are met. Humanitarian assistance and development aid needs to be delivered with no strings attached.

28. Member States should encourage respect for human rights and tolerance to ensure a society fit for all. Member States should recognize the universality of human rights and repeal laws that punish persons on the basis of sexual orientation, particularly LGBTQ persons.

29. Older women are critical providers of primary education, economic support and care for disabled and underage members of their families. Access to work should be ensured and their contributions to society must to be acknowledged. However, they may be in need of care and support themselves. They should be provided with meaningful assistance and financial security in order to improve their quality of life and guarantee ageing with dignity.

30. The International Criminal Court (ICC) recognized that rape, abduction and the use of girls as weapons of war and other armed conflicts is a crime against humanity. Member States should cooperate with: (a) ICC to bring perpetrators to court and end impunity for all forms of gender-based violence in war; (b) the new Special Representative of the UN Secretary-General on Violence in Armed Conflict, and the Victims' Trust Fund to ensure that survivors of these crimes receive comprehensive remedies; (c) the Special Rapporteur on Violence against women, its causes and consequences of the Human Rights Council; and (d) the United Nations system to implement gender-sensitive re-integration programmes for child soldiers into their families and societies should take into account the particular challenges that girls face.

Domestic work exposes women to violence and their being stripped of their rights; their passports are seized; they are denied food and refused access to health services, in addition to working round-the-clock in servitude.

The United Nations system should ensure better coordination between peacekeeping operations, the United Nations Security Council, the United Nations Secretariat, and the Human Rights Council so as to include women in conflict prevention, conflict resolution and post-conflict peace building.

31.   Engaging men and boys as partners to bring about women's empowerment is a critical component to advancing the status of women and girls and achieving gender equality and equity. While women's empowerment benefits men, programmes in positive masculinity provide skills training to men and boys, resulting in their individual development and the development of healthier societies at large.

Health and reproductive rights

32.   Women's health includes mental health and well-being, both which are influenced by their social and economic status. The lack of essential health services for women and girls keeps them in a revolving cycle of poverty, leaving them trapped in dire circumstances from one generation to another. Governments must ensure the prevention of conditions that lead to poor health – physical, social and mental – and into delivering on their commitments to women's health, as well as making access to health services universal for women throughout the life cycle.

33.   Ensuring women's health is not solely about delivering services, it involves changing gender norms. Women and girls often do not have the power to reject unwanted sex, which poses a great risk of HIV/AIDS and other infectious diseases, increases their chances of unplanned pregnancies and compromises their reproductive health. Education to end practices such as genital mutilations of girls and women must be a priority. Investing in adolescent girls is critical to their health and development. Keeping them in school and educating them about pregnancy, HIV/AIDS, and ways of negotiating sexual relationships, are steps that must be taken in all societies. Local organizations should engage with the United Nations Development Fund for Women (UNIFEM) and the United Nations Population Fund (UNFPA) to design comprehensive age-appropriate sex education programmes.

34.   In many areas, lack of human resources continues to increase child birth risks. Women should be involved in the delivery of public health-care services. Member States should develop and provide training for and strengthen support of health-care workers – doctors, nurses, midwives, social and community workers – specifically those who provide information and services to women and girls in rural areas.

[W]omen should not become hostage to perpetual expectations based on the gender division of roles in a patriarchal society... Discrimination against women and girls is grounded in patriarchy and affects them all... throughout the life cycle.

Particular attention should be given to services for girls subjected to early marriages. Owing to their young age, these girls are exposed to notably higher risks of complications and death at childbirth.

35.   Family planning saves women's lives and empowers women, and yet in many areas, funds for family planning services have been cut. Member States should establish a high-level task force on financing for women's health in order to achieve MDGs 3 and 5.

36.   Issues related to reproduction are extremely sensitive and value-laden, being linked to sexuality, control of women's bodies and fertility on the one hand, and to population size and composition, on the other. The complexity of ethics, politics, economics and religion has made the question a still more heated issue on the international agenda. After the 1994 Cairo UN Conference on Population and Development emphasized sexual health, the Beijing Platform for Action underscored the right of women "to have control over and decide freely and responsibly on matters related to their sexuality"(¶ 96).

37.   At the same time, all aspects of health-care for women – physical, mental and social – should be improved and not limited solely to obstetric and gynecological care and access to appropriately trained medical staff and physicians. Women and men differ in every system in their bodies, including the immune system, which can increase the risk and severity of infections from influenza to HIV/AIDS. Particularly during pregnancy, women's immune systems are compromised, exposing them to greater risks. Rapidly increasing around the globe are the rates of heart disease and cancer among women, including preventable cancer related to tobacco-use. Gender-sensitive medicine and equal access to all health-care systems must become standard practice throughout the world. The health of women and their access to health care are of paramount importance to the health and sustainability of society as a whole.

38.   The oppression of the world's women and girls stands in direct relationship to their mental health and social well-being. Among females of all ages, limited rights to control their own bodies is linked to unwanted pregnancies and an ever-increasing risk of HIV/AIDS. There is no subject that has been addressed during the CSDF 2010 that does not bear serious implications for the health and psycho-social well-being of women and girls. Social and cultural practices create further obstacles that would otherwise protect them against AIDS. Taboos against sex education, prevalent in many developed and developing countries, compound the situation. According to the World Health Organization, mental health is directly correlated with social and economic conditions. It is not surprising that women are the major sector of the

Mental health is directly correlated with social and economic conditions. It is not surprising that women are the major sector of the population at the greatest risk of non-psychotic depression and anxiety throughout the world.

population at the greatest risk of non-psychotic depression and anxiety throughout the world.

Concluding statement

39. This CSDF component was part of a series of *Co*NGO fora providing timely and organized civil society inputs to ECOSOC debates on the attainment of the MDGs . In 2007, CSDF participants met to debate on the overall theme "A Platform for Development: Countdown to 2015." They concluded that a "new narrative" – a new approach – is needed, that recognizes the emerging convergence of growth and development strategies with human rights norms, including gender equality and equity standards and "climate justice".

40. CSDF 2008 set out to highlight (i) the crucial role of the internationally agreed development goals / MDGs in the pursuit of a results-oriented global development strategy and (ii) the need for an assessment of the development community's efforts and achievements, so far, in meeting these goals. Specifically, its Outcome Document addressed issues germane to the then emergent crises – specifically the food crises – a manifestation of failed sustainable development policies.

41. Carefully chosen to be located within the same perspective as the theme of ECOSOC's Annual Ministerial Review, CSDF in 2009 focused on "Threats to the Health and Development of Nations (Civil Society Proposals on Global Public Health in the Context of the Global Economic Crisis)". Taking place during the far-ranging hardship caused by already ongoing multiple and interrelated global crises – food, energy, environment, finance, poverty and migration – CSDF participants concluded that the combined threats of the failure to achieve the MDGs, as cross-sectoral goals, are likely to harm the delicate interrelationship between global public health and development; threats to the good intentions to address the social determinants of health.

42. Closer to the target date and yet far from the timely attainment of the MDGs, participants at CSDF 2010 noted with concern that the failure of target realization by 2015 is now – more than ever – an imminent threat. Only under conditions of just and democratic governance within a holistic human rights framework, recognizing fully women's human rights and development via inclusion, participation and equality, will their realization be ensured.

[T]he combined threats of the failure to achieve the MDGs, as cross-sectoral goals, are likely to harm the delicate inter-relationship between global public health and development...

Women's Human Rights and Development: Inclusion, Participation and Equality

Introduction

1. The Civil Society Development Forum 2010 – Geneva Component was organized by the Conference of Non-Governmental Organizations in Consultative Relationship with the United Nations (*Co*NGO). It reviewed the outcome document of CSDF 2010 – New York Component, in conjunction with the conclusions and recommendation of ECOSOC's Annual Ministerial Review as reflected in the Ministerial Declaration (Ministerial Declaration of ECOSOC's 2010 High-Level Segment), focused on "Implementing the internationally agreed development goals and commitments in regard to gender equality and empowerment of women." The Outcome Document of the CSDF 2010 – New York Component was presented to ECOSOC.

2. Both the New York (May 4 and 5) and Geneva (September 30 and October 1) Components of CSDF 2010 had as their theme "Women's Human Rights and Development: Inclusion, Participation and Equality." The Geneva Component was held at the International Labour Office, at the courtesy of the Director General of ILO.

3. In preparation for CSDF 2010 – Geneva Component, *Co*NGO launched a discussion in which civil society organizations worldwide could participate.

4. The in-depth debates focused on the same five sub-themes as the New York Component:
   A. Legal and Institutional Mechanisms: Implementation and Enforcement;
   B. Women and Sustainable Development;
   C. Gender Discrimination: Multiple Layers and Multiple Forms;
   D. Women, Decent Work and Migration; and
   E. Women's Health and Reproductive Rights.

Action Points

5.	The Ministerial Declaration summarising the High-Level Segment of ECOSOC's 2010 Substantive Session (22 June – 2 July 2010, New York) re-affirmed the interconnected framework of the United Nations including the UN Millennium Declaration and the Millennium Development Goals (MDGs). A most significant statement in the Ministerial Declaration related to the establishment of the UN Entity for Gender Equality and the Empowerment of Women called UN Women. The Declaration pledged full support to its operationalization on the basis that "it will strengthen the United Nations to support the achievement of gender equality and the empowerment of women worldwide."

6.	There are several new measures proposed by the Ministerial Declaration as a result of the global crisis which includes financial and economic crisis, the food crisis, continuing food insecurity, and the energy crisis as well as the challenges presented by natural disasters and climate change. The Declaration recognises that women are disproportionately affected by these crises. It is recognised that women have a key leadership role to play including decision-making. The Declaration underlines the commitment to strengthen national policies and to make concerted efforts to remove the obstacles to the full realisation of the Rights of Women. The issues highlighted by the Declaration concern prevention and elimination of all forms of violence against women and move towards zero tolerance.

7.	The CSDF 2010 – Geneva Component heard thoughtful, challenging and often moving presentations from representatives of the United Nations System (International Labour Office, United Nations Office at Geneva, United Nations Conference on Trade and Development, UN Economic Commission for Europe) and from civil society leaders from Africa, Asia, Europe and North America. It was evident from the 26 plenary and panel presentations that a number of cross-cutting issues were of importance for all of the five substantive themes, including that:

- Women must accede without hindrance to decision-making positions at all levels of community, society, nation, and of international governance.
- Civil society organizations committed to gender equality and empowerment of women must increasingly take account of the inter-relatedness of both the challenges and the solutions. They must accordingly create and seize opportunities to share experience, to network, to enhance consensus, and to build on and "broadcast" good practices. Civil society organizations are catalysers: policy impact and influence will follow from responsibly working together, without in any way diluting

Women must accede without hindrance to decision-making positions at all levels of community, society, nation, and of international governance.

civil society commitment, enthusiasm and innovative imagination.

• For decades, within and outside the United Nations System, governments have adopted excellent Conventions and Treaties guaranteeing and extending women's rights. They have adopted Summit Declarations, Agreements and Programmes containing ringing promises of action to secure women's rights and expand women's role and opportunities in society. But in too many cases there is a lamentable gap in the implementation of these commitments and promises. Specific follow-up actions become mired in the thickets of traditionalism, dogmatism, bureaucracy, excuses of fiscal constraints, impenetrable legalisms, and perhaps often just sheer incomprehension of what women contribute to society when their energies are freed.

• It is therefore imperative that in every area of public policy, of international, national and local decision-making, civil society be ever more dynamic and adamant in its advocacy of Action Now For Women's Inclusion, Participation And Equality. No more excuses, no more sliding out of commitments, no more breaking of promises. Action Now!

8.   The CSDF accordingly adopted the following Action Points under each of the five themes, together with some overall conclusions. The Action Points are intended to foster and reinforce policy choices and programmatic decisions by the widest range of civil society actors, by the gamut of organizations of the United Nations System, and by governments individually and collectively. The CSDF recommends the Actions Points for timely, consistent and sustained implementation. In *Co*NGO's own context, we refer these action points to the *Co*NGO Substantive Committees that are deeply engaged in these key areas of human rights and development.

A.   Legal and Institutional Mechanisms: Implementation and Enforcement

Action Points for Civil Society

According to the Regional Review Meeting of Beijing +15 (2 - 3 November 2009), one of the recommendations emphasized: "The implementation of Human Rights principles is the core responsibility of all governments; they must underpin the development of all legislation and policy and ensure its implementation, as well as being accountable to civil society."

[D]espite laws against violence, the incidence in the intensity and degree of violence (against women) has not been reduced.

9.   Legal, economic or political status of women must be translated into positive practice in all countries. Attitudes of society, community and family that obstruct equality and equity being applied to women must be tempered and then eliminated, as must traditional practices where they continue to oppress women with the support of the state and religion. This dynamic naturally differs from country to country, community to community, and therefore it is essential that civil society organizations work together in solidarity at global, regional and local levels to enforce positive national policies, laws and regulations. The focus of advocacy and intervention needs to be specific and special according to local needs and sensitivities.

10.   The trade-union movements in many countries have historically protested against unequal remuneration between men and women in various occupations from time to time. These actions must be continued and extended to achieve the implementation of laws on equality of remuneration ("equal pay for equal value") and to build on cases where there have been judicial decisions in favor of women. We urge that these efforts be documented and compiled, to make a global case history on introducing gender equality and equity.

11.   The CSDF gives moral support to women's organizations in several countries that have rebelled against traditional practices such as Female Genital Mutilation (FGM) and successfully changed policy and legislation. Noting that there are currently 28 countries which have signed and ratified the Maputo Protocol and legally prohibited this practice and made it a punishable crime, the CSDF supports further pressure by all NGOs to eradicate these practices that so violently deny women's rights.

12.   The CSDF is disturbed at evidence of indirect correlation between women exercising their human rights and the resulting violence in their lives. The CSDF urges NGOs to examine national statistics and surveys on violence against women to determine needed public advocacy and action on this matter.

Action points for the United Nations

13.   The CSDF welcomes actions by the United Nations System, at the instance of NGOs, Women's Organizations and Governments, to introduce policy and legislation, particularly over the last four decades, to bring about change against the discrimination of women. Since the Declaration on the International Women's Year 1975 and the subsequent Declaration of the International Decade for Women from 1976 – 1985, this process has accelerated. Indeed, the United Nations System has acted as

2/3 of the world economy relies upon women's unpaid work and work in the informal sector.

an umbrella for a militant but non-violent revolution on equality between men and women through four UN conferences on women: Mexico (1975), Copenhagen (1980), Nairobi (1985) and Beijing (1995). Subsequently, the UN Reviews in 2000, 2005 and 2010 have reaffirmed the Beijing Platform for Action, the 12 components, of which consolidated earlier recommendations to empower women everywhere. The United Nations System must continue to involve and harness civil society, notably women's organizations in carrying this momentum forward energetically.

14. For the last half of the 20th century, legal and economic norms have been transformed to introduce gender equality at the highest levels in international law, the outstanding example of which is the Convention to Eliminate all Forms of Discrimination Against Women, signed in 1979 and to date ratified by 184 countries. There are several other international standards, resolutions and decisions that have been adapted at the national level into national law to make legal equality between men and women a reality. The United Nations System is asked to take all possible steps to incorporate civil society input to the implementation and monitoring of these processes.

15. The CSDF has however to note with deep regret that violence against women worldwide, irrespective of class, creed, race, or caste, has increased everywhere despite the adoption of new laws. The UN Special Rapporteur on Violence against Women visited more than 40 countries to analyze the causes and consequences of the violence against women in her report to the UN Human Rights Council in 2009. She concluded that despite laws against violence, the incidence in the intensity and degree of violence has not been reduced. The Human Rights Council must act with determination and coherence to give positive long-term follow up to this report.

16. The CSDF notes that thus far very few cases of discrimination against women have been dealt with under the CEDAW Optional Protocol, and requests the appropriate United Nations bodies to provide all necessary facilities to NGOs and victims to steer further cases through the process, noting that all cases constitute valuable precedents for bringing about true justice.

[W]ork with communities to increase productivity of local farms, and to promote terms of trade between rural and urban areas to ensure that women have better access to local, national and international markets and have adequate wages.

Action Points for Governments

17. The implementation and enforcement of International Conventions, International Standards and International Agreements on women's rights will irrevocably transform the daily lives of women. In many countries, developed and developing, the legal institutions and enforcement mechanisms are not yet strong enough to influence traditions and customs that continue to abuse and exploit women. In order to make the law have a concrete impact on the lives of citizens, we call on governments to publish reports on implementation, using indicators and benchmarking, as well as provide sufficient and predictable funding of relevant programmes and services. We call on governments of countries where plural legal systems exist to harmonize these systems to ensure respect for human rights and fundamental freedoms. Governments must be aware that this has particular significance where women's issues are concerned, in regard to customary law and practice.

18. We remind governments that where the rule of law is not generally applied, it is even more difficult to change the economic and social status of women. Governments cannot be satisfied with the non-application and the weak enforcement of legal provisions, resulting in the violation of almost all women's human rights and depriving them of basic human dignity in daily life. We draw governments' attention to the fact that the underlying principle has been reiterated in several UN standards and decisions and most recently underlined in the Beijing +15 Review (Geneva 2-3 November 2009): "Women's rights as human rights are not bargaining terms. Evidence shows that ensuring women's rights through policies enables a stronger impact on employment, economic growth, and the development of democratic societies and the lives of families."

19. We demand that governments introduce and/or apply legal provisions on equal remuneration and demonstrate the political will to enforce the provisions of the ILO Convention on equal remuneration in paid work, adopted as early as 1951 and subsequently incorporated in ILO Recommendations. Governments cannot be satisfied that in the beginning of the 21st century, even before the world economic crisis, equal remuneration principles were not implemented for different occupations in the national economy despite the fact that a series of ILO standards exist. Governments cannot accept that women's work continues to be invisible, underestimated and undervalued.

[B]iodiversity is being steadily decreased in the Global North and South. This calls for wide-ranging interation among and concerted action by, a range of civil society actors.

20.   Despite remarkable advances in the methodology of quantification, women's work in rural areas, the household and the informal sector remains undercounted. We ask governments to take steps in national employment structures, from recruitment to retirement levels, to eliminate specific traps such as "job grading and job evaluation" where they discriminate against women. In the process of quantification, recent estimates indicated that 2/3 of the world economy relies upon women's unpaid work and work in the informal sector. This means that low pay and no pay continues to be the norm of women's economic contribution. We ask governments to take all necessary legal measures, and introduce all necessary mechanisms, to overcome this patent and unacceptable discrimination.

B.   Women and Sustainable Development

Action Points for Civil Society

21.   Civil society has long recognized that women sustain and conserve the environment and that they have a direct relationship with forests, preservation of trees and longevity of plants. Civil society should work with communities to increase productivity of local farms, and to promote terms of trade between rural and urban areas to ensure that women have better access to local, national and international markets and have adequate wages. Civil society must attentively monitor the rules and regulations of transnational companies such that they include social responsibility for fair trade, and equitable prices for essential commodities for sustainable life. At the international level, NGOs need to encourage the UN Global Compact to foster such policies.

22.   The CSDF notes with regret that the Doha Development Round continues to be stalled due in large part to the fact that the global agricultural system is not sustainable in most developing countries and some developing countries, and that unequal government subsidies distort patterns of trade among countries. We call on civil society organizations to find ways to further support small-scale farmers particularly affected by these circumstances, noting with sadness that some have committed suicide due to debt burden. Civil society organizations should seek to support women to meet the basic needs of feeding the family during crises and higher food prices.

23.   In the rural areas of poor countries, women look after forests and gather wood for sale, fuel, and

Governments must base policy on the basic notion of sustainability, namely to preserve and develop all the economic, natural, financial, and ecological resources within a country for succeeding generations.

their livelihoods. Due to an unsustainable environment and ineffective government schemes, the number of poor who are not able to access food has increased. According to the World Summit on Food, hunger has become widespread. According to the World Bank, there are many cases where ownership of land is passing from the rural poor to international companies producing essential items particularly food items. These matters are interconnected and call for policy and programmatic interventions from civil society organizations.

24.   Civil Society recognizes that women have always contributed to biodiversity to preserve it. But now due to reduced activity of women and man-made intervention, particularly by national and international companies, biodiversity is being steadily decreased in the Global North and South. This calls for wide-ranging interaction among and concerted action by, a range of civil society actors.

Action Points for the UN

25.   Distribution of land must be re-organised to provide an equal share to women and agricultural systems should be improved to introduce new technologies, which reduce the workload of women and increase local production. In the Doha Round of Negotiations (currently stalled), equal and just rules must be instituted and applied to subsidies given to the farmers both in the Global North and Global South.

Action Points for Governments

26.   We ask governments to acknowledge that development as a concept has often been misunderstood. The adjective "sustainable" before development was the result of changes in concepts and terminology in different development models over time. Governments must base policy on the basic notion of sustainability, namely to preserve and develop all the economic, natural, financial, and ecological resources within a country for succeeding generations. Governments must therefore plan action to better re-distribute national wealth and achieve balanced consumption, according "to need and not greed." Since the natural wealth of almost all countries is unequally distributed between income-class, gender, and race, governments must adopt policies to avoid that most of the disadvantages fall on those who are vulnerable, mostly women.

Land is one of the main assets of an economy community, and family. Governments must take determined action to protect and support women who have become increasingly landless...

27.   Land is one of the main assets of an economy, community, and family. Governments must take determined action to protect and support women who have become increasingly landless despite the fact that they work long hours in agricultural production in rural areas. Particular attention must be given to indigenous women. Government action must specifically address issues of unequal distribution of land and abolish provisions that prevent women from owning property and inheriting equally with men. Governments in Asia, Africa and Latin America must no longer tolerate situations where women produce 2/3 of the food, but without the legal status of farmers, resulting in situations where they themselves often go hungry. We ask governments to recognize that widespread hunger is the result of unsustainable development, and that can be corrected by government action with involvement of all stakeholders.

28.   Since sustainable development is negated by conflict – whether internal or cross-border – we demand that governments put highest priority on prevention of conflicts and their peaceful resolution, with full involvement of women as contributors to such processes and negotiations. At the moment of the achievement and consolidation of peace, sustainable development will be most attainable if governments promote social justice and provide targeted opportunities for women to contribute fully to the regeneration of societal life through education and business development. Governments must recognize, and build upon, the potential of women of all ages – including of course women in villages and small communities – to take charge of their lives and livelihoods. Governments will best serve their people and best achieve sustainable development if they harness and release the energies of women in their multifaceted roles – entrepreneurs, farmers, mothers, educators, deciders, family providers and economic managers.

C.   Gender Discrimination: Multiple Layers and Multiple Forms

Action Points for Civil Society

29.   CSDF recalls with appreciation that it has basically been NGOs and women's organizations and some friendly governments who have been responsible for creating and expanding awareness globally on different types of discrimination suffered by women. They supported protests against discrimination in a variety of ways, which enlarged the area of awareness of ordinary citizens. They were also leaders in influencing public opinion to change public policies in favour of women. The first UN Conference on Women 1975 was also the result of pressure by NGOs on governments and the

Governments will best serve their people and best achieve sustainable development if they harness and release the energies of women in their multifaceted roles...

United Nations System to take serious action against discrimination and to draft new policies and legislation. Civil Society must continue to work against gender discrimination in all UN agencies and organizations in what is called mainstreaming by the United Nations System.

30.   Civil society organizations need to engage locally and nationally throughout the life-span of women, from birth to adolescence, before, during and after marriage, motherhood and old age to combat the layers and layers of discrimination against women. This includes combating discrimination in dimensions such as food, education, dress-code, type of work, treatment in the work-place, and inequality in decision making in private and public sectors.

31.   Furthermore, civil society organisations will need to focus on eliminating the perpetual state of poverty in which most women in developing countries live and which prevents them from fully developing themselves, educating their children and participating on their terms in the production and reproduction processes. Most of the violence against women can be ascribed to sexual abuse. Many women do not enjoy sexual freedom, nor have the right to choose their life-partner or the number of children. This type of disharmony in the family results in more and more conflict and violence. The interface between sex and race adds to more intensity and degree of violence. This applies very particularly to migrant women and domestic workers. In all of these areas, civil society has to lead in education, awareness building, putting in place and monitoring implementation mechanisms.

Action Points for UN

32.   It is to the honour of the United Nations System that discrimination against women has been defined and described by several international standards, notably the UN Convention on the Elimination of All Forms of Discrimination against Women, 1979, which has clearly listed the most significant discrimination experienced by women on which there is a global consensus. The United Nations must keep up pressure on the few countries that have not ratified the Convention and especially on those that have made significant reservations, which adversely affect women's human rights in almost all social, political and economic sectors.

33.   The United Nations System must keep its communication and information services focused on the varying degrees of discrimination in different regions, countries and communities, and particularly the most

United Nations spotlight must shine on the double standards that are applied to men and women where society and religion treat them differentially.

186

universal discrimination that stands out against women in the two areas of employment and sexuality. The job market is clearly disaggregated according to gender and there is visible and invisible discrimination and abuse against women in their sexual lives. The United Nations spotlight must shine on the double standards that are applied to men and women where society and religion treat them differently. There are multiple forms of discrimination, which result in physical, mental and emotional violence depriving women of their human dignity. All agencies of the United Nations System have a role in keeping these issues at the top of the international agenda.

34.   One particular area in which the United Nations can provide expertise and leadership is facilitating the expansion of access by women to information communication technologies. The long-term follow-up process to the World Summit of the Information Society provides an opportunity and a framework for action in this area.

Action Points for Governments

35.   Governments have primary responsibility in guaranteeing equal access of girls to education at all levels. In order to achieve gender equality in employment, it is essential to harmonise the system of education in universities with the system of selection in job interviews. In many cases, the entire process of recruitment in jobs is discriminatory and governments must introduce the necessary laws and regulations to remedy this situation. One set of measures must include introducing gender sensitivity in the terminology applied to jobs and professions, which may also create psychological conditions encouraging girls to enter professions previously dominated by men.

D.   Women, Decent Work and Migration

Action Points for Civil Society

36.   A wide range of civil society organizations work with women who are migrating to get better economic opportunities within countries and beyond borders. They work with women who leave rural areas for cities where they are usually offered work only in factories and households; and with women migrants who become domestic workers, whose conditions of work are uncertain and

[J]ob market for migrant women is inequitable, indecent, and without adequate protection of labour laws and trade unions, leading to abuse and maltreatment of women.

exploitative, whose wages are below the national average and whose work hours are not regulated. Noting that a large number of migrants become domestic workers, do not have any valid economic or social status, cross boundaries without papers and are classified as undocumented workers without any rights of citizenship. The CSDF calls upon civil society to intensify its involvement in programmes of protection, care and support for migrants, that they too many have conditions that conform to the ILO definitions of decent work.

Action Points for UN

37. ILO itself must intensify attention to problems associated with migration and movement of labour across the world and different regions, as more and more women are moving across borders to earn an adequate wage to escape the trap of poverty and discrimination. The definition of decent work proposed by ILO must apply to jobs available to women who are casual, uncertain, physically and mentally unsustainable, and low-paid. Since the job market for migrant women is inequitable, indecent, and without adequate protection of labour laws and trade unions, leading to abuse and maltreatment of women, ILO must continue to provide leadership to the United Nations System and the international community in responding to migrant women's needsv.

38. ILO leadership, analysis and monitoring are equally needed in relation to the further ratification and implementation of the International Conventions applicable to migrant workers and their families. As a reliable source of information and statistics, including on migrant workers, ILO must keep before governments the moral and legal obligation to undertake and implement commitments in this area.

39. Noting the historically new phenomenon of a concentration of highly skilled and highly technological jobs in which there are fewer women than men, the CSDF calls for UN programmes to gather statistics and to identify and propose solutions applicable in both public services and commercial enterprises. Moreover, similar action is needed from the United Nations System in regard to women displaced as a result of natural disasters and conflicts and needing protection and humanitarian aid.

Every country should be able to choose its own path to development in which the majority of its citizens should acquire basic education and training to protect and promote jobs at home and in rural areas.

Action Points for Governments

40. Every country should be able to choose its own path to development in which the majority of its citizens should acquire basic education and training to protect and promote jobs at home and in rural areas. This would prevent qualified people from going to other countries thus depriving the national economy from basic skills. In working towards these objectives, governments must undertake participatory consultations with civil society, including migrants associations and of course women's groups.

41. The CSDF recognizes that the reasons and motivation for migration for men and women are distinctly different. In addition to earning income, there are many cases of women persecuted in the family and forced to migrate within countries and beyond borders. In this context, the international definition of a refugee under the relevant UN Convention may need to be re-considered.

42. The CSDF recognizes that one of the main causes of increase in the movement of labour across the world is that those who move to find work or income do not have employment possibilities at home. This points to a big defect in the structure of the national economy in which governments have not made adequate investment to create jobs. The current decline in the world economy has exposed the need for government regulation encouraging investment and planning in small-scale and medium enterprises. In any case governments must invest enough in sectors where there is a majority of women at work.

E.   Women's Health and Reproductive Rights

Action Points for Civil Society

43. Civil society is fully aware that in most countries, the health of women is not given priority in the family, despite the fact that it is their energy and effort that determines the health of other members of the family. Civil society must continue to advocate energetically for prioritizing women's health needs in government policy at the national and local level, recognizing that a healthy woman is central to a healthy family, a healthy community, a healthy nation.

[W]omen's health is key to the production and reproduction processed, and that the well-being and health of a society rests upon these two issues.

44. Since the period of fertility of women is much shorter than their life-span, women themselves and society at large tend to give less attention and care to women's health during their reproductive years. Women themselves tend to give priority to their children and husband. Here too are causes requiring civil society education, awareness building and advocacy programmes.

45. According to estimates, a large number of women are malnourished and undernourished, particularly in developing countries. In some countries food distribution is unequal between men and boys and women and girls in the family with the result that women tend to eat least and last. Also in some countries, the medical system is structured in such a way that the decisions on women's health are taken by the male hierarchy. In developed countries, more and more women consume painkillers and anti-depressants. These issues are so complicated and so deeply affect women at all stages of life that they require civil society organizations to work cross-sectorally to reach all segments of the population.

Action Points for UN

46. CSDF welcomes the long-standing norm-setting of the United Nations System (Conferences, World Summits, Heads of State Declarations, etc.) establishing that Reproductive Rights should be considered as an individual human right and should not be regulated by family, tradition or state, which would result in women being deprived of choices and freedom in their personal life.

47. We ask that the United Nations System continue to proclaim that reproductive rights include a women's decision on all matters concerning her body, the right to have a child or not to have a child, the right to choose a partner with whom to have a child and the decision on the number of children. These decisions must be taken by women, not subordinated to family, religion, or state. United Nations agencies must promote education across all these issues.

48. We are aware that the UN Population Conference in 1994 in Cairo put reproductive rights on the international agenda. We welcome that since then a new term has been added to the vocabulary of women's issues – empowerment. To empower women means that they should be able to exercise all reproductive rights without any legal or moral opposition from their society. The United Nations System

Now is the time to move towards gender equality.

must uphold the principle that women's health is key to the production and reproduction processes, and that the well-being and health of a society rests upon these two issues.

49. We note that large numbers of people use alternative systems of medicines rather than allopathic and that due to reasons of poverty, a majority of women tend to use natural and alternative medicines. We call on WHO to conduct medical and drug-research on the diseases and illnesses that particularly affect women and on medical devices and remedies that are regularly used by them.

50. We call on WHO to give adequate attention to these issues at policy level. Recent research has indicated that the biological reaction to drugs differs according to the gender. This factor has not yet been largely recognized by the pharmaceutical companies, doctors and hospitals. Again this is a matter calling for adequate attention by WHO.

Action Points for Governments

51. We note that medical education in most countries is very expensive and less accessible to women. There are more women than men who are para-medicals, medical technicians and nurses, and the nursing profession is also low-paid. Moreover nurses are not everywhere respected and their conditions at the work-place are not very conducive to their health.

Conclusions

52. The journey to women's equality has been long and hazardous. The landscape of women's rights has been irrevocably transformed; the area of awareness is uneven and is changing at different levels and different speeds. Patriarchy as an institution is eroding and the structures that supported it are becoming weaker. Now is the time to move towards gender equity.

53. Civil society, which has many components including women's organizations, must continue to play a positive role in the future. Women's organizations must continue to lead the struggle against all layers of discrimination and must continue to learn to fully exercise their human rights. Governments need to continue to listen to the voices of women in order to implement policies and legislation in the future.

[T]he UN, UN Women and governments must continue to listen to women and to heed their voices, so as to consolidate the achievement of the last century.

54. The United Nations System must continue to work with governments to have international standards and norms implemented at the national level and introduce innovative mechanisms for them to put into practice. In this context, civil society and particularly women's organizations salute and enthusiastically welcome the creation of the new entity to be known as UN Women. The appointment of Michelle Bachelet as the new Under-Secretary-General to lead UN Women has also aroused much enthusiasm and eager anticipation.

55. It is now imperative that governments provide adequate, timely and long-term funding for the new entity. The necessary political and procedural decisions must also be taken immediately such that when the UN Women entity enters into being on 1 January 2011, the full and productive participation of all relevant NGOs is assured. In particular, the UN, UN Women and governments must continue to listen to women and to heed their voices, so as to consolidate the achievements of the last century.

[A] healthy woman is central to a healthy family, a healthy community, and a healthy nation.

Threats to the Health and Sustainable Development of Nations

1. We, representatives of member organizations of the Conference of Non-Governmental Organizations in Consultative Relationship with the United Nations (*Co*NGO), and other civil society groups, convened in Geneva, Switzerland, from 2 to 4 July 2009, for the Civil Society Development Forum (CSDF). We discussed issues germane to the agenda of the High-Level Segment of ECOSOC's Substantive Session – on global public health, to be held in Geneva from 6 to 9 July 2009. Our conclusions and recommendations were prepared for careful consideration by ECOSOC Member Governments in the course of their deliberations and decision-making at this Session.

2. We gathered at a time when the worldwide food, energy and environmental crises were reinforced by the devastating effects of the financial and economic crises. The combination of these crises is threatening the socio-economic roots and stability of the Global North and inflicts even greater burdens, with debilitating effects, on the Global South, cancelling momentary socio-economic gains achieved over the last three to five years.

3. Now, more than ever, UN Member States must reaffirm their commitment to fulfil the promises they made with regard to Official Development Assistance, and for member states and the international financial institutions to take into account the conclusions and recommendations of the UN Conference on the World Financial and Economic Crisis and Its Impact on Development held in June 2009 in New York. These recommendations reminded all States and international financial institutions to ensure adherence to the social and economic rights of the most vulnerable, especially their right to health.

Outcome Document

4.   Attaining the Millennium Development Goals (MDGs) by 2015 is in greater jeopardy ever since their promulgation by the leaders of the world nine years ago. The combined threats of the failure to achieve the MDGs, which are cross-sectoral goals, the current paralysis in foreign assistance policies, and the misallocation of national budgets to favour non-productive and military activities are likely to harm the delicate interrelationship between the pursuit of human rights and poverty eradication, global public health and development, and gender equality and the empowerment of women. These are threats to the good intentions to address the social determinants of health.

5.   In six workshops, CSDF 2009 delved deeply into its overarching theme of "Threats to the Health and Sustainable Development of Nations." Three keynote themes were also explored: (i) the social determinants of health; (ii) impacts of the global economic crisis on health; and (iii) threats to the achievement of the MDGs, especially those relating to global public health. Following are the major points arising out of those workshops, including the elements of a special report from the youth participants who attended these workshops:

Responding to Health Inequities at Local and International Levels

6.   Governments are increasingly aware of the value of competent civil society input for their policy deliberations and decision-making. In the public health field, the input of numerous international and national advocacy, scientific and community-based civil society organizations can enhance government policies. We call on governments and parliaments to take full advantage of these competencies. Meeting the full range of health needs requires partnership: civil society is ready and able to contribute constructively.

7.   The conversion of international agreements into national legislation and practical implementation mechanisms frequently reveals inadequacies. Civil society calls on governments to fulfil their obligations as the credibility of government institutions in this adoption process is at stake. A review of the internationally agreed development goals and commitments, including the MDGs relating to public health, is of key importance.

8.   It is critical for governments to adopt a human rights-based approach to health, which would contribute towards attaining the MDGs. This approach redefines health beyond being a mere state and

It is critical for governments to adopt a human rights-based approach to health, which would contribute towards attaining the MDGs

recognizes it as a potential for people to deal with challenges to their bodies and the social determinants of their health. It is a potential to become fully human and humane. Health care must be affordable, acceptable, accessible, and adaptable. It must also be socially responsive, policy-based, contextually-appropriate, and gender-sensitive. Primary health care should in itself be comprehensive, by focusing on all aspects of prevention, cure and care, and to healing and wholeness.

Dealing with the Shortage of Health Care Workers

9. Policies need to be designed to reduce the brain drain of health care workers and to achieve their equitable distribution compatible with community needs. Education and training must encompass all levels of health care personnel, including local and grassroots. Decent wages and working conditions are key to ensuring retention and a rationalized migration policy in both sending and receiving countries.

10. We stress the importance of a holistic approach to health and capacity building. The inclusion of indigenous medical specialists and traditional healers is essential for comprehensive health care delivery. Their marginalization in society and the discrimination of their expertise are directly linked to poor health services and endanger the availability and viability of health care at the local level.

11. We emphasize the importance, as does WHO, of defining health as encompassing mental, physical and social well-being. Depression is projected to be the greatest risk factor in terms of global disease burden, surpassing all physical illnesses combined by 2030. Women are already at greater risk for depression worldwide. Yet, mental health is missing from the global public health agenda.

Addressing the increase in non-communicable and chronic diseases

12. The increasing trend of non-communicable and chronic diseases is leading to a shift away from infectious communicable diseases in the overall global disease burden. The former diseases tend to be under-diagnosed, especially among the poorest, the most vulnerable and the ageing, thus endangering timely treatment among large population groups, often in an environment of inadequate health system infrastructure. The growing incidence of these diseases results in a reduction in the quality and length of life and in excessive actual costs and social opportunity costs. It is incumbent on governments

Policies need to be designed to reduce the brain drain of health care workers and to achieve their equitable distribution compatible with community needs.

to issue health-related regulations to meet and promote public health interests outside of industry's profit maximization strategies and to develop constructive public-private health policy partnerships.

13. The advance of non-communicable and chronic diseases must be stemmed by helping remove unhealthy life conditions and lifestyles. Conditions such as health illiteracy, toxic environments, impediments to treatment and care need to be eradicated. Harmful lifestyles such as inadequate nutrition, drug abuse, alcoholism, tobacco smoking, and the consumption of other toxic products, and dependencies need to be abandoned. Multi-sectoral, gender-based, comprehensive strategies pursued by civil society, including also health professionals, scientists, faith-based organizations, the private sector and policy-makers, must be set up for effective global action.

14. Concrete follow-up action should comprise (i) the inclusion, in the MDGs and UN agency programmes, of quantifiable action against the spreading of communicable, non-communicable and chronic diseases; (ii) the creation of a Global Fund to address such diseases that do not have such funding mechanisms; (iii) the adjustment of international health regulations to include a strengthened focus on such diseases and the management of risk-related factors; (iv) the revision of international trade agreements and legislation in favour of healthy food and decent labour-related productivity standards and markets; and (v) political action highlighting the right to health, including access to quality medicine and health care for all, the facilitating of the local manufacturing of safe medicine, covering also the development and production of generics and traditional medicine.

Financing Global Access to Health Including Health Technologies

15. Health financing by governments should go beyond financing health care systems but include investing in the preconditions of health, including freedom, education and economic welfare. In so doing, financing health should not be seen as an economic burden but an investment in people contributing to sustainable development and gross national product. Health systems function properly with several key elements, such as adequate numbers of skilled health workers, basic infrastructure and equipment, essential medicines and supplies and health financing systems. They underscore the importance of establishing effective health information systems.

16. Ancestral indigenous people's medicine must be recognized and respected, and adopt health policies

that take into account the particular realities in each country. The holistic approach of indigenous medicine complements western medicine and needs to be included when shaping national health policy and practice. A change of attitude, including an intercultural approach, should take place to overcome the hegemonic approach of modern medicine as the only existing answer to health care. Efforts should be made to shift towards a harmonious coexistence of both modern and ancestral medicine for the benefit of all peoples.

17. Communities as well as states should create their own programmes to make their health system more efficient. Public housing, spaces, and conveyances, including traffic facilities, should be made accessible so as to reduce medical and caregiving costs. Promotion of innovative user-oriented information and communications technology (ICT) could support independent living, especially for elderly and disabled persons. Skills and infrastructure for low-income countries need to be developed to enable them to use ICT, such as e-Health and m-Health for medical education and information systems. Use of ICT will reduce costs and lead to a better and more efficient health care system. As with all technologies, like wireless technologies, their use must be thoroughly evaluated for implications on health.

Ensuring the Right to Health for Women Throughout the Life-Cycle

18. Women's health, including reproductive health, must be promoted throughout their lifecycle by providing gender sensitive medical care. Healthy mothers and healthy babies make for healthy societies. Continuing and expanding financial and political support for MDG 5 is critical. We must break out of the scandalous lack of progress on this goal. Investing in maternal and child health is a precondition for the health of families, communities and nations and not only the health of half of humanity.

19. Most national budget allocations are used to cover curative services and the recurrent costs of health facilities and services; very few resources are deployed for prevention, promotion and rehabilitation. The availability and accessibility of essential health services are often inadequate. This has resulted in considerable inequalities in health-care provision and access, especially among women and other vulnerable groups.

20. Donor and recipient countries, as well as NGOs, must be supported in introducing good governance, efficient planning, accountability and responsible approaches of communities at regional and local levels.

Harmful lifestyles such as inadequate nutrition, drug abuse, alcoholism, tobacco smoking, and the consumption of other toxic products, and dependencies need to be abandoned.

Scientific research into gender medicine needs to be funded to provide data for optimal health programmes taking into account differences between men and women, age groups and ethnicity.

Promoting Prevention and Treatment of HIV/AIDS

21. Governments and intergovernmental agencies must broaden the concept of HIV/AIDS prevention and address the social determinants of health regarding vulnerable populations, including women and people who live in abject poverty and hunger. Resources for HIV/AIDS programmes are threatened by the financial crisis which should not be used as an excuse to stop funding them. Countries need to keep their commitment and allocate resources to address HIV/AIDS. The Global Fund should be made more accessible for HIV/AIDS resources and should work towards ensuring that resources get to the needy. HIV/AIDS programmes and policies should make scaling up possible at the national level.

22. Governments need to commit themselves to keep their promise of 0.7% of their GDP, which would help towards attaining the MDGs. Civil society needs to hold up that issue in ECOSOC's debates. Coherence within UN agencies must be encouraged to avoid duplication of services.

23. National health systems should be strengthened and measures taken expeditiously to confront the brain drain phenomenon. Governments should be urged to exercise pressure on pharmaceutical companies and laboratories to produce diagnostic tools, child-friendly medicines, and to provide universal access to antiretroviral drugs. The disbursement of funds for HIV/AIDS programmes at the global level should be closely monitored.

Youth Perspectives

24. Empowering youth is an investment for today and the future for their meaningful participation in decision-making for themselves and for society. Promoting youth participation in decision-making is a key element in ensuring the provision of youth-friendly health services, including opportunities for employment and decent wage, and thus a healthy and productive youth population. Increased funding and research must be allocated to attend to young people's health. Greater attention

Ancestral indigenous people's medicine must be recognized and respected, and adopt health policies that take into account the particular realities in each country.

must be given to the high disease burden among youth, including the high prevalence of depression and suicide rates. Health strategies must guarantee accessibility to health services for the youth.

25. Young people need a voice in global governance systems. It is crucial that they can feel a sense of purpose and respect. When encouraged to speak with their opinion being valued, recognizing that "youth speak truth," they are empowered to talk about their experiences. For young people, meaningful participation includes being immersed and knowledgeable about the issues they mostly only hear about. New approaches of communication and dialogue must be explored to relate the daily experience of young people. These dialogues can help initiate change in communities.

26. Many youth are faced with inadequate health care services and feel that the health care system needs to be taken beyond a monetary world. For youth, a new service-based health system should be seen as a social duty and a new global ethic. The idea of "design for all" services should encompass the development of a truly generally accessible global health network. Accessibility denotes prior access to the system, but what about those who have no access.

Cross-cutting Themes and Other Concerns

27. Civil society advocacy for the MDGs must redound to the betterment of life and living conditions of people around the world, especially the extremely poor and the hungry who are also the most deprived, oppressed and marginalized. In the economic downturn, we must not renege on ensuring their health and the health of the entire human community. A review of internationally agreed development goals is a reconsideration of humanity's commitments to life-giving and life-enhancing activities. It must give focus to combating activities and tendencies that deal with and peddle violence and death, especially wars.

28. CSDF 2009 reaffirmed the intersections and interdependence between human rights, peace and security, and sustainable development. These values undergird, enhance and sustain a healthy human life and the planet. Human right to health is equally the human right to a healthy and sustainable ecological system. Food, an essential element of health, must be ensured for all. Without food, health goals are meaningless. Profit entities and structures, especially those affecting the food production and distribution

Investing in maternal and child health is a precondition for the health of families, communities and nations and not only the health of half of humanity.

199

chain, must favour and ensure availability of safe, healthy and affordable food for all. No one should gain and make profit from making people sick.

29.   Global public health is a challenge to socio-economic policies. Health is not primarily an economic outlay but the foundation for productivity and the enjoyment of human rights and dignity. Public health cannot be a mere consumer good for it is a fundamental building block of society. The right to and equal access to health care implies a just and equitable health for vulnerable populations. Thus, society needs to ensure that public policies consider the implications of social and economic conditions--determinants that either increase or decrease the risk and vulnerability of specific populations.

30.   The use and abuse of alcohol is a global problem that spans both physical and mental health. It is multi-faceted with issues varying across cultures. The benefits connected with the production, sale and use of alcoholic beverages come at an enormous cost to society. Acute and chronic disease and psycho-social problems are integrally linked. Physical toxicity, intoxication, and dependence explain alcohol's ability to cause medical, psychological, and social harm. Like WHO, NGOs must be mobilized to promote alcohol policies which safeguard from the negative consequences of alcohol abuse and addiction, enjoining everyone to own the problem and help monitor alcohol marketing. NGOs must help foster political will to reduce the global burden of disease caused by alcohol.

31.   Health information for people and communities involves access to information for health promotion, health education, health literacy and awareness. These require consideration of legal and ethical aspects such as the quality and credibility of information, whether or not it is evidence-based, the source, conflicts of interest, and consent. Access to information across organizational and geographic boundaries should not limit access to health data and information, but must be managed through agreed protocols for data protection, privacy and authenticity.

32.   E-health is an emerging field in the intersection of medical informatics, public health and business, referring to health services and information delivered or enhanced through the internet and related technologies. E-health is more than a technical development, it is a way of and a commitment for networked and global thinking, to improve healthcare locally, regionally, and globally by using information and communications technology. A national e-Health legislative framework should provide the basis for protecting data, users and citizens from misuse.

Human right to health is equally the human right to a healthy and sustainable ecological system.... Health is not primarily an economic outlay but the foundation for productivity and the enjoyment of human rights and dignity.

Threats to the Health and Sustainable Development of Nations

Introduction

1. The Conference of Non-Governmental Organizations in Consultative Rela-tionship with the United Nations (*Co*NGO) organizes every year Civil Society Development Fora (CSDF) in New York and Geneva. These Fora advocate civil society positions towards United Nations Member States through the governments participating at the annual Substantive Sessions of the United Nations Economic and Social Council (ECOSOC). Specifically, the main CSDF event is held at the location of the Substantive Session (which alternates each year between New York and Geneva). The follow-up CSDF event is subsequently conducted at the other location.

2. The CSDF's Outcome Documents constitute the primary advocacy instrument for conveying the political content of civil society's positions to the United Nations System and to member governments.

3. The CSDF's main theme, while taking into account ECOSOC's central theme for its High-Level Segment (which, in 2009, was: "Implementing the Internationally Agreed Goals and Commitments in regard to Global Public Health") focused on: "Threats to the Health and Sustainable Development of Nations (Civil Society Proposals on Global Public Health in the Context of the Global Economic Crisis)."

4. The CSDF 2009 – Geneva Component was held from 2 to 4 July, the New York Component on 15 and 16 October 2009. The latter Forum examined ways and means for follow-up action to implement the earlier Geneva Outcome Document. It was attended by some 100 participants from civil society, the UN System and governments.

Action Points

5.   Both CSDF Components took place under the far-ranging hardship caused by ongoing multiple and interrelated world crises – food, energy, environment, finance, poverty and migration. The participants expressed deep concern that the failure to attain the Millennium Development Goals (MDGs) universally by their target date of 2015 was now a realistic threat. It was essential for civil society, the UN System, and, above all, governments to boost their efforts drastically and demonstrate unwavering commitment towards the attainment of the MDGs.

6.   The President of ECOSOC, other senior government and UN officials reiterated the importance of civil society organizations as advocates for, and partners in achieving a more socially just and equitable world. CSDF participants pledged to give even more impetus to their actions to respond to these calls and to attain these objectives.

7.   The participating civil society organizations agreed to advocate the implementation of the following Action Points at international and national levels in the coming months by civil society, the UN System and governments. The first follow-up for *Co*NGO will take place in Vienna from 9 to 11 November 2009, when the *Co*NGO Board will meet and the President conducts the CSDF Vienna Briefing.

Action Points for Civil Society

8.   On the matter of global public health civil society will take accountable action in the following areas and strongly urges governments to include in their national budgets specifically earmarked supportive funding to:
- refocus national institutional health structures towards prevention measures, which includes actively promoting healthy lifestyles and healthy nutrition practices,
- promote human rights learning for all stakeholders involved in physical and mental health care service delivery,
- build and expand the capacity of health and mental health personnel, including local and grassroots community workers and traditional healers,
- collect gender-specific data to ensure and upgrade health services for women of all ages,
- leverage all forms of media, including traditional communicators, to educate communities and promote health and mental health,

[P]rovide prevention, education on and treatment of HIV/AIDS, tuberculosis, malaria and sexually-transmitted diseases, recognizing the social determinants of health that affect vulnerable populations.

- support the development and appropriate use of information and communication health technology and encourage related exchange programmes as means of training and familiarization, and
- provide prevention, education on and treatment of HIV/AIDS, tuberculosis, malaria and sexually-transmitted diseases, recognizing the social determinants of health that affect vulnerable populations, especially women and children living in poverty.

9.   Dialogue must integrate older persons along with youth in order to achieve preventive health measures – to preserve traditional health care methods and adapt them in a time of changing technology. Dialogue is a means to bridge the digital divide, and should help encourage all stakeholders to revisit the outcomes of the two segments of the World Summit on the Information Society (WSIS).

Action Points for the United Nations

10. UN Systemwide communications and programmes should cover both physical and mental aspects of health. They should stress that physical and mental health are themselves rights and that access to them is also a right. The UN System should recognize that education and awareness-raising relating to the importance of health are broader than the traditional focus on health education. While primary health care should remain an essential priority, prevention of disease should be a principal focus of UN System health programmes. It is important to remember that while there are three specific health UN MDGs, health cuts across all eight MDGs. These considerations should be central to UN System campaigns to mobilize and educate public opinion on health issues.

11.   The UN System should cooperate with academic institutions to enhance global youth dialogue on public health so that youth can educate themselves on the immediate health care crisis and take ownership of long-term solutions.

12.   UN Treaty Monitoring Bodies should require States to include mental health aspects in their reporting. UN System programmes and projects should incorporate mental health considerations. The UN General Assembly should convene a Special Session on mental health and related issues.

13.   The UN Global Fund to Fight AIDS, Tuberculosis and Malaria must be strengthened. Civil society organizations must be given improved access and enhanced participatory roles. UN programmes to

UN Systemwide communications and programmes should cover both physical and mental aspects of health. They should stress that physical and mental health are themselves rights and that access to them is also a right

prevent early childhood diseases and address the causes of maternal mortality must be expanded. UN health programmes must address the entire range of all communicable and non-communicable diseases. They must bring together all stakeholders to end violence against women, cultural practices that are harmful to women's health, and all forms of sexual abuse.

14.   Early adoption by the UN General Assembly of the draft resolution currently in circulation on "Mobilizing Public Opinion for the Health of Nations" is strongly recommended. The purpose of this resolution is to achieve "Healthy People on a Healthy Planet by 2020."

Action Points for Governments

15.   Governments must give legitimacy to the voice of youth representatives by ensuring their full and unimpeded participation in the decision-making process on future health issues, including but not limited to the MDGs.

16.   As governments rebuild cities and urban centres, they must seize the opportunity to influence public health by, for example, creating spaces that foster physical activity, older persons' involvement, ecofriendly/green communities and social interaction. This facilitation of health through urbanization will require prospective planning and sustained leadership.

17.   Governments should recognize the role that climate change plays in increasing global conflict (e.g. Darfur) and its associated disorders (e.g. post-traumatic stress disorders). They must also recognize the ensuing increases in global disparities/inequities and the grave impediments for states, especially fragile states, to create sustainable societies.

18.   As part of their ongoing work on migration and immigration, governments need to investigate and document the role of climate change in influencing migration and creating new refugee flow patterns. Governments should accept their responsibility to guarantee the rights of those affected by climate change including the recognition of the resettlement rights of people who are becoming known as environmental migrants and climate refugees.

19.   In light of the fact that 80 percent of the world's disease burden results from preventable causes,

Governments should accept their responsibility to guarantee the rights of those affected by climate change including the recognition of the resettlement rights of people who are becoming known as environmental migrants and climate refugees.

governments are strongly urged to shift their focus and resources from a preoccupation with the treatment of non-communicable disease to a focus on public health and prevention by enacting policies that directly target the root causes of non-communicable disease, which include physical inactivity, tobacco use and other dependencies, and inadequate nutrition.

20.   In support of such policies, governments should mobilize resources for the promotion of health awareness campaigns. They should encourage their countries' parliaments to embed in their legislations and in their constitutions the concept of the right to health, and to legislate standards for informing and educating the public on the human right to health.

21.   Governments should develop patient-centred national health legislation with the full participation of civil society, should work cooperatively with civil society to shift the impetus from health care to health promotion and disease prevention, and should provide constructive and financial support for family policy.

22.   Governments should mobilize disease prevention and health promotion funding. They should reallocate resources foreseen for military expenditures for the development of poverty-stricken societies to help ensure an adequate level of economic development.

23.   We call on governments to enhance accountability and implementation mechanisms to ensure allocations of resources in accordance with intended purposes. We adamantly call on governments to fulfil their obligations and commitments to ratify and act on international treaties. We lay particular focus on the universal ratification of the International Covenant on Economic, Social and Cultural Rights, and of all the principal international Human Rights Instruments. Governments are morally obliged to implement the Concluding Comments that are issued by the UN Treaty Monitoring Bodies after examination of each national report.

Governments are strongly urged to shift their focus and resources from a preoccupation with the treatment of non-communicable disease to a focus on public health and prevention by enacting policies that directly target the root causes of non-communicable disease....

Conclusion

24. The Civil Society Development Forum participants were only too well aware that achieving any and all of the goals and aspirations set out in this document will require leadership, imagination, wisdom, courage, determination and resources. It will require political will, which is another way of saying "moral will". Civil society is ready for the redoubled efforts that are required. We will work in partnership with the United Nations System and responsible governments to improve global public health today, tomorrow and for the years to come.

[A]chieving any and all of the goals and aspirations set out in this document will require leadership, imagination, wisdom, courage, determination and resources.

Implementing the Internationally Agreed Development Goals and Commitments in Regard to Sustainable Development

We, representatives of member organizations of the Conference of Non-Governmental Organizations in Consultative Relationship with the United Nations (*Co*NGO), convened in New York from 27 to 29 June 2008. We discussed issues germane to the agenda of the High-Level Segment of ECOSOC's Substantive Session, to be held in New York from 30 June to 3 July 2008. Our conclusions and recommendations were prepared for consideration by ECOSOC member Governments in the course of their deliberations and decision-making at this Session.

1.   We gathered at a time of confrontation with a series of crises – food crises – a manifestation of failed sustainable development policies, leading to riots in many countries; energy prices driving the cost of food, other commodities and services even higher; climate change having adverse effects worldwide; increasingly destructive weather patterns and occurrences; more extensive desertification, increased drying up of critical water resources, rising sea levels threatening the survival of populations on low-lying coastlines and islands; global financial turmoil and uncertainty; and the many ongoing conflicts around the world.

In light of the above,

2.   We request Governments to substantially increase their investments in the sector of agriculture, to strengthen the position of small landholders, to stop the non-sustainable import of products grown far away and of genetically modified products, and to enhance the use of local and indigenous agricultural knowledge, practices and inputs.

Conclusions and Recommendations

3.   We urge that agricultural workers have the opportunity to work in cooperatives, to earn the benefits of the value they add to the processing of food products, and to have access to capacity-building opportunities. Land ownership is crucial to agricultural workers. We encourage land redistribution measures to make this possible. In particular, land tenure rights for women must be legally recognized and enforced.

4.   We reaffirm the human right to food and recognize the importance of food sovereignty. We urge Governments and civil society to reach agreement and to implement national level food sovereignty strategies and measures.

5.   We note the pervasive role of international financial institutions in influencing national development strategies. We urge these institutions to redesign their strategies with a view to assisting countries in defining their priorities at home by using home-grown expertise and products of these countries. WTO's role in negotiations on agricultural matters should be re-examined. Measures should be taken at multilateral and bilateral levels to prevent speculative trading of staple food items and energy fuels.

6.   National decision-making should respect human rights, encompassing food security considerations, especially those affecting children, and should contribute to the eradication of poverty and famine.

7.   We recognize the need to end lifestyle trends embracing high resource, high energy, and other unsustainable consumption patterns. We urge governments to collaborate with civil society in halting and reversing these trends.

8.   We strongly encourage corporate social responsibility that contributes to participatory and sustainable development that precludes the exploitation of natural resources, that helps end the violation of human rights, and that promotes the human right to decent work and to adequate compensation and social protection.

9.   We recognize full employment and decent work as essential to poverty eradication and in achieving sustainable development. We call on Governments to integrate the decent work agenda in international and national development strategies.

10.   We assert that the achievement of sustainable development goes with the realization of human rights. We urge Governments and intergovernmental entities to include the realization of human rights

National decision-making should respect human rights, encompassing food security considerations, especially those affecting children, and should contribute to the eradication of poverty and famine.

in their development strategies. They must act in accordance with the mutually reinforcing relationship of human rights and sustainable development and the interdependence and equal importance of civil, political, economic, social and cultural rights.

11.   We support a holistic approach to human rights and call on multilateral and bilateral donors to reinvigorate and not renege on this approach. We strongly urge UN agencies, Funds and Programmes to continue the explicit reference to human rights in Common Country Assessments, UN Development Assistance Frameworks and other UN development planning instruments.

12.   We regret the absence of consensus with regard to the concept of development as a human right. We urge Governments to accept the mutual obligations implied by the human right to development, which is part of the Internationally Agreed Development Goals (IADGs) that include sustainability of development.

13.   We ask that the realization of human rights be introduced as a guideline for the attainment of the Millennium Development Goals (MDGs) and Poverty Reduction Strategies (PRS), as well as in the mitigation of and adaptation to climate change, especially ensuring that the most vulnerable and marginalized populations receive priority attention.

14.   We call on Governments to ensure the genuine participation of people experiencing extreme poverty in the development, implementation and evaluation of policies and programmes for sustainable development and poverty eradication.

15.   We note the legitimate demand of aid recipient countries to be given more "policy space" in determining the use of aid. This demand should not be used as a pretext to disregard the obligations these countries have accepted to have women, men, youth and children realize their human rights and attain sustainable development.

16.   We support efforts in the preparation of the Accra High-Level Forum on Aid Effectiveness to devote more attention to gender equality, human rights and environmental sustainability. We call for a more balanced economic policy agenda that promotes participatory and gender responsive budgets as tools for including the voices of the poor and of women in fiscal policy. Specifically, we urge Governments,

We recognize full employment and decent work as essential to poverty eradication and in achieving sustainable development.

and public and private entities, to support gender mainstreaming and promote gender balance in the agricultural sector.

17. We recommend to public institutions the development and publicizing of human rights instruments for sustainable development and of best practices in good governance. These mechanisms must demonstrate close cooperation and linkages among local, national, regional and international levels.

18. We assert that effective sustainable development should be people-centred. This requires effective local capacity building, capitalizing on the innate strengths and resources of the people themselves.

19. We call on Governments to bring youth and children into the discussion and action around sustainable development. Programmes for formal and non-formal education and training, including educator/teacher training, must be designed, established and sustained at every developmental and educational level.

20. Finally, *Co*NGO and its member NGOs wish to reaffirm to Governments that implementing Internationally Agreed Development Goals, including the MDGs, is a vital long-term process. Its success can only be ensured in conditions of just and democratic governance within a holistic human rights framework and in the adherence to and the realization of the rule of law. National governments based on these inalienable principles should know that they can count on the support of organized civil society, nationally and internationally.

[E]ffective sustainable development should be people-centered. This requires effective local capacity building, capitalizing on the innate strength and resources of the people themselves.

AIDS	Acquired Immunodeficiency Syndrome
AMR	Annual Ministerial Review
CEDAW	Convention on the Elimination of Discrimination Against Women
CoNGO	Conference of Non-Governmental Organizations in Consultative Relationship with the United Nations
CSDF	Civil Society Development Forum
CSW	Commission on Status of Women
ECOSOC	Economic and Social Council
FEMNET	African Women's Development and Communication Network
FGM	Female Genital Mutilation
GBCS	General Board of Church and Society
GBGM	General Board of Global Ministries
IADG	Internationally Agreed Development Goals
ICC	International Criminal Court
IFI	International Financial Institutions
ILO	International Labor Organization
LGBTQ	Lesbian, Gay, Bisexual, Transgender and Queer
MDG	Millennium Development Goals
NGO	Non-Governmental Organization
NIGH	Nightingale Initiative for Global Health
ODA	Official Development Aid
UMC	The United Methodist Church
UMYF	United Methodist Youth Fellowship
UMCOR	United Methodist Committee on Relief
UMW	United Methodist Women
UN	United Nations
UNAIDS	Joint United Nations Programme on HIV and AIDS

List of Abbreviations

UNICEF	United Nations Children's Fund
UNDP	United Nations Development Programme
UNESCO	United Nations Educational, Scientific, and Cultural Organization
UNIFEM	United Nations Fund for Women
UNFPA	United Nations Population Fund
USAID	United States Agency for International Development
WHO	World Health Organization

SCRIPTURE SOURCES

AKJV	Authorized King James Version
ASV	American Standard Version
CEB	Common English Bible
CEV	Contemporary English Version
ERV	English Revised Version
ESV	English Standard Version
GNB	Good News Bible
GNT	Good News Translation
KJV	King James Version
MSG	The Message Bible
NAS/NASV	New American Standard/New American Standard Version
NKJV	New King James Version
NIV	New International Version
NLT	New Living Translation
NRS/NRSV	New Revised Standard Version
TNIV	Today's New International Version